CW00348341

Sir Herbert Lloyd

PETERWELL

The History of a Mansion and its Infamous Squire

BETHAN PHILLIPS

CYMDEITHAS LYFRAU CEREDIGION Gyf.

First Impression – November 1983 (ISBN 0 86383 026 9)
Second Impression (as facsimile) – November 1997

ISBN 0 948930 59 4

Published by Cymdeithas Lyfrau Ceredigion Gyf
Bryn Awel, Y Stryd Fawr, Aberystwyth SY23 1DR

Printed by Cambrian Printers
Ffordd Llanbadarn, Aberystwyth, Ceredigion SY23 3TN

I'M TEULU,
JOHN
GERAINT A CATRIN

AUTHOR'S NOTE

The seeds of this book were sown in childhood. Fear evokes its own fascination and for a child growing up in the town of Lampeter the sad and neglected ruins of Peterwell proved to be both fascinating and frightening. This fascination has continued into adulthood for it is well rooted in a folk memory that has survived over two centuries. It took the form of a long held belief in the locality that this once magnificent mansion was doomed and that it suffered the effects of a curse placed upon some of the stones used in its construction. Inextricably linked with its downfall is Sir Herbert Lloyd, its most infamous squire, whose name has become a byword for evil and tyranny. Yet, little is known of the man behind the legend and this book seeks to discover whether or not the vilification of his character over the years has been justified. It is the product of many years research into the history of eighteenth century Cardiganshire and relies in the main on contemporary letters and documents. All spelling, capitalisation, punctuation and use of italics have been modernised throughout and new style dating has been used.

My researches led me to seek the assistance of many institutions and I wish to record a particular debt to the members of staff of the following: the British Library; the National Library of Wales; the National Museum of Wales; the Dyfed Library, Aberystwyth; Dyfed Record Office; Jesus College, Oxford; the Public Record Office; St. David's University College Library, Lampeter; the Parochial Church Council, Lampeter; the Victoria Art Gallery, Bath. I wish to thank the West Wales Association for the Arts, and Lampeter Town Council for their financial assistance towards the publication of this book.

My gratitude is also due to many individuals and I must acknowledge the encouragement and the assistance I have received over the years from Miss Elizabeth Inglis-Jones, Major Herbert Lloyd Johnes, Professor P. D. G. Thomas and Dr. D. A. Rees, Jesus College, Oxford. I am greatly in debt to Mr. Robert Blayney for his willingness to provide illustrations for the book; to Miss Anne James for providing many of the photographs; and to Mr. Alun Williams, N.M.W. for his assistance with the portraits.

Bu Miss Rhiannon Roberts a Mrs. Emrys Williams o'r Llyfrgell Genedlaethol yn gefn i mi, a bûm yn ffodus i fedru manteisio ar wybodaeth eang Dr. Euronwy James o achau a hanes Ceredigion. Dymunaf ddatgan fy niolchiadau hefyd i Mrs. Gwenda Davies o Lyfrgell Coleg Prifysgol Dewi Sant, Mr. William Howells, Llyfrgell Aberystwyth, a Miss Susan S. Roberts, Ysgol Gyfun Aberaeron, am eu cymorth parod; ac yn arbennig i Dyfed Elis Gruffydd a Gwasg Gomer am y gofal a'r llu o gynghorion a gafwyd wrth lywio'r gwaith drwy'r wasg. Diolch hefyd i lu o bobl Llanbedr am fod mor barod i rannu eu gwybodaeth â mi ac yn enwedig i Mr. John Penry Davies, Castell. Rwy'n ddyledus hefyd i'r Canon Bertie Lewis, cyn Ficer y plwy, a'r Parch. Tim Morgan, y Ficer presennol, am lawer cymwynas. Yn olaf, hoffwn gydnabod y gefnogaeth a gefais gan fy ngŵr a'm teulu, heblaw am eu goddefgarwch hwy ni fyddai'r gwaith wedi ei gwblhau.—Without the support of my husband and the tolerance of my family, I should never have stayed the course.

I hope that the reader will derive as much pleasure from reading the book as I had from writing it.

Bethan Phillips

Castellan
Maesyllan
Lampeter

October 1983

NOTE TO SECOND IMPRESSION

I am greatly indebted to Cymdeithas Lyfrau Ceredigion Gyf. for undertaking the second impression of this book and in particular to Dylan Williams for his invaluable assistance, and also to the Cambrian Printers for their co-operation.

CONTENTS

	Page
Author's Note	vii
List of Illustrations	xii
Owners of Peterwell	xvi
The Descent of Sir Herbert Lloyd	xvii
Map of the Mansions	xviii
Foreword by Miss Elizabeth Inglis-Jones	xix

Chapter:

1	A Curious Story	1
2	The Rise of Peterwell	14
3	'Ye Great Fabric at Peterwell'	21
4	The Young Gentry	33
5	The Methodist Connection	46
6	'A Rioting Justice'	63
7	Mournful Houses	72
8	Lord of the Manor	82
9	Face to Face with the Poor	97
10	An Uneasy Inheritance	113
11	The Road to Westminster	120
12	The Vulture Knight	139
13	The Black Ram	151
14	'A Most Sickly and Irritable Time'	165
15	'There is Nothing He Will Not Attempt'	180
16	'A Noble Nine Days Fight'	193
17	An Enigmatic End	203
18	The Aftermath	214

APPENDICES

A.	Miscellaneous Accounts relating to Sir Herbert Lloyd	228
B.	Medical Records of John Lloyd, Peterwell	234
C.	A Rental of the Peterwell Estate	238
D.	Inventory from the sale of Peterwell, 1781	242
E.	Lampeter Parish and its Poor	253

Printed Primary Sources 276
Printed Books 277
Abbreviations 278

INDEX
Persons 279
Places 282
Subjects 283

LIST OF ILLUSTRATIONS

Page

Sir Herbert Lloyd (Frontispiece)
Painted by Allan Ramsay. Reproduced by permission of the Paul Mellon Foundation Centre for Studies in British Art. (Wrongly described as Sir Lucius Lloyd by Steegman.)

Sir Marmaduke Lloyd of Maesyfelin 3
Anon. 1642. By kind permission of Major Herbert Lloyd Johnes.

Vicar Prichard's House, Llandovery 6

Peterwell Avenue 12
Photo: Anne James, Lampeter

Walter Lloyd of Peterwell 24
Attributed to J. Richardson.
By kind permission of Major Herbert Lloyd Johnes.

Thomas Johnes of Llanfair and Croft Castle 26
By kind permission of the N.M.W.

Black Lion Royal Hotel, Lampeter 28
(At the turn of the century)
By kind permission of the owner, Mr. Glyn Jones.

Thomas Powell of Nanteos and his wife Mary 30
(G. E. Evans, *Aberystwyth and its Court Leet.)*

Nanteos 31
By kind permission of the Dyfed Library, Aberystwyth.

Jesus College, Oxford 34
By kind permission of the Archivist.

Croft Castle 40
From an eighteenth century drawing in the ownership of Major Herbert Lloyd Johnes.

Foelallt 42
A reconstruction by Robert Blayney based on a sketch in the N.L.W.

John Lloyd of Peterwell 43
By T. Hudson, 1750. Reproduced by kind permission of the N.M.W.

Communion Vessels 44
By kind permission of the Vicar and the Parochial Church Council,
St. Peter's Church.
Photo: Anne James, Lampeter.

Daniel Rowland 48
By kind permission of the N.L.W.

Howel Harris 50
By kind permission of the N.L.W.

Dame Anne Lloyd 56
Anon. 1730. By kind permission of Major Herbert Lloyd Johnes.

Memorial to the daughters of Anne Lloyd 58
at Strata Florida Church.
By kind permission of the Vicar of Tregaron.
Photo: Lluniau Bro.

Great Abbey Farm, Strata Florida 61
Photo: Lluniau Bro.

Lewis Morris 66
By kind permission of the N.M.W.

Henblas Abermâd 68
Drawn by Elizabeth Parrott, the present owner,
and published with her kind consent.

Dr. William Powell, Nanteos 70
G. E. Evans, *Aberystwyth and its Court Leet.*

Gogerddan 75
By kind permission of the Dyfed Library, Aberystwyth.

Memorial Ring of John Lloyd 80
By kind permission of Major H. Lloyd Johnes.

Old Brongest 85
From a painting by A. Davies.
By kind permission of Miss L. Thomas, Lampeter.

Lampeter Court Leet Records 87
By kind permission of the N.L.W.

Stocks and Whipping Post 91
From a sketch by the late John T. Williams, Cwmann.

Eighteenth Century Punishment 92
A sketch by Robert Blayney.

Comforts of Bath 94
By Thomas Rowlandson.
Reproduced by kind permission of the Victoria Art Gallery, Bath.

A Cardiganshire Cottage 97
By kind permission of the Dyfed Library, Aberystwyth.

The Parish Vestry Book: extract 99

The Parish Vestry Book: extract 100

The Parish Vestry 101
A sketch by Robert Blayney.

Driven from the Parish 104
A sketch by Robert Blayney.

The Medieval Church, Lampeter 106
Reproduction of a sketch by H. C. Harford in 1820.
By kind permission of the Vicar and the P.C.C., Lampeter.
Photo: Mr. Roy Davies.

An Eighteenth Century Vagrant 108

Cockfighting 109
From a 1759 engraving.

Medieval Font, Maestir Church 110
Photo: Anne James, Lampeter.

Letter from Sir Herbert Lloyd to John Johnes, Dolaucothi 115
By kind permission of the N.L.W.

Sir Charles Lloyd of Maesyfelin 117
By kind permission of the N.M.W.

Trawsgoed 121
By kind permission of the Dyfed Library, Aberystwyth.

Wilmot Vaughan of Trawsgoed 123
By kind permission of the N.M.W.

Dolaucothi 130
Reproduced from a water colour owned by Anne Robertson,
and published with her consent.

An Election Entertainment 135
Hogarth.
By kind permission of the Trustees, Sir John Soane's Museum, London.

Chairing of the Member 136
Hogarth.
By kind permission of the Trustees, Sir John Soane's Museum, London.

Siôn Philip's Cottage 152
A sketch by Robert Blayney.

An Eighteenth Century Constable 154
Drawing by Robert Blayney.

Map showing location of Cae Siôn Philip 156
By kind permission of J. Lloyd Davies, Pontfaen Farm, Lampeter.

The Bench 159
Hogarth.
By kind permission of the Fitzwilliam Museum, Cambridge.

Hanging of Siôn Philip 161
An artist's impression: Robert Blayney.

Clay pipe unearthed in Cae Siôn Philip 163
Found by Roy Heath, Pontfaen Cottage.
Photo: Anne James, Lampeter.

Wine bottles bearing the name of Sir Herbert Lloyd 165
By kind permission of Major H. Lloyd Johnes.

Comforts of Bath: Suffering from Gout 169
By Thomas Rowlandson.
Reproduced by kind permission of the Victoria Art Gallery, Bath.

Comforts of Bath: A Card Party 170
By Thomas Rowlandson.
Reproduced by kind permission of the Victoria Art Gallery, Bath.

Comforts of Bath: A Concert 173
By Thomas Rowlandson.
Reproduced by kind permission of the Victoria Art Gallery, Bath.

Bath Gamblers 174
By Matthew and Mary Darley.
Reproduced by kind permission of the Victoria Art Gallery, Bath.

Wilmot Vaughan. The Fourth Viscount Lisburne 185
Reproduced by kind permission of the N.M.W.

Pryse Campbell of Stackpole Court 188
Anon. c. 1755. By kind permission of the N.M.W.

Mabws 189
From an etching by J. Slater.
Reproduced by kind permission of the owner, Mrs. Winifred Gunton.

Thomas Johnes, son of Thomas Johnes the Custos 194
From an engraving by Worthington.
By kind permission of the N.M.W.

Lampeter Court Leet Record 196
By permission of the N.L.W.

An Election Scene 199
Hogarth.
By kind permission of Sir John Soane's Museum, London.

Burial entry of Sir Herbert Lloyd 211
From the Lampeter Church Register.
By kind permission of the Vicar and the P.C.C., Lampeter.

The unmarked grave 212
Photo: Anne James, Lampeter.

A claim for expenses 220
By kind permission of the N.L.W.

Book Plate of Sir Herbert Lloyd 221
G. E. Evans, *Lampeter.*

Falcondale 224
By kind permission of Mr. S. B. Smith, owner of Falcondale Hotel.

Parish Vestry Record 225
The removal of the Peterwell stones.
By kind permission of the Vicar and P.C.C., Lampeter.

Peterwell ruins 226
Photo: Anne James, Lampeter.

OWNERS OF PETERWELL 1642-1781

DAVID EVANS	1642-1646
THOMAS EVANS	1646-1669
DAVID EVANS	1669-1675
DANIEL EVANS	1675-1696
MARY EVANS (LLOYD)	1696-1722
WALTER LLOYD	1722-1747
JOHN LLOYD	1747-1755
SIR HERBERT LLOYD	1755-1769
JOHN ADAMS	1769-1781

THE DESCENT OF SIR HERBERT LLOYD, PETERWELL

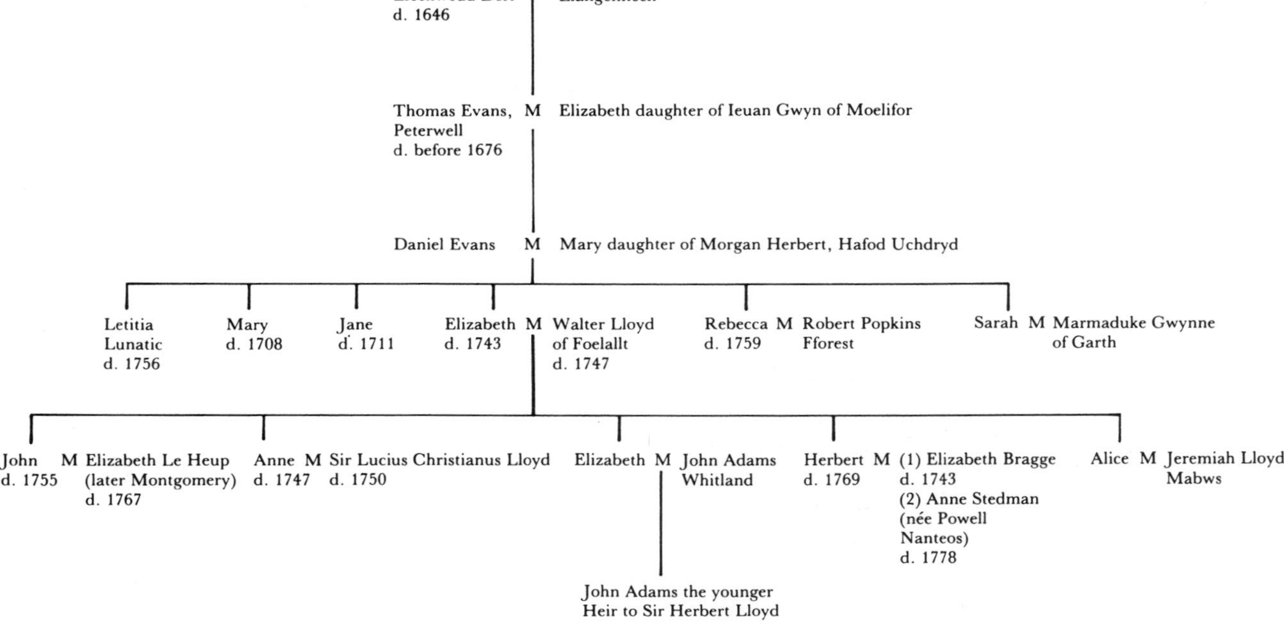

MAP SHOWING THE LOCATION OF THE HOUSES OF THE GENTRY

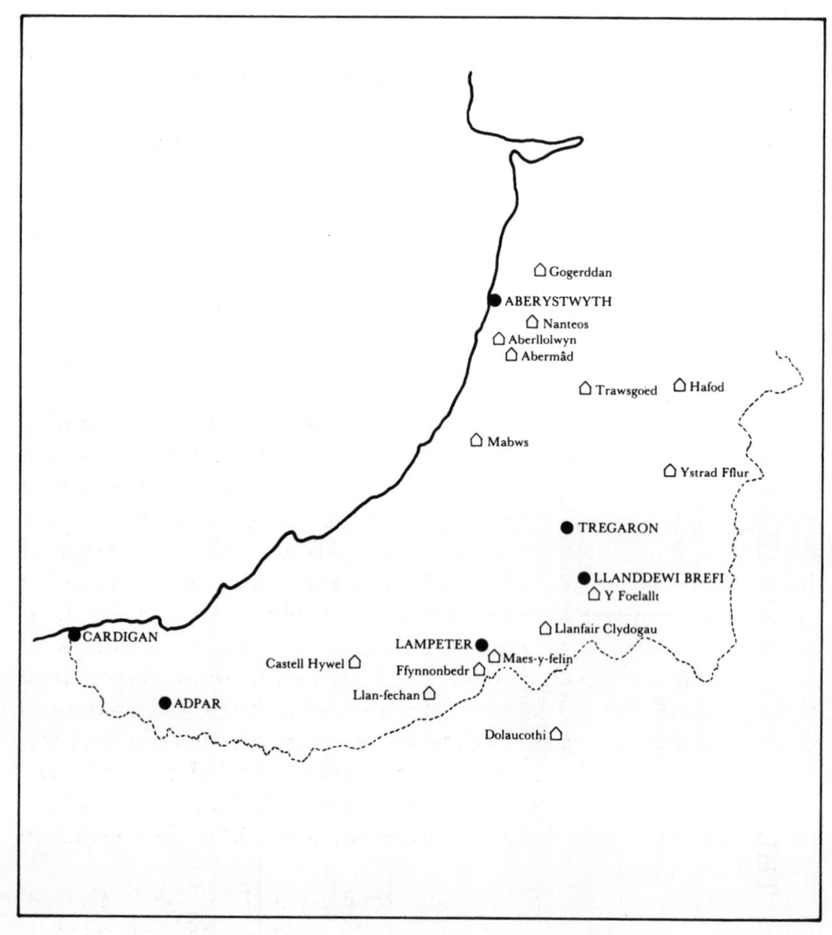

FOREWORD

Overshadowed by its ancient aura of evil-doing, the pitiful remnants of the once great house of Peterwell, hidden among trees at the end of a once stately avenue, have for long been a source of speculation and romantic imagining.

As long as I can recall Sir Herbert Lloyd has loomed in one's fancy as the very embodiment of wickedness whose excesses led him at last to suicide, an event that has been described in lurid detail by a somewhat less scrupulous local historian than Mrs. Phillips. Now in this meticulously researched and well-documented book, she clears up legendary accretions that hitherto have been accepted as truths and tells us all that there is to tell about his life and character as he was seen through the eyes of his contemporaries in gleanings from letters and county records.

Never it seems was a man more generally disliked, spoken of with contempt and hatred by his relations and his acquaintances alike—a sombre though necessarily incomplete portrait of a mendacious and unscrupulous scoundrel. For since there are no personal papers available to enlighten us further, none of those intimate letters and diaries that are so invaluable to a biographer for getting inside his subject, we only get glimpses and not the whole. One cannot help suspecting that in his younger days at any rate, there was another side to his violent, uncontrolled nature, a fundamental sense of insecurity perhaps, a striving after something better, which may have accounted for his marriage to a pious widow many years older than he was and his friendship with that great and good man Howel Harris, who undoubtedly at one time had hopes of saving him. Although it was a light which did not last for long, nevertheless, it would be interesting to know more about it.

Particularly interesting to many readers will be the lively and detailed picture Mrs. Phillips paints of the social and political scene in Cardiganshire in the mid-eighteenth century. Cut off from the outside world by great tracts of impassable bogs and ranges of desolate hills, it was the least accessible of the Welsh counties. Here a tyrannical and quarrelsome squirearchy ruled the roost, lording it over their tenants like petty potentates, even as we shall see when the need arose leading them forth to battle against their opponents. For others less favoured by fortune—farmers struggling against the poor soil and climate, labourers and craftsmen existing on a pittance—it was an era of unrewarding toil and grinding poverty, while the living conditions generally were appalling. Horrifying are the accounts we read here of deaths due to starvation and whole families decimated by fevers. Charity and compassion were singularly lacking among their betters who seem to have accepted this state of affairs with indifference. 'They never think of other people starving if they do but eat themselves' as later on in the century Jane Johnes wrote indignantly from Hafod.

Though rumbustious sports and merrymaking occasionally enlivened the scene, the overall picture is a grim one. Around Lampeter it was made worse still by the heavy shadows Peterwell cast across the Teify Valley and the menacing proximity of Herbert Lloyd. Always short of money to support his grandiose schemes and as the years passed by getting more and more involved with his lawsuits and debts, if it profited him he was ready, as everyone knew, to resort to any violence or trickery.

Although his reign at Peterwell was comparatively short, lasting only fourteen years, so indelible was the dreadful impression he created that even today, we are told, many believe that his evil emanations are still lurking in its avenue and ruins. That may well be so but we must also be obliged to him for providing the motif for this excellent book.

ELISABETH INGLIS-JONES

FFYNNONBEDR

Dy ryfedd rin edwinodd – a harddwch
Dy erddi ddiflannodd;
Du dy ffawd, dy hud a ffodd
A nos dy dranc ddynesodd.

WJP

Chapter 1

A CURIOUS STORY

A mile or so outside the town of Lampeter can still be seen the vestiges of an avenue of stately trees. To-day, they lead to a heap of forlorn stones, the wreckage of what was once the magnificent mansion of Ffynnonbedr or, in English, Peterwell. The old house has long gone, its stout walls split asunder and ravaged by time. What now remains harmonises with nature; moss and lichen embroider its dark stones, small green ferns and straggling nettles sprout from the gaping cavities, and each passing year adds a little to the vesture of decay and neglect which now encompasses the place.

In the last century a traveller visiting these ruins remarked: 'It is a curious story . . . the race that ruled here is long extinct and the house was abandoned in the freshness of its prime and pride'.[1] This story of Peterwell, whose glory blazed across the Teifi valley, has been echoed on the hearths of the locality for many generations, and it is a tale rooted in evil and tangled with superstition. Once, the four great towers, crowned with their golden domes, glowed in the setting sun, and its magnificent roof-top garden displayed a profusion of shrubs and flowers amid cascading fountains. But to-day there is little to attract the passing visitor. Even in the height of summer, the long leafy avenue is plunged into perpetual shadow, and the artificial canals fringing it are densely silted up, choked by the dead leaves of countless autumns. Yet the story of its decline remains to fascinate us.

Local tradition has, over the centuries, ascribed the misfortunes of Peterwell and its owners to the 'Curse of Maesyfelin'. From the turn of the seventeenth century Maesyfelin, or Millfield, was the seat of the Lloyd family formerly of Llanllŷr. We know little of the mansion itself except that it was a Jacobean edifice built in the pointed style and that it stood to the east of the town of Lampeter close to the town rugby field. During the years preceding the Civil War (1642-9) between King and Parliament the head of the family was an illustrious jurist, Sir Marmaduke Lloyd, (1585-1651) noted by his contemporaries as a man of great piety and rectitude. Educated at Oriel College, Oxford, and called to the Bar at the Middle Temple, he became Chief Justice for Breconshire and lived for most of the year at Ludlow. His eldest son Sir Francis Lloyd was in effect the Master of Maesyfelin, but he does not appear to have been cast in the same mould as his father for a contemporary described him as 'one who seems to love his private ease above public affairs'.[2] We do know that he was prepared to flout the conventions of his time, to forsake his wife Mary, daughter of the Earl of Carbery, and to live openly at Maesyfelin with his mistress Bridget Leigh who bore him two sons out of wedlock. On his wife's death, he eventually married Bridget Leigh and as there was no issue from his first marriage, the children born of his affair with his mistress became heirs to Maesyfelin.

The Lloyd family were on extremely friendly terms with the family of Rees Prichard, Vicar of Llandovery, a notable divine and the author of popular religious rhymes. In simple verse which appealed to the sense of poetry and rhythm of the Welsh, he exhorted his fellow men to follow the true path and to abandon their sinful ways. These were collected and published after his death under the title *Canwyll y Cymry* (The Welshmen's Candle). A devout Anglican such as Sir Marmaduke Lloyd had a great deal in common with the Vicar, for he was also obsessed with the moral laxity of the age and forthright in his condemnation of it. In a letter to Rees Prichard written from Ludlow Castle in 1626, he addressed the Vicar as his 'very worthy friend' and recognised the power of his writing. 'Your golden pen', he congratulated the Vicar, 'hath gotten victory'. He also acknowledged his influence upon his own life and work and promised to act as 'you graciously direct me to do'. The letter ended with 'kind salutations' to the Vicar and to his 'hopeful son'.[3] These last words were to have a bitter and ironic significance if we are to believe the tale, that has over the centuries been linked with the misfortunes and downfall of Maesyfelin.

The 'hopeful son' to whom Sir Marmaduke addressed his salutations was in fact Samuel Prichard, the Vicar's only son. Born in 1605, he was, like his father, educated at Jesus College, Oxford, and on graduating he also entered the Church. His wayward behaviour while a student must have worried his father very much for in a letter home he confessed that his 'precipitant courses have caused so many storms of vexation'; yet he promised that his 'reformed life' would now allow his father's grey hairs to 'reobtain their former lustre'.[4] But if we are to believe tradition, Samuel's eventual fate was to poison

Sir Marmaduke Lloyd of Maesyfelin

his father's very existence and to turn this rhymester for God into a man obsessed with a desire for vengeance. This was to take the form of a curse uttered against the House of Maesyfelin which is said to have blighted the future fortunes of that family and to lead to its eventual destruction. It is contained in the following lines attributed to Vicar Prichard:[5]

Melltith Duw fo ar Maesyfelin,
Ar bob carreg a phob gwreiddyn,
Am daflu blodyn tre' Llandyfri
Ar ei ben i Dywi i foddi.*

The story associated with the Vicar's curse was very much alive in the localities of Llandovery and Lampeter at the turn of the last century. It has as its basis the friendship that existed between the Maesyfelin family and that of Vicar Prichard. During Sir Marmaduke's long absences at far away Ludlow, his son Sir Francis Lloyd indulged himself in those wordly pleasures which would have proved anathema to his ascetic father. A frequent visitor to Maesyfelin was the young Samuel Prichard, who found the atmosphere at his father's house stifling after the gay abandon of a student's life at Oxford. The attractions of Maesyfelin were such that he was prepared to endure the dangerous and tedious journey along tortuous tracks from Llandovery to Lampeter in order to indulge himself in the pleasures of wine and women.

During these visits, the young Samuel was to overreach himself for he became attracted to a young lady of the Maesyfelin family reputed to be one of Sir Francis's sisters. Although the Vicar's son could be accepted as a friend and a vivacious companion, his social standing was merely that of a lowly cleric and his designs upon a daughter of the household would not be well received. The affair was frowned upon; feelings of jealousy crept in, and there was a fear that Prichard might appropriate a measure of the wealth of Maesyfelin since the daughter was a favourite of Sir Marmaduke Lloyd. Everything was done to discourage the courtship, but this only served to fuel the passion of the

*May God's curse be upon Maesyfelin
On every stone and every root,
For casting the flower of Llandovery town
Headlong into the Towy to drown.

lovers. Contemptuous of warnings they continued to meet in stealth and secret; sometimes along the banks of the Teifi, sometimes amid the shady clumps overlooking the Dulas, and when chance permitted, even within the dark walls of Maesyfelin itself.

Spurred by his amorous desires, Samuel Prichard would gallop recklessly along the narrow corkscrew lanes twisting the twenty one miles which separated Lampeter from Llandovery to see his lover. Fully reciprocating his love, the young daughter would signal to him with a fluttering handkerchief from one of the mansion's windows whether or not it was safe for him to approach, for the great mansion of Maesyfelin was visible from afar. The family, well aware of his persistent visits and deceit, despised the whole illicit affair; the sense of betrayal felt by Sir Francis Lloyd turned into a wild hatred for this feckless youth, and it was decided to end the relationship once and for all. Soon, a terrible conspiracy was conceived to murder the Vicar's son.

One evening, as he approached unsuspectingly to keep a clandestine assignation, his enemies lay in wait for him. They set a trap by allowing him to enter the portals of Maesyfelin and meet the young girl in her bedroom. There, suddenly they set upon him and ruthlessly smothered him to death between two feather beds. Great care was taken to ensure that there was not a mark made upon his body; then, still in his travelling clothes, he was carried out into the night, placed in a woolsack which was packed with wool so as to disguise its shape, and slung over the saddle of his horse waiting outside the mansion walls. Four servants, sworn to secrecy, were instructed to lead the animal with its macabre burden out of Lampeter back along the leafy winding path to Llandovery. Although it was by now a late hour of the night, the light of a full moon flooded across the whole countryside showing up clearly the little knot of men furtively wending their way along tracks ribbed by tall trees and flanked by thick bushes. Only the rhythmic clopping of the horses' hooves broke the silence of the eerie journey.

As dawn was breaking they were within three miles of the town of Llandovery, but near a farm called Gwinten they were surprised by the approach of another traveller whose curiosity was very much aroused. Clearly intrigued by the odd shape of their load and inquisitive as to the nature of their business at such an early hour, he asked what it was that they were transporting. On being told that it was a load of wool, he approached the sack and on striking it casually with his fist, he felt a sharp metallic object which he later realised was Samuel Prichard's spur. Before the traveller could pursue the matter further, the agitated party hurried away into the dawn until they reached a narrow stone bridge near Nant yr Hogfaen. Here, the body was taken out of the woolsack and hurled unceremoniously into the dark waters of the Tywi so as to give the impression that Samuel Prichard had met his end accidentally, thrown from his horse and drowned in the fast flowing river. But the whole incident was witnessed by a young maid servant from Pantyweil who happened to be out on an early morning errand for her mistress. She was so horrified and severely afflicted by what she had seen that she was said to have died two days afterwards.

Samuel Prichard's horse was then released and, sharply whipped, was sent galloping in the direction of the now waking town. As it careered through the empty streets its hooves clattering on the cobbles, the people peering through their windows realised that something was amiss for they immediately recognised it as belonging

Vicar Prichard's House, Llandovery

to the Vicar's son. Wild eyed and foam flecked it slithered to a stop outside the Vicar's house where its frantic whinnying aroused the household. As soon as he saw the empty saddle, Rees Prichard knew instinctively that there was something seriously wrong, for he had strongly disapproved of his son's excursions to Maesyfelin. A search was organised and when his body was discovered, the old Vicar's worst fears were realised. But he was not to be deceived by the attempt to conceal the murder of his son. He had long feared that his son's companionship with Sir Francis Lloyd and his obsession with temporal pleasures would eventually lead to a bitter fate. His grief at the loss of his only son was inconsolable, but it soon congealed into a terrible hatred. There was no question of turning the other cheek; his rage became ungovernable and, consumed with loathing and hell bent on revenge, he called down the curse of God on Maesyfelin, on its every stone and every root. This curse was to resound throughout the centuries and every misfortune that befell the Lloyd family was to be attributed to it.

Such is the tale as related in the 1841 edition of *Canwyll y Cymry* and is the tradition as it existed in Llandovery. A similar version existed in Lampeter except that Samuel Prichard's body was cast into the Teifi and not the Tywi. In 1828 a different version of the tale appeared in *The Adventures and Vagaries of Twm Shon Catti* by T. J. Ll. Prichard; it appears in ballad form. This was republished many times during the course of the century and a Welsh narrative version was printed in 1872. This account is much embellished, taking the form of a Gothic murder story. It contains many historical inaccuracies; the Maesyfelin family are known as the Vaughans, the tragic heiress, the object of Samuel's love is called Ellen. She is portrayed as an orphan who is to inherit all, and constantly under threat from her evil brothers who have been disinherited. Samuel Prichard is depicted as a star crossed youth, 'Llandovery's Flower', waiting on Pencarreg hill for his love's signal, a red silken handkerchief to tell him that it was safe for them to meet. Trapped by the brothers his end is described in horrendous detail:[6]

His hands they fasten'd behind his back,
And over his head they drew a sack,
They jump on his body—his rib bones crack,
Till a corse on the ground they find him.

The body was then taken and thrown into a pool in the Teifi. The demented Ellen, distraught with grief, eluded her brothers, wandered to the Vicar's house in Llandovery where she died within a fortnight, and was buried in her lover's grave. The horrific climax to the story was the discovery of Maesyfelin alight: in the charred ruins the bloodstained bodies of the brothers were found, and hanging from a beam was the body of the eldest still with the blood of his brothers on his hands.

Versions of the story must have been known in other parts of Wales during the nineteenth century. In 1871 Francis Kilvert, the diarist, heard a version in Clyro in Radnorshire.[7] In this account 'Sammy' was murdered by the two half brothers of the heiress for money, and it is Kilvert who relates the incident of the maidservant from Pantyweil.

But to what extent are these stories to be believed?

Although much adorned with the passage of time, many folk traditions are founded on a modicum of historical truth. Rees Prichard, his son Samuel and Sir Francis Lloyd were indeed historical figures and we know that a real friendship existed between the two families. A verse written in the style of the Vicar exists uttering its strange curse upon Maesyfelin and one could easily conjecture that some misfortune befell Samuel Prichard and that the Lloyd family were in some way implicated. All the versions of the story rely upon a portrayal of him as an impetuous lover cut down in his youthful prime. But what do we know of the real Samuel Prichard? We have already seen that he graduated at Oxford on 10 October 1623 at the age of eighteen and that he took holy orders. It is likely that he became his father's curate and that he was not the Samuel Prichard, Rector of Llanynys, near Builth, as is suggested in the *Alumni Oxonienses.*[8]

We do know that when Samuel Prichard returned from Oxford he was already a married man, having taken as wife Frances Harding, a young lady of that city. It is also probable that she bore him a son and a daughter early in the marriage. We can with some certainty determine the date of his death and that he died before his father. He was alive on 13 October 1642, for a bond was drawn up on that date in the names of 'Rees and Samuel Prichard of Llandovery, clerks'.[9] This confirms the belief that he was his father's curate and a resident of Llandovery. A year later, on 19 October 1643, Rees Prichard signed a deed transfering a substantial portion of his estate to his grandson

Rice Prichard of Stroud Water, Gloucester, whom he refers to as his heir.[10] It is almost certain, therefore, that Samuel Prichard had died between October 1642 and October 1643.

At this time the Vicar was in failing health for 'sick in body' he drew up his will on 2 December 1644,[11] and he died soon after. In the will no mention is made of his son, and most of the estate is bequeathed to his grand-daughter Elizabeth, who had married Thomas, son of Roger Mainwaring, Bishop of St David's. It is probable that his grandson had also died, for the estate bequeathed to him previously is now included in the will. The Vicar also makes provision for his daughter in law, Frances Prichard. Thus, far from dying in his youth, Samuel Prichard died at the age of thirty eight years or so, survived by a wife and two teenage children, a reality far removed from the tragic figure portrayed in the tale.

Tradition has attached much of the odium for the supposed murder of Samuel Prichard to Sir Francis Lloyd of Maesyfelin, and as evidence of his depraved nature, much has been made of his association with his concubine Bridget Leigh. But at the time of Samuel Prichard's death, Sir Francis Lloyd was Member of Parliament for Carmarthen, a member of the Long Parliament and he held the office of 'Comptroller of the Household' in the court of King Charles I. During the Civil War he fought loyally for the King, was taken prisoner on two occasions, and fined heavily by Parliament for his adherence to the Crown. Following the return of Charles II to the throne in 1660, he was reinstated at court and appointed a Gentleman of the Privy Chamber. Once again, the historical Sir Francis bears no real similarity to the character pictured in the tradition as being responsible for the murder of Samuel Prichard.

The supposed object of Samuel Prichard's affections was, according to tradition, the daughter of Maesyfelin, and we know that Sir Marmaduke Lloyd had six daughters, all of whom eventually married respectably into prominent families. We know that the youngest daughter Penelope was still unmarried in 1645, but she would have been quite young in 1642-3 and hardly likely to have become involved with a middle aged man. A favoured theory was that it was Samuel Prichard's involvement with Bridget Leigh which led to his downfall at the hands of Sir Francis Lloyd but, although she moved into Maesyfelin as a concubine, it is highly unlikely that she had done so at the time of the alleged murder. In 1645 when Sir Marmaduke Lloyd drew up his will, Sir Francis and his wife Dame Mary are mentioned and the common bequest made to them suggests that they were at that time living together. We know that Bridget Leigh bore him two sons out of wedlock and that the second son, Charles, was born in 1662. Thus, it appears that Sir Francis's affair with Bridget Leigh and his abandonment of his wife Mary occurred much later than the date of Samuel Prichard's death.

It is extremely difficult to adduce any firm historical evidence to substantiate the tradition of the Curse of Maesyfelin. Perhaps William Edmunds, a local historian, has come closest to explaining the origin of this strange tale in his series of articles entitled *On Some Old Families in the Neighbourhood of Lampeter* published in 1861. He suggests that Samuel Prichard could have died through some mischance while on a visit to Maesyfelin or while returning from such a visit,[12] and in Theophilus Jones's *History of Brecknockshire,* first published in 1805, it is stated that he was drowned in the river Towy.[13] The years 1642-43 were the early years of the Civil War when the country was split in its allegiances, when erstwhile friends became foes, when whispers and rumours were rife. Both the Lloyd family of Maesyfelin and Vicar Prichard were ardent Royalists, and Edmunds suggested that those who wished to divide the supporters of the King sought to incriminate Maesyfelin in Samuel Prichard's death.

As time passed misfortunes befell the family such as the suicide of Lucius, Sir Francis's elder son and the premature deaths of male heirs led to the line becoming extinct in less than one hundred years after the death of Sir Marmaduke Lloyd in 1651. Such tragic happenings could have fuelled the story of the curse, becoming connected in folk memory with the enigma of Samuel Prichard's death. During the latter half of the eighteenth century Maesyfelin itself became a ruin, thus providing in the minds of people positive proof of the truth of the prophecy. A similar fate was soon to befall Peterwell leading to the popular belief that it also had been damned because stones from Maesyfelin had been used in its renovation, thus transferring the effect of the curse to that mansion.

Whatever the origin of the tradition itself, we are still left with the verse, supposedly the work of Rees Prichard, predicting the downfall of Maesyfelin. This seems to authenticate the account of Samuel Prichard's tragic end and to confirm that Maesyfelin played some part in it. It remains the source from which the tradition springs.

D. Gwenallt Jones in his study of the Vicar's life and work[14] was convinced that he was not the author and he pointed out that it never appeared in any edition of *Canwyll y Cymry*. But this in itself is not strange, for it would have been more surprising if Stephen Hughes, the devout Puritan who published the 1659 edition of *Canwyll y Cymry*, had included such an irreligious verse in a volume of the Vicar's sacred works. At this time Maesyfelin was poised to re-emerge as a family of influence, following Cromwell's death a year earlier, and it would have been unwise to publish anything which constituted a gross libel against it. In fact, the verse did not appear in print until 1841 with the publication of Rice Rees's edition of *Canwyll y Cymry*. In the book, an account of the Vicar's life is given, and the story of Samuel Prichard's death as it was related at that time in Lampeter and Llandovery is included.

It is probable that the verse was integral to the story as it existed in those localities, a story which must have developed as part of an oral tradition over a number of years. In the process there must have been many accretions and embellishments, and it would have been natural for the curse to have appeared in rhyme, for it was in this manner that the Vicar had, over the years, addressed the people of Wales. The verse is so out of character with what we know of Rees Prichard that we must also conclude that it is not his work, but that it was composed to accompany the tradition and to make the story more credible.

To the people, however, the curse was a reality with the sad ruins of Maesyfelin and Peterwell providing ample proof of the disastrous consequences. In 1802 Eliezer Williams, Vicar of Lampeter, wrote thus of the Maesyfelin family:

> The country people will have it that the family never throve since the curse; that the place was soon a heap of ruins and when the estate fell into the hands of the Lloyds of Peterwell, that they too, soon felt the effects of the same malediction, and every family that subsequently came into possession of these obnoxious lands; in proof whereof, they show the modern built House of Peterwell a mass of rubbish.[15]

If, as the cottagers of Lampeter believed, the fall of Peterwell was the inevitable consequence of the curse, they must also have felt that nowhere could the old Vicar have found a more suitable instrument for its fulfilment than Sir Herbert Lloyd, the last of the Lloyds to be

Peterwell Avenue

master of the house. Here, indeed, was a man born to destruction. During his turbulent life the fortunes of Peterwell reached a zenith, but his excesses and his recklessness led to its eventual perdition. His name became a byword for tyranny, sending thunderclaps of fear throughout Cardiganshire. It is his association with Peterwell that evokes a sense of fear and dread which is still linked with its sombre ruins. Over the years, some maintain that they have seen his ghost riding in the avenue; others claim to have momentarily lost control of their cars whilst driving past the entrance to the ruins; many people react with an instinctive feeling of revulsion and apprehension at the very sound of his name. His career is the story of naked ambition, of greed, of cruelty, and of injustice. As though impelled by destiny, he took a course which led to the destruction of himself and the celebrated mansion which once was Peterwell.

NOTES

[1] Bradley, p. 256.
[2] *Cambrian Register,* p. 165.
[3] *Lloyd Letters,* p. 27.
[4] Rice Rees, p. 304.
[5] ibid., p. 308.
[6] T. J. Llewelyn Prichard, p. 148.
[7] F. Kilvert, p. 118.
[8] A Samuel Prichard was appointed Rector of Llanynys in 1631 and according to Theophilus Jones, the Breconshire historian, continued until 1646. There is also evidence that he remained there until 1650 when he was ejected by the Puritans. It is probable that our Samuel Prichard died before 1646.
[9] D.R.O. Cawdor-Lort 10/508.
[10] Rice Rees, p. 315.
[11] ibid.
[12] Edmunds, *Arch. Camb.,* 1861, p. 24.
[13] ibid., p. 25.
[14] D. Gwenallt Jones, p. 16.

Chapter Two

THE RISE OF PETERWELL

In the summer of 1720 at Peterwell, a son was born to the squire Walter Lloyd and his wife Elizabeth. The cleric who recorded his baptism in the Lampeter Church Register on 22 July could not have foreseen that the squalling infant, named Herbert, would become one of the most infamous country squires who ever galloped across Cardiganshire.

He was fortunate to have survived the ordeal of being born, for in those days the struggle for existence was at its most fierce during the early stages of life. Two of his brothers, Walter (d. 1714), and Thomas (d. 1717), had already succumbed to the rigours of infancy, and he was yet to lose another brother Daniel and a sister Mary in childhood. The appalling rate of child mortality is poignantly mirrored in the Church records of the day and the name of Peterwell appears with touching regularity.

The young Herbert was born into a world of affluence and influence, for his father was a prominent lawyer, and the Attorney General for the counties of Carmarthenshire, Cardiganshire and Pembrokeshire. The mansion of Peterwell was a 'very handsome house' overlooking the Teifi and set among the lush water meadows. At the time of Herbert Lloyd's birth, it was less than eighty years old, for the Peterwell family had risen to wealth and power during the conflict and confusion which marked the Civil War between the King and Parliament in the previous century.

The founder of the House of Peterwell was an impecunious freeholder, David Evans of Llechwedd Deri in the parish of Llanwnnen, some three miles from Lampeter. In 1632 he was fined for failing to attend the coronation of Charles I. The King had revived an old law summoning all freeholders with an income of forty pounds or more from lands or rents, to present themselves at his coronation and to purchase a knighthood. David Evans had declined the honour, claiming that he 'had not forty pounds yearly rent . . . and had a great charge of children'.[1] The next decade seems to have seen some improvement in his financial affairs, for in 1641 he attained the office of High Sheriff for Cardiganshire. It was he who launched the Peterwell family on the first rung of the social ladder which was to culminate, a century or so later, in the granting of the baronetcy to his great, great, grandson Sir Herbert Lloyd.

Shortly after becoming High Sheriff, David Evans decided to move from Llechwedd Deri and build a dwelling house more appropriate to his new found status. He chose an idyllic spot set amid emerald meadows edging the silver Teifi and close to an ancient well called Ffynnonbedr or Peterwell. This well can still be found; although it is now almost totally concealed by rushes and long grass, its clear water continues to trickle over the cold grey stones. David Evans was destined to enjoy his more opulent surroundings for only a few more years: on his death in 1646 at the age of forty nine, his estate passed to his son Thomas Evans.

It is he who can properly be described as the true architect of the later prosperity of Peterwell. A man of little scruple and of overriding ambition, he was to exploit every situation to advance his own fortunes. His character foreshadowed in its ruthlessness that of his great grandson Sir Herbert Lloyd. It was a time when the country was convulsed by the Civil War: family was set against family, and disorder reigned. In and around Lampeter, the most prominent and influential families were the Lloyds of Maesyfelin and the Lloyds of Llanfair Clydogau. These were long established and well connected, being represented at Westminster by Sir Francis Lloyd of Maesyfelin as M.P. for Carmarthen borough, and Walter Lloyd of Llanfair as M.P. for Cardiganshire. Sir Francis Lloyd also held the position of Comptroller of the King's Household and he had received his knighthood from Charles I, an honour which the King was also to bestow on Walter Lloyd for his service to the crown during the conflict.

In comparison, the Evans family of Peterwell were mere upstarts. During the early years of the Civil War, the Lampeter gentry supported the King, and no-one declared himself more vigorously for the royalist cause than Thomas Evans. It was he, who in January 1645 'mustered the inhabitants of Llanbeder Co. Cardigan and charged them to be ready to assist the King against Parliament'.[2] Like Sir Francis Lloyd, he took an active part in the fighting which now rent west Wales, serving under Colonel Gerard, the King's commander during the Pembrokeshire campaign. The area around Tregaron and

Lampeter suffered much from the depradations of the royalist army under Gerard, who 'plundered much and swept away the provisions'.[3]

But the tide soon began to turn in favour of Cromwell. On 18 December 1645, Sir Francis Lloyd and his father Sir Marmaduke Lloyd were taken prisoners at Hereford. Six months later Cromwell's forces laid siege to the castle of Aberystwyth and over the next two years the royalist cause petered out in Cardiganshire. On 1 March 1648, a meeting was held at Lampeter and the royalist forces in Cardiganshire assembled in the town to be paid off, so that the 'county was cleared of free quarter and other impositions'. There was a brief revival of royalist fortunes, but the King's forces suffered a decisive defeat at St Fagans on 8 May 1648. Once again the names of Sir Francis and his father appear in the list of prisoners. It is probable that Thomas Evans took part in this battle but, as his name does not appear in the list, it is likely that he evaded capture.

There soon followed a period of retribution when the adherents to the royalist cause, now termed 'delinquents', were to be punished for their so called delinquency. Heavy fines were imposed and estates sequestered. Sir Francis Lloyd was fined the sum of £1003,[4] and Sir Walter Lloyd of Llanfair was obliged to pay the sum of £1033-9s-0d.[5] Thomas Evans was also required to account for his delinquency, and the commissioners were requested to 'examine witnesses' against him and to 'seize and secure his estate'.[6] Thomas Evans, however, succeeded in turning what could have been a time of disaster, into a period of personal profit. There is no evidence that the Peterwell family had to compound for their estates. Thomas Evans simply changed sides; he bounded easily from one regime to another, forsook his erstwhile allegiances, and gladly adopted Cromwell's banner.

Henceforth, Thomas Evans channelled his undoubted vigour for the cause of Parliament. He is described as being an 'active captain of horse', and his son David 'a captain of foot' under the Committee of Safety, and it has been suggested that he served with Cromwell during the Irish campaign of 1648-49.[7] The Protector had appointed committees in each county to make assessments of royalist possessions and to confiscate the estates of those gentry who had been loyal to the King. This was indeed fertile ground for the avaricious and self seeking, and it is no surprise to discover that Thomas Evans was involved in much dubious work on behalf of the Commonwealth.

Many unscrupulous men grew rich on the spoils unfairly wrung from former Cavaliers, and Thomas Evans did not shrink from exploiting his new found authority. Very soon, desirable farms and fertile lands were being acquired by Peterwell, and he was not above using a measure of ruthlessness in fulfilling his purpose. In 1660, after the Restoration of the Monarchy, the freeholders of Cardiganshire petitioned Parliament, complaining that in 1649 Thomas Evans had confiscated lands 'using excessive amercements, fines and threats', and that the alienated manors had unlawfully become 'the possessions of private men'.[8]

Thomas Evans had judged with precision the ebb and flow of political power, and this acumen, coupled with a high degree of severity, made him a man to be reckoned with. An anonymous survey of the Welsh gentry written after the Restoration in 1660 sums up his character thus: 'Passionately violent in anything . . . impatient without an office and tyrannical in it'.[9] Such was his mercenary cunning that even his new allies treated him with suspicion. On 10 November 1652, the County Commissioners for Cardigan, who were charged with the collection of fines and dues, were unhappy about the state of the financial returns. They wrote to their superior body, the Committee for the Advance of Money in London, stating that Thomas Evans, Registrar to the late Sub-committee of Accounts in the County, had been called before them for an investigation into his affairs. Never one to succumb meekly, he had refused to be 'examined about his papers and acquittances or to deliver them up'.[10]

The Commissioners then ordered Oliver Lloyd, the Mayor of Tregaron, to apprehend the intractable Thomas Evans and to take him into custody; but Lloyd refused to execute the order. The reluctance of Lloyd to arrest Thomas Evans may have been due to his fear of him, for these were violent times when the seat of government was a long way off. The Committee in London again instructed Lloyd to 'produce Evans and commit him to custody until he conforms'.[11] The outcome we do not know, but the incident amply illustrates that Thomas Evans was a character not easily quelled. The same blood was to course through the veins of his descendant, Sir Herbert Lloyd, who was to show the same irreverence for the law.

His grasping disposition profited Thomas Evans well: the fortunes of Peterwell flourished as he plundered the estates of men who had previously been his *confrères*. One source even claims that he 'ammassed great riches by robbing and despoiling churches'.[12] Certainly, it was the ideal time for such plunder. Cromwell's men regarded church treasures as idolatrous trappings, and it is said that many a goblet and silver plate found its way to Peterwell. One tradition holds that the later misfortune which befell the family resulted from the sacrilegious conduct of Thomas Evans at this time.

Despite his early lawlessness and reprehensible behaviour, Thomas Evans was promoted to the list of Commissioners for the Monthly Assessment in the County of Cardigan on 12 August 1653. Such a position now gave him greater authority for amassing personal wealth. At this time, he also sought to add some lustre to his social prestige in Cardiganshire by aspiring to the office of High Sheriff for the county. On 10 November 1653, a list of sheriffs for every county in England and Wales was published, but strangely, Cardiganshire was omitted. Five days later, the following decision of Parliament was recorded:[13]

> Resolved upon the question by Parliament that Thomas Evans Esquire, should be, and is nominated and approved to be Sheriff of the County of Cardigan for the ensuing year.

Why it was necessary to make a specific resolution for Cardiganshire when all other names had been announced five days previously is not clear, and it must remain a matter for conjecture. Could it be that his past record and dubious conduct had brought a degree of controversy into the proposal to appoint him sheriff? Whatever the reason, Thomas Evans again showed his amazing resilience, for he now had sufficient influence under the Commonwealth to ensure that any objections to his appointment to the shrievalty did not succeed. This influence was to continue for the remainder of the Protectorate under Cromwell; for on 2 March 1658, he was appointed Commissioner of Assessment for the counties of Carmarthen and Cardigan.

With the death of Cromwell on 3 September 1658, the days of the Commonwealth were drawing to a close, and already initiatives were being taken to secure the return of Charles II to the throne. This prospect must have been greeted with alarm by Thomas Evans, for although he was a supreme survivor, even he must have realised that the return of the monarchy would mean a restoration of the fortunes of Maesyfelin and Llanfair, who had suffered for their loyalty to the crown. At the very least, his own influence would be diminished; but he must also have feared greater retribution for the relentless manner in which he had sequestered the estates of his fellow gentry in order to ingratiate himself with Cromwell and augment his own wealth. It was natural that he opposed the restoration of Charles II and, when General Monk was actively negotiating for the King's return, Thomas Evans was prepared in April 1660 'to incite men . . . to take arms against him'.[14]

With the return of the King, the fortunes of Sir Francis Lloyd of Maesyfelin flourished and his influence at court was restored. Sir Walter Lloyd preferred to spend his remaining years cloistered at Llanfair, not seeking to establish himself under the new regime. Of Thomas Evans little is heard, but it does not appear that he suffered unduly for his work on behalf of Cromwell. One cynical contemporary bitterly remarked of him soon after the Restoration: 'He has the luck to continue Justice of Peace and Commissioner for the Assessment in the two counties at this day'. It appears that once again he had managed to reach an accommodation with the new order, and that, chameleon like, he was prepared to change his colours to accord with the new political situation.

By fair means or foul, Thomas Evans had hoisted the Peterwell family from the comparative obscurity of Llechwedd Deri to a new prominence within Cardiganshire. We do not know the exact date of his death, but it must have occurred prior to 1670 because the Hearth Tax returns for that year refer to Elizabeth Evans of Peterwell as a 'widow'. During the reign of Charles II, Parliament imposed a tax of sixty pence on every hearth and the returns give an indication of the size of the various dwellings. Peterwell was assessed for seven hearths; Maesyfelin had eleven hearths, whereas Llanfair had thirteen.[15] Enshrouded as it was by mists from the Teifi each night, Peterwell would have had need of its seven hearths but, in the years to come, it was destined to have many more.

If towards the end of his earthly existence Thomas Evans had the time to reflect upon the landscape of his life, he must have felt well satisfied with his achievements. All around him, belonging to Peterwell were fecund acres cloaked in thick green rolling gently to the Teifi; but far beyond extended huge tracts of territories, estates, mills, and farms which added greatly to the meagre inheritance left by his father. His life had been a time of building and he had been a man of action; ever on the rampage, he had ridden abroad first for the King, then for Cromwell, but above all for himself.

NOTES

[1] W. J. Lewis, 'Some Freeholders . . .', *Ceredigion,* Vol. 3, p. 32.
[2] *Cal. Advance of Money,* 1642-56, Pt. 2, p. 894.
[3] ibid.
[4] *Arch. Camb.,* 1887, p. 127.
[5] *T.C.A.S.,* Vol. 6., p. 40.
[6] *Cal. State Papers,* Domestic. Pt. 2, p. 894.
[7] *Cambrian Register,* p. 166.
[8] *Y Cymmrodor,* Vol. 15, p. 4.
[9] *Cambrian Register,* p. 166.
[10] *Cal. State Papers,* Pt. I, p. 107.
[11] ibid.
[12] Isaac, *Hanes Llanbedr,* p. 99.
[13] *J.H.C.,* Vol. 7, p. 350.
[14] E. D. Jones, *N.L.W.J.,* Vol. 2, p. 144.
[15] P.R.O. Hearth Tax, 179, 219/94.

Chapter Three

'YE GREAT FABRIC AT PETERWELL'

Thomas Evans had married Elizabeth the daughter of Ieuan Gwyn Fychan of Moelifor, Llanrhystud, in the county of Cardigan. Three sons had been born to them; David, Erasmus and Daniel. David Evans, as we have seen, was captain of a body of infantry and had served alongside his father in the Civil War; he was, however, to die young. Erasmus, the second son, attended Jesus College, Oxford, and subsequently entered the Church. He was Vicar of Lampeter in 1662 and later became Rector of Burton in Pembrokeshire. He also died at a comparatively early age in 1670. The estate, therefore, fell to the youngest son Daniel, who had married Mary the only daughter of Morgan Herbert of Hafod Uchtryd.

Daniel Evans was educated in a manner deemed appropriate for the scions of the minor gentry at this time. He entered Jesus College, Oxford on 1 April 1664, aged seventeen and graduated in 1669. It was also customary for the sons of the gentry to receive a legal training, and 'Daniel Evans of Lampeter, Gentleman',[1] enrolled at Gray's Inn in 1671 before returning to Cardiganshire to pursue a career in law.

He proved a worthy successor to his father, for under him the upward trend in the fortunes of Peterwell continued, but this time without the ruthlessness and chicanery of Thomas Evans. The Restoration of the Monarchy had brought with it a new age; gone was the flux and turmoil of the years of the Civil War: a certain serenity had settled over the land, and Daniel Evans's acumen was a fitting attribute to promote the power of Peterwell. He shrewdly acquired mortgages and negotiated profitable land deals, doing so peaceably and legally. In 1691 he followed in the footsteps of his father and grandfather and became High Sheriff of the county.

Having added acre after acre to his patrimony in many different counties, he now decided that the original house built by his grandfather in the 1640s was no longer adequate for his substantially enriched station in life. A new imposing edifice was needed to symbolise his wealth; public stature was measured not only in acres, of which Peterwell now had a plenitude, but also by a distinctive residence. The old home with only seven hearths had long presented too mean a seat; therefore, in 1695 he embarked upon an undertaking to build what the Golden Grove Book described as 'Ye great fabric of Peterwell'.[2] A new stately mansion appeared, breathtakingly magnificent, adorned by ornamental gardens, small lakes, exotic shrubs and trees, having a dovecote, warrens, coach house and stabling for twenty five horses.

Within a year of transforming his mansion, Daniel Evans's vanity was cut short by fate and he died in 1696, 'before it was finished', at the age of forty nine.[3] At his death, Daniel Evans was described as being 'seized of a great real estate . . . of considerable value',[4] and his daughters were to benefit handsomely from his legacy. His epitaph originally stood in the porch of St Peter's Church, Lampeter, where he was described as:

> Prudent, ingenious, affable and just,
> True to his friend and active to his trust.

Daniel Evans's one regret must have been that he had produced no sons, for with his death the male line of the Evanses of Peterwell came to an end. Six daughters were born of his marriage to Mary, and she was now left to bring up these small girls ranging from Sarah aged one month to Letitia aged ten years, later to be declared a lunatic. Prescient of his impending death, he had drawn up his will a week or so before he died. He left the bulk of his personal estate, goods and chattels to his wife Mary in trust for his daughters. Mary was also to have the house and demesne of Peterwell together with an income of £300; the residue of the estate was to be divided between the daughters as soon as they attained the age of sixteen or on their marriage.[5]

But it was Mary Evans herself who was first to the altar. The huge estate of Peterwell was possibly too much for matriarchal control; her six little daughters were too young to be of any assistance and within a year or so of the death of Daniel Evans she took a second husband, John Lloyd of Llangennech, and four more children were born to her. Peterwell, in the closing years of the seventeenth century was never without the echo of young children in its stately halls.

The dawn of the new century saw the six daughters of Mary and Daniel Evans grow to womanhood, but not without some loss. In 1707 Mary, the second daughter, died, and in 1711 Jane. Ironically, the eldest daughter Letitia, the least able to cope, was to continue to live at the mansion up to the time of Herbert Lloyd. The three remaining daughters all married into prominent families. Sarah married Marmaduke Gwynne of Garth (it was their daughter, Sarah, who later married Charles Wesley); Rebecca married Thomas Popkins of Fforest; and Elizabeth married Walter Lloyd of Foelallt who was a descendant of the prestigious Llanfair Clydogau family. It was with this last union that the future of Peterwell lay.

Daniel Evans had left a vast estate consisting of over one hundred farms, mills, cottages and messuages extending over hundreds of acres in west Wales. In 1724, after some legal wrangling, this great legacy was broken up and divided among his daughters according to the terms of his will, and Peterwell entered, for the first time, a period of dismemberment rather than aggrandisement.[6] Each of his four daughters received lands reputed to be worth thirty thousand pounds apiece. To Walter and Elizabeth Lloyd fell Peterwell, Llechwedd Deri and surrounding possessions including some sixty farms in Lampeter and nearby parishes. Letitia, the lunatic daughter, also received her fair share of her father's legacy which later became known as 'Stâd Madam Let', this being administered, first by her mother and afterwards by other members of her family.

Walter Lloyd, the new lord of Peterwell, proved to be an eminently suitable husband for Elizabeth and an ideal successor to Daniel Evans; he brought to Peterwell's wealth a welcome measure of the nobility and good breeding of the Llanfair family. He was a lawyer by profession, having been called to the Bar in 1711; in addition, he was a political activist who espoused the Whig cause and courted public offices to advance his own ambitions. He served as Mayor of Cardigan in 1710, 1711, 1718 and 1721.[7] In 1715 he acted in the vital role of returning officer in the Cardigan election, and, following the Whig take over on the accession of George I, he was rewarded with the influential office of Attorney General for South Wales in January 1715 at a salary of £300 a year. This was a key post in the administration of Justice in west Wales.

Nine children were born to Walter and Elizabeth Lloyd; the last generation destined to emerge from Peterwell. Of these, the following five survived: John, born 1718; Anne, born 1719; Herbert, born 1720; Elizabeth, born 1721 and Alice, born 1724.[8] All, in one way or another, were to be involved in the final act of the history of the House of Peterwell. Their father, Walter Lloyd, had played an active role in the affairs of the county, doing all he could to promote his own high

Walter Lloyd of Peterwell

political ambition, which was to gain a seat at Westminster. His efforts were rewarded in 1734 when he was returned as the Whig M.P. for the County of Cardigan. It was a significant signpost in the history of the family: at last the wealth of Peterwell had been translated into real political power, and this mansion had now superseded both Llanfair and Maesyfelin to take its place alongside other influential and well established Cardiganshire families such as Gogerddan, Nanteos and Trawsgoed.

In the eighteenth century a seat in Parliament provided the apex of power for a country squire, and it now gave Walter Lloyd a firm foothold in the corridors of influence, providing him with access to the Prime Minister, Sir Robert Walpole and his circle of privilege which was at this time at the very height of its authority and corruption. Lloyd must have felt truly pleased with his achievement as, for the first time ever, the Peterwell coach rolled out of the sylvan avenue bound for London and Parliament. Henceforth, he could play his part in dispensing privileges, controlling church appointments, providing sinecures and, most importantly, appointing members to the Bench; he quickly made his two sons Justices of the Peace at an early age.

But all good things come to an end; by 1741 his seven year tenure of the county seat was over, and he was faced with the hurdle of re-election to Westminster. Having tasted the sweet fruits of power he was most desirous of retaining his seat, but he unexpectedly found himself challenged by a newcomer to the Whig scene in the person of Thomas Johnes of Llanfair. This Thomas Johnes was destined to be closely linked with the history of Peterwell up to the final years. He hailed originally from Penybont, Tregaron, but had inherited Llanfair from his uncle in 1733. He later became Custos Rotulorum for the County of Cardigan and his son, also named Thomas Johnes, was to become famous for his efforts to transform Hafod into a paradise. In 1741 Thomas Johnes of Llanfair was an ambitious and flamboyant young squire looking to augment his station in life by seeking admittance to Westminster. In this, he was aided and abetted by Lord Lisburne of Trawsgoed, who was opposed to Peterwell. Thomas Johnes's challenge to Walter Lloyd was a serious blow to his cause for it split the Whig faction in the county; although Johnes later withdrew from the contest, the damage had already been done. Walter Lloyd was now faced with a challenge from Thomas Powell of Nanteos,

Thomas Johnes of Llanfair and Croft Castle

whose decision to stand as the Tory candidate meant a costly contested general election for both candidates.

The other Whig candidate for the borough seat was Richard Lloyd of Mabws, facing a Tory challenge from Thomas Pryse of Gogerddan supported by the Nanteos family. Eighteenth century elections could be rough and brutal conflicts. Politics were shamelessly corrupt: there was no general franchise or mass electorate: there was no secret ballot, voting took place under the glare of the contestants. The only persons allowed to vote were freemen, forty shilling freeholders and, in the case of borough seats, burgesses. In reality, political power was vested in the rich county families. The 1741 contest between Walter Lloyd of Peterwell and Thomas Powell of Nanteos highlights much of the corruption and sharp practice which characterized Cardiganshire politics in the eighteenth century. Powerful landlords were able to control the supply of voters for the borough seat by creating their own selected burgesses at the Court Leet. They were presented, sworn in, and given a voting ticket costing one pound twelve shillings and six pence in readiness for the coming election.

Walter Lloyd, anxious to promote the Whig cause and prove the political strength of Peterwell, immediately embarked upon a vigorous campaign of burgess making. This took place at the Black Lion Inn at Lampeter, which housed the Court Leet. Many came from outside the county, since non resident burgesses were allowed to vote in the Cardiganshire elections. A significant number of local burgesses were servants from the Peterwell mansion and included the butler, footmen, coachmen, grooms, gardeners, and ploughmen. They were sworn in for the sole purpose of supporting Peterwell and swelling the ranks of the Whigs.

On the Tory side, Walter Lloyd's opponents, Gogerddan and Nanteos campaigned no less vigorously, adopting the same tactics. At one Easter sitting of the Aberystwyth Court Leet in 1740, upwards of one hundred and thirty four burgesses were created by Pryse of Gogerddan.[9] But Walter Lloyd of Peterwell was determined to match their numbers, and Lampeter Court Leet continued to be the hub of frenetic political activity as burgesses were admitted in great numbers up to the first day of polling in 1741. An observer, Lloyd of Ffos, remarked on the second day of the election at Cardigan: 'three hundred people were yesterday sworn in at Lampeter, . . . and they will continue as long as they can get men to swear'.[10]

Black Lion Royal Hotel, Lampeter
(The Court Leet and Parish Vestry met here in the eighteenth century)

Elections were always held at Cardigan where the burgesses were obliged to attend in order to record their votes at the hustings. This 1741 election between Lloyd and Powell proved to be redolent of many of the malpractices which typified electoral contests of the time. The Mayor of Cardigan acted as the returning officer having the power of determining which votes to accept or reject: as such, he was in a prime position to influence the election result. It was, therefore, of vital importance for the candidate to procure the election of a mayor of his own choice. The Mayor of Cardigan in 1741 was Daniel Bowen, a friend and supporter of Walter Lloyd, who now exerted every kind of pressure at the open polling booth on Lloyd's behalf.

As it happened the year 1741 seems to have been a notorious one for malpractice throughout the whole of Wales. In Denbighshire, William Myddelton, the sheriff, acting for his cousin, disallowed as many as five hundred and ninety four votes for Sir Watkin Williams Wynn. At Pembroke, the Owens of Orielton, friends of the Peterwell family, actually had men wielding pitchforks to prevent the opposition approaching the polls. At Cardigan, Daniel Bowen blatantly acted for Walter Lloyd, 'having behaved with the most partial and determined manner, being entirely influenced through the whole course of the poll by the said Mr Lloyd . . . at whose pleasure and desire he openly rejected several electors for Thomas Powell and admitted several others for Mr Lloyd who had no sort of right'.[11]

Despite Bowen's overt collusion with Lloyd, when the final count was taken, it showed that Thomas Powell had obtained a majority of three hundred and fifty two to three hundred and forty two. Walter Lloyd, however, refused to accept the result. Bowen then resorted to the practice of pretending to examine the poll books and, in so doing, struck out twelve votes for Powell and two for Lloyd and secretly returned the latter as officially elected when Thomas Powell and his supporters had retired to a nearby inn.

The result was a bombshell for Powell, but he was not to be so outrageously outwitted by Lloyd. It was common practice in the eighteenth century to petition against unfavourable election results and on 15 December 1741, Powell appealed to the Committee of Elections and Privileges claiming that Daniel Bowen, the Mayor had acted with 'extreme partiality' towards Lloyd causing him to be unfairly elected.[12]

Normally, such a petition, however justified, would have received short shrift during Sir Robert Walpole's ministry but, at last, the reins of power were slipping from his grasp. The shock waves caused by his fall from power vibrated as far as Cardiganshire and, in particular, Peterwell; for Walpole's opponents now took advantage of Thomas Powell's petition to unseat Walter Lloyd. The Committee of Elections and Privileges decided that Lloyd had not been fairly elected and the seat was awarded to Thomas Powell on 22 March 1742.[13]

It was a bitter defeat for Lloyd, all the months of campaigning and heavy expense were negated at one fell blow. He again tried for Parliament when he unsuccessfully contested the Cardigan boroughs by-election on 20 March, 1746, which was won by John Symmons, Llanstinan, for the Tories.

Meanwhile, back at Peterwell, the political defeat of 1742 was to be followed by the death of his wife Elizabeth in February 1743. The following month, Walter Lloyd drew up his will bequeathing the Peterwell estate to his elder son John, and Foelallt with its surroun-

Thomas Powell of Nanteos and Mary his wife

ding lands to Herbert, his second son; the three sisters Anne, Elizabeth and Alice were to receive money. Appended to the will is an interesting codicil which signals later storms; in it, Walter Lloyd set out categorically that if Herbert his son should 'at any time claim any right of property or interest' to which he was not entitled, 'the devise made by me . . . unto my said son Herbert concerning Voelallt shall cease and be utterly frustrated and void'.[14] Clearly, Walter Lloyd was unhappy about the grasping nature of his son Herbert and, as we shall see, his fears were well founded.

Nanteos

NOTES

[1]Foster, Vol. I, p. 468.
[2]D.R.O. Cawdor Mss., Bk. A., p. 28.
[3]ibid.
[4]Pet.Mss. No. II.
[5]P.R.O. Prob. II/435.
[6]Pet. Mss. II.
[7]Meyrick, p. 344.
[8]L.P.R.
[9]Evans, *Aberystwyth . . . Leet.,* p. 145.
[10]N.L.W., 13492, C.
[11]N.L.W., 17080, E., (A.126).
[12]ibid.
[13]*J.H.C.* Vol. 24, p. 144.
[14]Pet. Mss., 26, Box I, No. 5.

Chapter Four

THE YOUNG GENTRY

While Walter Lloyd spent his time struggling to fulfil his social and political ambitions, his two young sons John and Herbert grew up in an atmosphere of privilege and comparative opulence. Their mansion home with its imposing towers and roof garden lay only a few hundred yards from the Teifi; here, shoals of minnows and silver trout darted beneath dipping fronds of willow trees, offering an ideal playground for the young boys. Nearby, were rook haunted woods where they could go hunting and nesting; for a wilder scene they had the vast mountain stretches of Foelallt made more exciting by mysterious grey crags and hare filled bracken, all of which were enough to gild and gladden the childhood of any boy. We know little about these early years, but it is likely that their education was the responsibility of the local parson Erasmus Lewes. He was admirably qualified to instruct them, a poet and scholar of some distinction who had assisted with the compilation of John Rhydderch's English-Welsh Dictionary published in 1725. Lewes himself became very much an established part of the Lampeter scene serving as Vicar from 1695 to 1743.

After early instruction at Peterwell both boys went to Oxford, entering Jesus College, a favourite among the Cardiganshire gentry. This College had significant connections with Cardiganshire, for its second principal, Griffith Lloyd was a member of the Maesyfelin family. On his death, he bequeathed to Jesus College farms in the parishes of Llanddewi and Nantcwnlle which have been sold only recently.[1]

Students usually set out for university at the age of sixteen or seventeen. John Lloyd, as the elder brother, was the first to leave the serenity of Peterwell for the towers and spires of Oxford, setting out in April 1735 at the age of seventeen. Two years later, he was followed by his brother Herbert who entered Jesus College in the spring of 1737 to be educated in the mould of a gentleman of the day. Exactly what that mould offered is questionable. The standard of education at both Oxford and Cambridge universities in the eighteenth century had sunk to an all time low. Instead of enlightenment, the prevailing climate tended to be one of immorality, drunkenness and indolence,

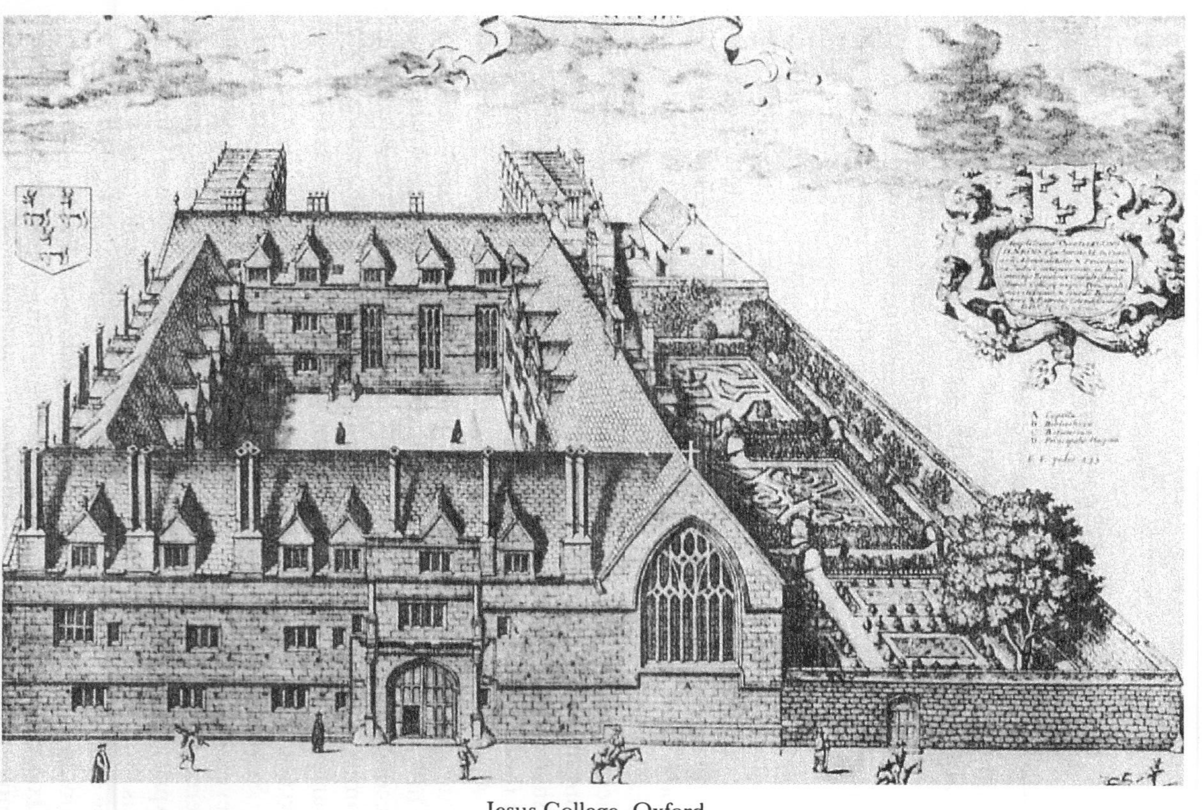

Jesus College, Oxford

with constant diversions such as racing, gambling, cockfighting and prize fighting to take the place of academic study. One contemporary observer noted that Oxford undergraduates were 'courageous fighters and generous spenders'. Jesus College was the 'home of the brutal athlete' and 'housed heroes that vanquished bargemen'.[2] Such a training proved a fitting apprenticeship for Herbert Lloyd's later violent propensities in Cardiganshire. It is likely that the young Herbert Lloyd did not so much sharpen his intellect at Oxford as broaden his experience in the coarser aspects of life; and, after the seclusion of Peterwell, he must have welcomed the opportunity of socializing with the sons of the leading and privileged families of the land.

Howell Harris, the Methodist Revivalist, a few years previously had found Oxford quite intolerable and quit the place after only a very short time on encountering the irregularities and the wickedness which surrounded him. He wrote, 'I soon became weary of the place and cried to God to deliver me from thence'. George Whitefield, his fellow evangelist, expressed a similar sentiment. 'It has', he sighed, 'often grieved my soul to see so many students spending their sustenance on extravagant living'. Whitefield's concern was undoubtedly genuine, for he entered Oxford as an impecunious servitor having to wait upon the likes of Herbert Lloyd. While Whitefield struggled on a small allowance of thirty pounds a year from the magnanimous Sir John Philipps of Picton Castle, Herbert Lloyd, on the other hand, entered Oxford on a ticket of wealth and privilege as a 'Gentleman', with the financial means to indulge in all the readily available pleasures. Lloyd's room as an undergraduate would have been plain and his fare simple, but it is likely that his food was occasionally supplemented by hares, venison and salmon sent up from Wales by carriers, as was the custom of the time.

Whilst many students indulged in dissipation and prodigality at Oxford, there were others who were excessively conscientious. John Wesley, whose brother Charles was soon to marry Sarah, first cousin of Herbert Lloyd, studied hard. But in general, there was little emphasis on academic work and guidance from the top was lacking. Adam Smith, a student at Balliol, complained that, 'Professors have given up altogether the pretence of teaching'. Gibbon declared that, 'Dons have absolved their conscience from the toil of reading, thinking or writing'. One foreign visitor noted that the Bodleian was 'dusty and intolerably noisy'. Such then was the milieu which surrounded Herbert Lloyd as a student but, for a young man such as himself, without academic propensities, Oxford presented an ideal interlude for the drinking of port or claret and absorbing some of the new and urbane habits of high society. The person responsible for his moral wellbeing and his studies was David Price, a Carmarthenshire man who acted as tutor to both Herbert Lloyd and his brother John.[3]

From the evidence of his subsequent correspondence we must conclude that his years at Oxford did not do a great deal for Herbert Lloyd. Throughout his life he showed no love of learning. Whereas his father, his brother and Sir Lucius Christianus Lloyd of Maesyfelin all subscribed towards Theophilus Evans's *Drych y Prif Oesoedd,* the name of Herbert Lloyd was conspicuously absent. His later letters suggest a man uneasy with the quill, whose spidery scrawl is often painful to read, whereas his brother John wrote in a neat civilized hand which is much easier on the eye. Neither John nor Herbert Lloyd took a degree at Oxford, but this was not unusual for the time. John Lloyd on his departure presented Jesus College with gifts of silver. The college has today in its possession a silver tankard and a silver stand containing a set of silver casters and cruets. The cruet exhibits the college arms and the donor's arms, and one dredger has the following inscription: 'Dono dedit Johannes Lloyd, Gualteri Lloyd de Peterwell in Com. Cardigan Armigeri, Filius Natu maximus et huius Collegi Sociommensalis 1738'.[4]

After Oxford, the Lloyd brothers, following the family inclination for the law, went to study at the Inns of Court. Like their father before them both boys entered the Inner Temple. Life at the Inns of Court provided no more of a challenge than had confronted them at Oxford; the same intellectual torpor prevailed. Residence in itself was sufficient to qualify as lawyers without the need to prove any legal competence by serious examination. John and Herbert Lloyd merely kept their terms by dining in hall, at the same time, no doubt, enjoying the excitement and vitality of eighteenth century London life before being called to the Bar.

Thus equipped, the Lloyd brothers returned to Cardiganshire ready to play their part as the sons of Walter Lloyd whose social, legal and political prominence ensured that they had an advantageous start in life. Almost immediately, in 1740, they were elevated to that enviable position of authority, Justice of the Peace. Such an office in the eighteenth century carried considerable power. Justices were drawn almost exclusively from the gentry; an Act of 1731 had raised the property qualification for the Bench from an estate of twenty pounds to one hundred pounds. This ensured that no poor ordinary tenant farmer became eligible for the office. Promotion to the Bench was considered a natural step for the sons of the gentry and, in an age when the power of central government was still undeveloped, it meant that John and Herbert Lloyd could become virtual local despots enjoying absolute power. This is exactly what Herbert Lloyd was to seek; we shall later see how he grossly abused his privilege, bringing upon his head the odium of many in the county by his overbearing behaviour and savage treatment of others.

To John and Herbert Lloyd, along with the other J.P.s, fell the task of dispensing justice in the county. Their power was such that they could inflict summary fines, transport poachers or arsonists, and order offenders to be whipped or placed in the stocks for such minor offences as vagrancy, swearing or drunkenness. The magistrates meted out their justice at various venues; sometimes Peterwell was used, but more often they sat in alehouses at Tregaron or Lampeter issuing their admonitions and fines. Their real authority lay in the Quarter Sessions which met four times a year in each county; here, they were also responsible for the maintenance of bridges and roads, the administration of Houses of Correction, the licensing of ale houses and drovers, and the control of wages, prices and many other aspects of eighteenth century life.

The Peterwell brothers welcomed this power vested in them and enjoyed the influence that went with sitting on the Bench; but, having tasted the fruits of cosmopolitan life at Oxford and London, the remote Cardiganshire mansions and the simple pleasures of mid-eighteenth century life in Lampeter must have seemed dull and unexciting to the young and by now sophisticated gentlemen. There was some compensation in the fact that they had as their companion the up and coming Thomas Johnes of Llanfair Clydogau. He was regarded as a fashionable courtier and something of a playboy in his early years. Gambling and drinking were the primary pleasures of the leisured class, and the Lloyd brothers were able to indulge themselves to the full at Thomas Johnes's country house at Llanfair. Such was its reputation as a gaming venue, that it drew to this sequestered corner of Cardiganshire some of the leading personalities of the London social and gambling scene. No less a person than Henry Fox, the notable politician who later became leader of the House of Commons and Paymaster General of the Forces, and was alleged to have been a defrauder of public millions, endured the long bone-shaking journey to Llanfair just to gamble at Thomas Johnes's tables. Another famous politician of equally dubious character who presented himself at Llanfair was Richard Rigby, M.P.; he later became House of Commons spokesman for the Duke of Bedford's party. But among the most distinguished visitors to Llanfair was Sir Charles Hanbury Williams, M.P., a notable literateur and a famous diplomat. To have attracted such an impressive guest list was a significant social achievement for Thomas Johnes, but not without gain did they endure the jolts and hazards of that endless journey from London all the way to Llanfair. The wily London gentlemen profited enormously from their visits; Thomas Johnes and John and Herbert Lloyd were no match for these seasoned gamblers and consequently lost thousands of pounds. 'The country gentlemen', wrote one historian, 'were much cut up'.[5]

It is probable that Thomas Johnes and the Lloyd brothers made their acquaintance with Sir Charles Hanbury Williams at Bath in the early 1740s. In a letter to Henry Fox dated 17 June 1742, Hanbury Williams stated that he had met a 'young man certain to come in for Cardiganshire'.[6] This refers to Thomas Johnes and his recent challenge to Walter Lloyd for the county seat. In addition, the game-books at Coldbrooke, Monmouthshire, the home of Hanbury Williams, record that he and Henry Fox shot grouse on the 'moors of Cardiganshire'.[7] Evidently, it was not only the clatter of dice and the twist of cards that lured these men to the 'hospitable seat' at Llanfair; the surrounding hills, harbouring an abundance of game, also provided a healthy and bracing attraction after long enervating nights spent at the gaming tables.

Gambling for the young gentry was not the only activity; they indulged themselves in any pleasure they wished and they considered that their exalted station in life gave them a prescriptive right to pursue whatever whim or fancy they chose. Wenching was common, and the Llanwennog Register contains this record of the birth of an illegitimate daughter to Herbert Lloyd: '5 March 1742 Anne a bastard child of Herbert Lloyd and Mary Evan Hugh was privately half baptised'.[8] This was an expression for a baptism that took place when a child was in danger of dying before a priest could arrive. Infant mortality was so prevalent in the eighteenth century that it was often a race against time. It was recognised in an emergency that laymen could baptise, and midwives were enjoined by the Bishop in no wise to neglect baptism if the child was sickly. Even George III's condition as an infant had precipitated the same emergency baptism: an entry in Lord Egmont's diary for 4 June reads, 'The Princess of Wales was brought to bed of a boy, which the same night received private baptism—there being a doubt if he would live'. As it turned out the royal infant not only survived, but suffered his hand to be kissed on at least three occasions by Herbert Lloyd in the 1760s.

In the eighteenth century marriage was one way of securing wealth, and financial reward took precedence over emotional attachment. The young Lampeter gentry sought profitable marriages. Sir Lucius Christianus Lloyd, the young owner of Maesyfelin, married Anne, the widowed sister of John and Herbert Lloyd of Peterwell. The other squires were to go further afield in their choice of wives, marrying heiresses from English families who brought with them substantial dowries. Thomas Johnes more than made up for his gambling losses by marrying Elizabeth Knight, the only child and heiress of the wealthy ironmaster Richard Knight of Croft Castle in Herefordshire. She brought a dowry of seventy thousand pounds and Thomas Johnes was soon to bid farewell to the wild and barren climes of Llanfair Clydogau to reside at Croft Castle, situated among the more fecund acres of Herefordshire. But he never severed his Cardiganshire connections; he always retained the Llanfair and Hafod Uchtryd estates and continued to play a prominent role in the affairs of the county. To his great personal satisfaction, he was appointed Custos Rotulorum of the county in 1741. This was a prestigious position which mainly involved nominating the Clerk of the Peace, keeping the king informed on the views of the gentlemen of the county, determining the composition of the Courts of Justice and issuing peremptory orders to Justices in times of national emergency. This office furnished Thomas Johnes with a distinctive status in Cardiganshire and for the rest of his life he became known as 'Thomas Johnes the Custos'.

Herbert Lloyd, the youngest of the squires, married at the early age of twenty two in 1742. He chose an English heiress, Elizabeth Bragge of Essex, and like all good eighteenth century brides she brought with her a dowry reputed to be fifteen thousand pounds. After their

Croft Castle

marriage she accompanied Herbert Lloyd to Foelallt, where they made their home. What her reactions must have been to this beautiful but rugged and distant seat in deepest Cardiganshire, we shall never know. She did not even live to see the first spring sweep across the hills, for she died in March 1743. It was the all too common story of a young bride dying in childbirth; the sadness of the occasion is poignantly noted in Lampeter Church Register: 'Buried March the 30. Elizabeth the wife of Mr Herbert Lloyd of Peterwell', and is added to by the fact that their baby daughter, Elizabeth, had been buried five days previously.

Herbert Lloyd was to remarry within two years. This time he went only a dozen miles or so north of Foelallt to Strata Florida and chose Anne Stedman, the daughter of William Powell of Nanteos and the widow of Richard Stedman of Great Abbey. It was a remarkable and perplexing match. She was eighteen years his senior but, most crucial of all, no material gain accrued to Herbert Lloyd from this marriage. After Richard Stedman's death the whole of the Stedman estate passed to Anne's brother, Thomas Powell, Nanteos, who was the principal mortgagor and executor of the will.[9]

Meanwhile, at Peterwell, the old order was changing. Walter Lloyd died in 1747 and was buried alongside his wife Elizabeth in the family vault of her ancestors at St Peter's Church. John Lloyd, as the eldest son inherited Peterwell; he also succeeded his father as Attorney General for the counties of Carmarthen, Cardigan and Pembroke. Like his father, he was ambitious and he determined to reassert the prestige of the family by attempting to regain the county seat for Peterwell. Thomas Johnes the Custos had also entertained the idea of the county seat for himself; supported by Lord Lisburne, he again came forward, as he had previously done against Walter Lloyd. Once again, he decided to withdraw from the contest, resigning the seat to John Lloyd by a 'private pact'. The field was now wide open for Peterwell. Thomas Powell, Nanteos, who had successfully wrested the seat from Walter Lloyd by means of petition in 1742, was no longer interested in the county seat; he had decided to switch his candidature to the boroughs seat. The other big potential threat, Gogerddan, no longer had a candidate to field, for Thomas Pryse of Gogerddan had died on 21 May 1745, leaving only a seven year old minor, John Pugh Pryse. He would later grow up to play a prominent part in Cardiganshire politics, but for the time being Gogerddan

Foelallt, Llanddewibrefi

could only exercise its political power by supporting other selected candidates. Fortunately for John Lloyd, the powerful Gogerddan trustees, Sir John Philipps, Sir Watkin Williams Wynn and the Reverend John Lloyd of Rug all decided to support the claim of John Lloyd of Peterwell 'for the interest and quiet of the county'.[10] As a result of this compromise, Peterwell gained the county seat for the Whigs, and Thomas Powell gained the boroughs seat for the Tories; both parties being spared the crippling cost of a contested election.

John Lloyd of Peterwell

Peterwell's political star was once again in the ascendancy and a triumphant John Lloyd showed his pleasure at being elected by contributing twenty five pounds towards the cost of restoring Cardigan Church tower. Of the young gentry, he alone had remained unmarried. He was perhaps the most eligible, being handsome, successful and rich. Attendance at Westminster now brought him into contact with influential persons at court; there he met his future wife, Elizabeth le Heup. She was a lady in waiting to the Queen and the daughter of Isaac le Heup M.P. of Gunthorpe Manor, Norfolk. They were married on 24 March 1750, and George II blessed them with a pair of gold wine coolers as a wedding gift.

It was an auspicious union, and in the spring of 1750 John Lloyd brought to Peterwell his young and well connected bride armed with a very welcome dowry of eighty thousand pounds. As his wife, she became Lady of the Manor of Lampeter and St Peter's Church still

Communion Vessels
(The gift of Elizabeth Lloyd of Peterwell to St Peter's Church in 1751)

bears testimony to her generosity. In 1751 she donated a magnificent silver chalice and communion plate which are still in use at the Church. It was also rumoured that George II intended to elevate John Lloyd to the peerage and he had apparently already chosen a title, Lord of Brynhywel, which was the name of the ancient seat of the Lords of Lampeter. Thus, exactly half way through the century, the Peterwell family, replete with political power, wealth and social prestige, seemed to be in an unassailable position. And John Lloyd appeared to have all that man desired.

NOTES

[1] Jesus College Archives.
[2] Godley, p. 40.
[3] Jesus College Archives.
[4] ibid.
[5] *Arch. Camb.,* 1861, p. 157-8.
[6] Ilchester and Brooke, pp. 49, 58-9.
[7] ibid.
[8] N.L.W. 149, 29, E.
[9] Stedman Thomas Ms. 7290, Nanteos Mss. Will of Richard Stedman.
[10] Gog. Mss., Rev. J. Lloyd to Thos. Lloyd, 20 June 1747.

Chapter Five

THE METHODIST CONNECTION

Politics were the key to worldly success, but amid all the ferment of political intrigue and pursuit of prestige, the Peterwell family also involved itself with another dimension, that of religion. The Methodist Revival was at this time sweeping across Wales taking Cardiganshire by storm and, contrary to expectations, Herbert Lloyd became closely associated with its most powerful leader, Howel Harris. It seems an unlikely relationship, but the evidence in the diaries and letters of Howel Harris clearly shows that for a few years Herbert Lloyd fell under the influence of the Revival. We shall never really know what prompted him to seek the hand of the spiritual Anne Stedman in marriage, but a possible explanation could be his fleeting interest in religion at this time. His character was fissured with inconsistencies; he was to swing violently from one extreme to another but during the early 1740s he was strangely fired by the fervour of Harris and the other evangelists.

In 1742 John and Herbert Lloyd of Peterwell had been appointed Church Wardens, but it was to a Church which fell far short of the needs of the people. Even in 1626, Sir Marmaduke Lloyd of Maesyfelin had ruefully remarked to Vicar Prichard of Llandovery that the 'light of the gospel is grown dim'.[1] A century or so later, while Herbert Lloyd was a young man in his twenties, the light was to shine again with a new lustre, fanned by the great preachers of the Methodist Revival which transformed Welsh religious attitudes and ultimately moulded the mores of modern Welsh society.

Reform was long overdue; the Church had wallowed in a state of spiritual torpor for many decades. Lampeter was fortunate in having a man of the calibre of Erasmus Lewes as its vicar, for a previous incumbent, Rees Meredith, had been 'ejected for drunkenness and selling ale at the Church gate'.[2] Generally speaking, the clergy were desperately poor; Lewis Morris recorded that the Cardiganshire clergy were 'ignorant wretches . . . of despicable appearance'. Many were inadequate and, in 1739, Howel Harris complained that 'ministers were oft so drunk as not to be able to marry or bury';[3] clerics were described as being 'most conspicuous in a cockpit or an ale house'.

Much of the blame lay with the Church hierarchy; appointments were often redolent of corruption and alien absentee English bishops drained away Church revenues without scruple. Many Church buildings had crumbled into decay, 'which if not converted into barns or stables', served 'only . . . for solitary habitations of owls or jackdaws'.[4] Lampeter Church itself needed structural attention, 'cows roamed in and out' of her sister Church at Betws Bledrws, and Llanddewibrefi Church was described as 'ruinous'.[5] Services were irregular, and in some places had been totally abandoned: such was the climate of religion prevailing during Herbert Lloyd's youth. It was one of extreme apathy, a failure to meet the needs of the ordinary people.

These needs were to be met by the Methodist Revival, which in the 1740s had reached a high tide in Cardiganshire with its leaders proclaiming a message of salvation for all, bringing new hope and solace to the labouring poor, the neglected and the underprivileged. This form of evangelism with its 'enthusiasm' and its levelling tendencies was generally treated with hostility by the landed gentry, yet the Peterwell and Maesyfelin families chose to sympathise with rather than oppose the cause of Methodism. But the greatest paradox of all was Herbert Loyd's involvement, for it is difficult to conceive of him being caught up in this great purging wave which swept away so many worldly pleasures, for its adherents frowned upon such amusements as cockfighting, fairs, wakes, interludes and many other recreational activities of the eighteenth century.

Various factors may have accounted for Lloyd's attraction to this religious awakening. Living at Foelallt, near Llanddewibrefi, he was very close to the epicentre of the movement, for Methodism made a deep and very powerful impact upon this part of the county. It was at Llanddewi Church that Daniel Rowland, the curate of Llangeitho, was, at the age of twenty three, converted by Griffith Jones. The seed fell on fertile ground; Daniel Rowland with thundering sermons was to shake the Welsh out of their spiritual apathy. Vast crowds gravitated to Llangeitho and Llanddewi, drawn by the eloquence of Rowland. George Whitefield was amazed by the scenes in this part of Wales; 'I have seen', he said, 'at seven in the morning some ten thousand people breaking forth into the most ecstatic strains in the middle of a sermon, shouting "glory" and "hallelujah" and jumping with lively joy under the divine power'.[6] Llanddewi Church, because

Howel Harris

it was larger in size than Llangeitho Church, became the venue for huge congregations and Daniel Rowland was described as having 'about two thousand communicants there'. Foelallt was almost within shouting distance of Llanddewi, and any religious propensities which might have been within the personality of the young Herbert Lloyd would certainly have been well nurtured in this place at this time. These preachers were nothing if not audible; Howel Harris claimed that he had 'uncommon power to make an outcry like a gale'; it is small wonder that he suffered from a perpetual hoarseness in his voice. In short, the whole locality surrounding Herbert Lloyd's home throbbed with the intensity of this new enthusiasm, whipped up by the itinerant preachers who, even when the Churches were closed to them, fearlessly proclaimed their message to mighty hillside congregations.

One of the most dynamic of these preachers was Howel Harris who campaigned in Cardiganshire on no less than forty seven occasions and who was to stay at Foelallt a number of times. As far as we know his first visit there occurred on 9 February 1739. The hospitality afforded by Herbert Lloyd in cold mid February amid the bleak Llanddewi hills would have been more than welcomed by Harris. The surrounding habitations were little more than dark and airless cottages providing the meanest form of shelter. At Foelallt, Howel Harris engaged the young Herbert Lloyd in intense religious discussion; the inveterate campaigner for Christ was always looking for converts, and here was the rare chance of reaching a young member of the gentry. From his diary we learn that Harris 'had last night, great liberty and freedom with God for the young counsellor [Herbert Lloyd] . . . and had instantaneous love and pity and bowels of affection given me to him so that I felt my soul hanging on his Soul'.[7] These are stirring words even for Howel Harris, especially when we remember that Herbert Lloyd was at this time at the impressionable age of nineteen.

This spiritual evening at Foelallt must have been particularly appreciated by Harris, because we learn from his diary that he had previously had a difficult time with his persecutors and prayed 'with God that he would chain those dogs his enemies'.[8] His was a tortuous path, and he was often cruelly beaten and once left for dead. Yet he wrote, 'I'll preach Christ till to pieces I fall'. At Carmarthen a man drew his sword to kill him; at Bala the local vicar provided the mob with a barrel of beer to incite the people against him, but his reaction to all this was, 'I am no more concerned to hear their threats than a fly'. No amount of physical brutality inflicted on his person deflected him from his calling and he warned the other evangelists, Daniel Rowland and William Williams, that 'Satan's teeth water for you'. Therefore, the night of 9 February, spent in the warmth and comfort of Foelallt in the company of a young person prepared to listen must have been, to quote Harris's own words, 'walking in the suburbs of heaven'. 'I am', he wrote, 'grieved every moment I am not preaching Christ'.

At Foelallt the seed fell on shallow ground, but it took root briefly. Tradition has it that, soon after this, Herbert Lloyd invited George Whitefield to Lampeter where he preached to a large congregation in the street on a Sunday afternoon.[9] Another source claims that it was Walter Lloyd who asked Whitefield to campaign at Lampeter and that he came, accompanied by Handel; and after a religious service they all rode to Llangeitho to hear the celebrated Daniel Rowland preach.[10] On 8 January 1739, Harris had informed Whitefield, 'There is a great revival in Cardiganshire through Mr D. Rowlands a Church minister'. Having visited Wales, Whitefield formed a favourable opinion of the Welsh for, on 5 April 1739, he wrote in his *Journals*: 'I could spend many months in Wales. The longer I am in it, the more

I like it. To me they seem a people sweetly disposed to receive the Gospel'.[11]

Many of the Welsh did indeed receive the gospel and Howel Harris soon became a familiar figure in Cardiganshire, riding indefatigably from one village to another, sometimes half dead with fatigue but never too exhausted to exploit any opportunity of spreading the message. Herbert Lloyd had become one of his committed supporters, which must have been a source of deep gratification to Harris. On 12 January 1742, Harris set out from Llangeitho to Lampeter where he was met by Herbert Lloyd who rode out part of the way to welcome him. This reception must have heartened Harris, for on this occasion, amidst his many other afflictions, he was troubled by two throbbing thumbs. An entry in his diary two days previously reads: 'In going to Church at Llangeitho . . . in cutting some Spanish liquorice, I did cut

Daniel Rowland, Llangeitho

both my thumbs so that I fainted and swooned and did not recover to past 11. O, the pain was sore'.[12] The next entry reads: 'Came to Lampeter past 10, there met by Mr Herbert Lloyd of Peterwell coming to meet me'.[13]

Once arrived in the town, Harris embarked on one of his marathon sermons which he described in his diary as: 'Another trial, great power in discoursing [preaching]. Luke 9, 10 to 11'.[14] The people of Lampeter listening to him would have been subjected to a sermon lasting a few hours; some meetings were known to have gone on for six hours. Harris had the power to transfix his congregations; he often spoke about hell as though he himself had been there, so that his listeners cried out for mercy while he preached. Herbert Lloyd evidently responded to Harris on this day, for the diary confirms: 'Some conference with him [Herbert Lloyd]—parted with the gentleman'.[15]

Also present at this meeting held at Lampeter was Daniel Rowland. We learn that Harris discussed with him the political crisis which was brewing in Walpole's cabinet, and they were clearly anxious lest changes in the government might adversely affect their campaign: 'Was with Brother Rowlands conversing', wrote Harris, '. . . hearing that persecution is like to come on the Tories gaining ground'.[16] The following day Harris again preached at Lampeter, and once again Herbert Lloyd was among those who attended this meeting: '13 January . . . discoursed to above 1,000 . . . there being many young ladies and Mr Lloyd, to past 12 with them'.[17]

Herbert Lloyd was not the only member of the Peterwell family interested in Methodism: Marmaduke Gwynne, who had married Sarah Evans of Peterwell, was also firmly committed to supporting Harris. He acted as an intermediary between Harris and Lloyd on at least one occasion. Initially, Marmaduke Gwynne had been hostile to the Methodists and had stood with the Riot Act in his pocket near Llanwrtyd Church determined to arrest Harris, 'not doubting that he was a madman'.[18] But so impressive was Harris that one 'who came to scoff remained to pray'; at the close, he grasped Howel Harris's hand, besought his pardon and took him home to Garth. Thereafter, began a friendship which was to last a lifetime. An even closer link was forged between the Peterwell family and the leaders of Methodism when Sarah, the daughter of Marmaduke Gwynne and Sarah Evans of Peterwell, married Charles Wesley on 7 April 1749 at Garth. Also prominent among the South Wales Methodists was Thomas Popkins of Fforest who had married Rebecca Evans of Peterwell.

This interest and support was in marked contrast to the behaviour of most of the other gentry towards the early Methodists. Although George Whitefield had waxed in dulcet tones regarding the Welsh, remarking that they were 'sweetly disposed' and 'thought nothing of walking twenty miles to hear a sermon',[19] the Cardiganshire gentry often treated these itinerant preachers in a callous fashion. Howel Harris frequently found himself running the gauntlet as he travelled between villages of the county. On 2 March 1739, after rejoicing in a 'good day at Tregaron', he was 'surprised by a sudden news that there was an attachment to take [him] immediately to prison, at the instigation of one of the gentry'.[20] In 1740, Harris went so far as to say: 'The Gentlemen hunt us like partridges, but the work must go on'.[21] He firmly believed that he had been divinely called, saying, 'I was given a commission to rend and break sinners . . . I thundered greatly denouncing the gentry, carnal clergy and everybody . . . God opened my mouth filling it with terrors and threatenings'. His friend and fellow evangelist William Seward was brutally stoned to death at Hay, and they all preached under this constant shadow of danger. 'I am put in court for discoursing at an ale house', wrote Daniel Rowland to Howel Harris in 1742, 'Bro. Williams [Pantycelyn] is put in too, I trust we shall have him out before long'.[22] A year later, the tiny village of Tresaith on the Cardiganshire coast witnessed a savage attack on Rowland and Williams, when 'ruffians with guns and staves beat them unmercifully, set on them by a gentleman of the neighbourhood; Rowland had a wound in his head'.[23]

In the same year, 1743, the Peterwell family not only abstained from harrassing the Methodists but acted positively on their behalf, becoming involved in the defence of a prominent Cardiganshire Methodist Counsellor named Morgan Hughes, who was set upon and badly beaten near Ffair Rhos by a mob incited by Richard Stedman,[24] whose widow Herbert Lloyd married. On 8 March 1743, Stedman arrested Morgan Hughes on a trumped up charge of being 'a vagrant and a wanderer and of keeping an unlawful assembly'.[25] This was a serious blow to the cause of Methodism in Cardiganshire, and it so alarmed Howel Harris that he immediately visited Hughes in Cardigan gaol. The following day, 9 March, he wrote to Daniel Rowland stating: 'It is a case I must make my own. If he is stopped, all our liberty will be taken from us alike'.[26] Harris tried in vain to get legal representation for Hughes; he even attempted to seek help from prominent members of the gentry 'sitting in a Cardigan Coffee House' on 10 March, but none of them wished to become involved in so controversial a case.

Harris, desperate for help, then turned to Herbert Lloyd's uncle, Marmaduke Gwynne of Garth. In a plea to Gwynne he asked, 'I know it shall be a matter of prayer with you and you'll give directions what is right to do'.[27] Marmaduke Gwynne, loyal as ever to Harris, responded by contacting his nephew John Lloyd of Peterwell who was to act as foreman of the jury in the trial of Hughes at Cardigan. Harris recorded the events in his diary: '31 March 1743. I went past 10 to Court and stayed there to past 1 . . . I had great respect shown me all arising from Mr Ll . . . [of Peterwell]. Instrumentally, he himself being foreman stopped their proceedings'.[28] It was a triumph for Harris; this intervention on the part of John Lloyd led to the case against Morgan Hughes being quashed. He was freed, much to the chagrin of Stedman, who now feared an action against him for false imprisonment, which Hughes had threatened on the advice of Gwynne. However, matters were peaceably settled, in Howel Harris's own words, 'To show him the Christian spirit', and proceedings against Stedman were dropped provided he paid all the expenses. This incident shows the willingness of the Peterwell family to intercede on behalf of the Methodists, who were afterwards enabled to worship freely in Cardiganshire.

Meanwhile, Herbert Lloyd was evidently in the thoughts of Howel Harris, for in July 1742 he wrote him a long letter containing a sermon which he had preached in the presence of the king. Harris often preached to the ruling class: Frederick, the Prince of Wales, held him in high regard. What was good enough for the king was good enough for Herbert Lloyd; thus, a long letter crammed with moral precepts penned in Harris's small, almost illegible writing was sent to Foelallt. From it, we learn that Marmaduke Gwynne had encouraged Harris to write to Lloyd: 'Hearing you would not have taken it unkind to have a line from me', wrote Harris, 'I intended much sooner—but had no direction till I met your dear and worthy uncle Mr Gwynne'. Harris then launched into an impassioned appeal urging Lloyd to lead a good and virtuous life. 'I hope this shall find you seeking for the pearl of great price, the Lord Jesus, who is a friend worth while to leave all to follow', implored Harris. 'Those, and only those, are truly happy . . . who are made willing by the spirit of God to renounce the pleasures and vanities of this world'. Such lines are distinctly ironic when considered in the light of Herbert Lloyd's later obsession for worldly goods. But Harris was not to know what the future held; he had high hopes for Herbert Lloyd, concluding on the note: 'Till we seek him, we shall not find him, this is a hard saying, but I trust Sir he gives you a heart to receive it . . . Most affectionately in all, Howel Harris'.[29]

Herbert Lloyd had recently married his first wife Elizabeth Bragge, but the following year his faith was to be tested when both his wife and his infant daughter died. However, his association with Harris seems to have strengthened. By 1744 his personal committment was such that Harris was now convinced that Lloyd had undergone a genuine conversion to the faith. On 19 February 1744 an exultant Howel Harris wrote to James Erskine, a Scottish M.P. and a prominent Methodist, conveying the glad tidings regarding Herbert Lloyd: 'Some few months ago, a young counsellor, a late Member of Parliament's son—was, I trust effectually awakened—I have discoursed at his house—which is now open to all that preach our dear Lord Jesus—and I think I had never more signs of the divine presence than there—he seems to have the usual good tokens of a real work. Time will confirm'.[30] Time, in fact, was to confirm the exact opposite.

During these years the Methodist Revival continued to grow apace. Harris diligently trekked the Lampeter-Llanddewi circuit and his congregations overflowed across meadows and hills. On 13 August 1744, we find him at Cwmann near Lampeter, where he stood preaching 'on block to a great crowd—there being many ladies and Sir Lucius too'.[31] Evidently, Sir Lucius Lloyd of Maesyfelin regarded Howel Harris as being sufficiently interesting to attend his meetings, for his name crops up frequently in the diaries. Lampeter Church, like many of the other established Churches in Wales, had closed its door to Harris, who recorded in his diary: 'Saw I was not wanted there in the Church'.[32] The Vicar of Lampeter was not a Methodist sympathiser, and in any case Harris was not allowed to minister within a church since he had twice been refused ordination. His bitterness showed: 'Many who wear the cloth . . .', he expostulated, '. . . what good they do I know not . . . I am called a madman . . . they are more contemptible than ordinary businessmen . . . I despise these niggardly professors'.

While Harris's zeal continued unabated, doubts began to creep in concerning the position of his convert Herbert Lloyd. The diary for 8 February 1745 reveals that Harris feared that Lloyd appeared to be drifting: 'Glyncorrwg. I met here Mr Herbert Lloyd, the young counsellor lately converted', wrote Harris, 'yet had been under convictions and got loose'.[33] But on this occasion Daniel Rowland came to the rescue and prevailed upon Lloyd to return to the fold; in the same entry Harris recorded that Herbert Lloyd was, 'now I trust, touched effectually through means of Brother Rowlands'. Harris breathed a sigh of relief and the whole incident seems to have drawn them together once again. The power of Harris over the other two is apparent when we read his entry: 'My heart was broken in hearing Brother Rowlands and Mr Lloyd saying how much good I had instrumentally done'. The reconciliation was further cemented by Harris's return to Foelallt to stay the night. There, Lloyd and Harris resumed their custom of fellowship and prayer to be followed by a sermon from Daniel Rowland: 'Foelallt, in Llanddewi. Great freedom for the young counsellor', recorded Harris, 'To Llangeitho Church to hear Brother Rowlands', and his diary reveals that he was even persuaded to remain a second night.[34]

Secure again in the lap of the Methodists, Herbert Lloyd once more allowed Foelallt to be used as an open house for the evangelists, but it had the need of a woman to take charge of its affairs. That woman was destined to be Anne Stedman, the widow of Richard Stedman who now became the second wife of Herbert Lloyd. It was an incredible match; he was twenty five and she was forty three, and it is difficult to understand what impelled a young squire like Herbert Lloyd to ride along the tortuous road skirting the dark and brackish Cors Caron to pay his respects to this pious but matronly widow of Strata Florida.

Anne was reputed to have been a local beauty; she had caught the eye of Edward Richard, the distinguished scholar, poet and school master at that celebrated seat of classical learning, Ystrad Meurig. His admiration of her found expression in one of his pastorals when he describes her radiance making the parish of Llanddewi flower:[35]

> Daw Anna i dywynnu cyn nemawr, cân i mi,
> Di weli blwy Dewi'n blodeuo.

Dame Anne Lloyd, wife of Sir Herbert Lloyd

He speaks of the heart's frequent desire to see her and recalls her virtues of comeliness, purity and generosity.

Er mynych ddymuniad o'r galon ei gweled,
Mor luniaidd, mor laned, a haeled yw hon.

But Edward Richard sang in vain when that most unlikely of suitors Herbert Lloyd appeared on the horizon.

Anne was one of life's unfortunates who was destined to tread a sad and lonely path; even before she met Herbert Lloyd, her life had been tinctured with sorrow. Two daughters had been born to her from Richard Stedman, both of whom had died young. Their loss can still be felt in the little church at Strata Florida. Here, Anne, describing herself as an 'afflicted mother', had a stone monument erected to their memory. One named Averina died at the age of eight months in 1726; the other named Elizabeth, described as 'sensitive and intelligent', died at the age of ten years in 1734. Their names, now dimmed by the years, remain on the wall of Strata Florida Church evoking the sadness of Anne's life; her faith, spanning the centuries, shows her conviction that she would be reunited with them 'through the merits of our Redeemer'.

Possibly, it was this piety that attracted Herbert Lloyd to Anne at this time; his thoughts, coloured by the teachings of Harris, found Anne a fitting wife for the mood of the moment. But knowing Herbert Lloyd, it is also likely that he hoped to come in for a share of the wealth of the Stedmans. Such hopes, if they were ever entertained, were never realized. Anne had been widowed a mere six months but she found Herbert Lloyd a sufficiently attractive proposition and a notice of their intended marriage was recorded by a 'fiat' at Tregaron on 27 December 1745.[36]

On her marriage, Anne left the cloistered surroundings of Strata Florida with its poignant memories to become mistress of Foelallt, which lay in the shadow of the massive crag from whence it took its name. To Llanddewibrefi she brought the light of kindness, showing a sincere concern for the less fortunate persons around her. No stranger to suffering and sorrow, she now made her life worthwhile by practising those Christian precepts which made her much loved by the poor of the parish. At Foelallt was accommodated one of Griffith Jones's Circulating Schools with the local inhabitants being

Memorial to the daughters of Dame Anne Lloyd
(Strata Florida Church)

encouraged to attend. It is significant to note that in 1764 Foelallt had forty eight pupils on its roll, whereas the numbers in the village school of Llanddewi had fallen from one hundred and seven in 1739, to a mere twenty seven in 1764.

Although her philanthropy was much in evidence, her marriage was doomed. Within a short time more sorrow lay in store for her. The very virtues which had attracted her to Herbert Lloyd soon grew stale as he began to tire of his Christian commitment. His character and temperament had never quite fitted him for the role of Methodist convert; Howel Harris had shown unease about his loyalty, and it was only a matter of time before he thrust aside all Harris's pleas and exhortations and went his own way. Towards the end of the decade Harris himself no longer proved an anchorage for him, for he was experiencing his own difficulties. Friction had developed between him and Daniel Rowland, which meant that Harris ceased to visit Cardiganshire for a number of years, and no longer called at Foelallt. Adrift from the radiating zeal and compelling personality of Harris, Lloyd's faith and marriage foundered. What had always been a fragile union, dissolved completely when his enthusiasm for religion waned, for this seems to have been their only common bond.

In 1755, changing fortunes were to place Lampeter under the dominance of Herbert Lloyd, but by then his conduct showed little trace of the influence of Harris. Indeed, the evangelist's early hopes for his 'young counsellor' were to be cruelly dashed in more ways than one. Within a few years, Lloyd had quarrelled with Daniel Rowland. Gone was the fellowship of the 1740s when he and Rowland had been moved to tears by Harris's preaching; he now acted for the opposite camp. The ecclesiastical hierarchy, embarrassed by Rowland's enthusiasm and power to attract vast crowds, had long desired to jettison him from their ranks. One tradition holds that Herbert Lloyd 'was the man who laid a complaint against the celebrated Daniel Rowland before Bishop Squire of St David's. The Bishop was an Englishman who had no sympathy with the Welsh, and he gave a willing ear to Rowland's enemies.[37] Correspondence shows that Herbert Lloyd was on close terms with Bishop Squire, whose support he canvassed in order to influence appointments in Cardiganshire. In 1763 Rowland lost his curacy at Llangeitho and was ejected from the Church.

After something of a lull in the tide of their affairs, the Methodists rode the crest of another wave in Cardiganshire in 1762. This was brought about partly by the publication of Williams Pantycelyn's hymns and Rowland's power of preaching. This second revival centred around Llangeitho and Bishop Squire, irritated by it all, would have particularly welcomed Herbert Lloyd's denouncement to get rid of Rowland at this time. The great preacher survived his ejectment remarkably well. One observer, the Reverend John Lloyd of Alltyrodyn, described to his brother Posthumus the healthy state of Methodism in Cardiganshire: 'Rowland is now turned out of his cures by the Bishop . . . but he had the satisfaction of drawing the crowd after him and of seeing his late churches almost vacant'. In the same letter we get a sharp impression of the *antics* of the Methodists who were reported to have spent 'whole nights singing, capering, bawling, fainting, thumping and a variety of other exercises'.[38]

By now Howel Harris had healed his rift with Rowland; after an absence of some twelve years he once again returned to preach in Cardiganshire. On 5 May 1763 he went to Lledrod where he held a thanksgiving service for the Peace of Paris, which had ended the Seven Years War; the following day he rode to Lampeter where he came face to face with his quondam convert, Herbert Lloyd. But it was a very different Lloyd from the young man he had known at Foelallt. He was now a baronet and a hardened man of the world whose many dark deeds had distanced him irretrievably from Harris. The years between had been a negation of all the evangelist's teaching and Harris's disappointment in his former protege is summed up in his diary entry which reads: '6 May 1763. Cried for Sir Herbert Lloyd who comes to hear me today'.[39] Almost certainly, news of Lloyd's dubious acts, especially his part in the hanging of Sion Philip and the betrayal of Daniel Rowland, would have reached Harris's ears giving good reason for his tears. What is surprising is that Sir Herbert Lloyd bothered to turn out at all to listen to Harris. Could he have been curious to see how time had dealt with his erstwhile mentor, or were there still within him some faint stirrings of that old spiritual hunger?

There is a second reference to Lloyd's name in a further entry in Harris's diary which reads: 'To Lampeter where I discoursed to a vast crowd of several thousands in the street, Sir Herbert Lloyd's wife hearing too; much in English'. Evidently, both husband and wife heard Harris speak on that day: for all three, there must have been

Great Abbey Farm, Strata Florida
(Home of Richard Stedman and Anne)

recollections of happier days. Harris continued to labour sporadically in the vineyard of Cardiganshire, but he never again referred to the name of Herbert Lloyd in his diaries. The following year, on 25 July 1764, John Wesley came to Lampeter,[40] but no mention is made of Herbert Lloyd in his account of the visit. Herbert Lloyd's connection with Methodism had been but a brief flirtation, easily sundered when it no longer benefited his social and political aspirations.

NOTES

[1]*Lloyd Family Records*, p. 28.
[2]Richards, p. 123.
[3]*C.C.H.M.C.*, Vol. 29, p. 97.
[4]Saunders, p. 23.
[5]ibid., pp. 14 and 22.
[6]Inglis-Jones, p. 43.
[7]Trevecka Mss. No. 115B.
[8]ibid.
[9]Hughes, Vol. 2, p. 76.
[10]Worthington, p. 96.
[11]Whitefield *Journals*, p. 245.
[12]*C.C.H.M.C.*, Vol. 30, p. 49.
[13]ibid., p. 51.
[14]ibid.
[15]ibid.
[16]ibid.
[17]ibid.
[18]Jones, *History of Brec.*, unpag.
[19]Whitefield, *Journals*, p. 231.
[20]*C.C.H.M.C.*, Vol. 30, p. 96.
[21]Morgan, *Life and Times*, p. 154.
[22]M. H. Jones, *Trevecka Letters*, p. 78.
[23]op.cit., p. 79.
[24]G. Roberts, 'Methodistiaeth . . .' *Ceredigion*, Vol. 5, p. 5.
[25]ibid.
[26]M. H. Jones, op.cit., p. 73.
[27]*C.C.H.M.C.*, Vol. 55, p. 68.
[28]ibid., Vol. 30, p. 102.
[29]Trevecka Mss., No. 574.
[30]Trevecka Mss., No. 1295.
[31]*C.C.H.M.C.*, Vol. 31, p. 22.
[32]ibid.
[33]ibid.
[34]ibid., p. 24.
[35]Gwenallt Jones, *Blodeugerdd*, p. 32.
[36]*West Wales Hist. Trans.*, Vol. 5, p. 127.
[37]*Pembs. Guardian*, 14 Jan. 1888.
[38]*Lloyd Letters*, 1754-96, p. 52.
[39]*C.C.H.M.C.*, Vol. 32, p. 38.
[40]A. H. Williams, p. 96.

Chapter Six

'A RIOTING JUSTICE'

In his youth Herbert Lloyd had mingled with the titans of the Revival, showing an unexpected interest in Methodism: the Quarter Sessions Records disclose another aspect of his many faceted personality. Instead of a spiritual 'young Counsellor', the picture which emerges is that of a despicable tyrant riding roughshod over the inhabitants of the county. The opportunity for bullying behaviour was there, for J.P.s were vested with a wide authority over the people at large, giving ample scope for unfair pressure or sadistic whims. Herbert Lloyd had so exploited his position, that by 1750 he had become the most unpopular magistrate sitting on the Bench in Cardiganshire. In all four corners of the county people were goaded into protesting against his unreasonable conduct.

It took a lot of provocation to produce objections against a J.P., who represented the forces of law and order. Yet, the Court Records give evidence of several clashes between Herbert Lloyd and others. One such confrontation occurred between Herbert Lloyd and a yeoman farmer named John Lloyd of Llanddewi. This farmer not only had the daring to oppose him, but he was sufficiently intrepid as to threaten violence to his person. It was a brave but futile stance, for Herbert Lloyd had all the protection of his rank and position: the pluck of the unfortunate John Lloyd was rewarded by a spell in Cardigan gaol. He was made to appear before an august assembly of J.P.s at the 'house of Evan Jones of Tregaron' on 18 July 1745. Among those sitting on the Bench at this time were Lord Lisburne, Sir Lucius Christianus Lloyd of Maesyfelin, Thomas Johnes the Custos, and John and Herbert Lloyd of Peterwell. Clearly, the farmer stood no chance and 'It was order'd that . . . John Lloyd of Llanddewi be committed to the custody of the gaoler for uttering several menaces against Herbert Lloyd Esq. . . . and threatening to run him through with a pitchfork'.[1]

Herbert Lloyd's antagonists were obliged to act from an impossible position, yet still they persisted in their protests against him. Sometimes tempers reached flashpoint, as happened to Richard Jones, 'Gent'. On 14 July, at the dwelling house of John Hughes, Innkeeper of Tregaron, Jones was meted the usual punishment of being 'committed to the County Gaol for insulting and abusing Herbert Lloyd Esq. . . . for calling him a scoundrelly dog and making other indecent expressions'.[2]

Hatred of Herbert Lloyd as a Justice became widespread. On 10 January 1747, at the Guild Hall, Aberystwyth, 'John Pugh, gentleman and attorney at law' was fined fifty shillings 'for insolent behaviour . . . in open court . . . to Herbert Lloyd Esq. . . . and stands committed in the custody of the gaoler until such time as he pays his fine'.[3] That so many dared to question his actions, when they could so easily fall victim to his prejudice and revenge, speaks volumes for his conduct.

Not surprisingly, Lloyd's treatment of offenders was merciless. Ann Morgan, a poor vagrant felt the full force of his judgment when on October 1750 she was dragged before the Court for being 'idle and disorderly'. He ordered that she be stripped 'from the waiste upwards and whipped in the open market between the hours of ten in the morning and three in the afternoon in the Town of Lampeter and back again until her body be bloody'.[4] This was normal punishment for such offences in the eighteenth century, but Lloyd's severity as a magistrate is highlighted by the fact that he further ordered that this woman be 'likewise whipped on 15 October in the town of Aberystwyth from the Market House to the bridge and back again and that in the meantime she be kept in the custody of the Gaoler'. Punishment in the eighteenth century was always public and was considered as being part of the normal entertainment of the age. Hangings were a time of boisterous merriment; men went to their deaths in a carnival atmosphere of drinking and merriment. Similarly, at Lampeter and Aberystwyth, jeering crowds would have thronged the whipping route to torment the hapless Ann.

But Herbert Lloyd embraced or discarded the law as it best suited his interests; sometimes he placed himself totally above the law, as in one dramatic incident which became known as the Esgair Mwyn Affair in 1753. The part played by Lloyd at Esgair Mwyn made a nonsense of his standing as a J.P., and ultimately became an event of considerable political significance involving many of the prominent gentry of the county. To understand it fully it is necessary to outline the background of events which led up to the affair. Cardiganshire was a county rich in mineral deposits which had been mined since time immemorial. Originally, the Crown had laid claim to all mining deposits of gold, silver and lead in the county but, over the years, intense rivalry had developed between the Crown and local landowners over these rights. In 1693, Sir Carbery Pryse of Gogerddan obtained an Act of Parliament enabling him to mine the rich silver and lead ore deposits discovered on his land. This opened the way for other prominent families to follow suit, namely, the Powells of Nanteos and the Vaughans of Trawsgoed.[5]

To prevent loss of revenue, the Crown resisted the attempts of these families to exploit mineral finds on their lands. In 1746, Lewis Morris, one of the famous Morris brothers from Anglesey, was appointed Deputy Steward of the Crown Manors in Cardiganshire and took up residence at Galltfadog, some seven miles from Aberystwyth. Morris himself was a notable antiquary and poet, whose prolific correspondence has since proved one of our richest sources of history for that period; but, as the King's representative, he soon became a ready target for the wrath of the gentry intent on pressing their own claims to mines.

Throughout the 1740s chronic hostility and a constant state of tension existed between the landowners and the Crown; by 1751 a crisis was reached with the discovery of rich deposits of ore at Esgair Mwyn, south of Ysbyty Ystwyth. It was a profitable prospect and the gentry looked to increase their fortunes by investing in it, but Lewis Morris kept a tight hold on this mine for the Crown. He had by now been appointed Crown Steward, in which capacity he let this mine for a term of one year from 1 July 1751 to three working miners, Evan Williams, and John and David Morgan. In October 1751 Lewis Morris himself entered into partnership with the lessees in order, as he claimed, 'to secure the mine from several riotous persons who had a view to taking it by force'.[6] It proved a lucrative enterprise, for Morris and his lessees were reputed to have cleared £1,300 each. No wonder the local squires were up in arms!

On 15 July, Lewis Morris had been appointed Agent and Superintendent of the mine to safeguard its interests, but the gentry were not inclined to submit meekly to his authority. Over the next two years relationships between them deteriorated to such an extent that Morris nervously wrote to Thomas Evans, a London attorney, asking 'whether an injunction from any Court of Law can or ought to stop me working these mines for the Crown?'[7] Lewis Morris need not have concerned himself about such legal niceties, for at this juncture

Lewis Morris

Herbert Lloyd dramatically entered the picture. Four days after the letter, on 23 February 1753, he appeared at Esgair Mwyn brandishing a cocked pistol and leading a mob of 'several hundred armed and tumultuous people'.[8] He was accompanied by his brother in law, William Powell, Nanteos, also a magistrate, who had promised Herbert Lloyd payment of one hundred pounds if he would assist him in forcibly ejecting Lewis Morris from Esgair Mwyn and claim possession of the mine for the benefit of Nanteos.

This encounter among the bleak north Cardiganshire hills had all the ingredients of the violence of the Wild West: and it was a bizarre situation which involved two of the leading county magistrates deliberately inciting an armed rabble to swarm up the banks in order to turn out the hapless miners. Being the conscientious officer that he was, Lewis Morris tried to resist this attack by Lloyd, who threatened not only Morris, 'but also the lives of his agents and miners on refusal to deliver up possession of the mine'. Matters quickly came to a climax when Herbert Lloyd 'presented a cocked pistol to the head of Lewis Morris and threatened to shoot him'.[9] Very wisely, Morris submitted, and he was conveyed to Cardigan Gaol by Herbert Lloyd. Here, he was obliged to sweat it out for six weeks until 4 April, when he was granted bail on his own recognizances.

Meanwhile, this precipitate action by Herbert Lloyd triggered off other consequences. To confuse matters further, a violent and unruly member of the gentry named Thomas Johnes of Abermâd now entered the dispute, taking up arms on behalf of the Crown. He had at his disposal a militant mob, which he used to wrest the Esgair Mwyn mine back from Herbert Lloyd and William Powell and return it to Lewis Morris for the Crown. For this service, Thomas Johnes of Abermâd was rewarded with the sum of twenty one pounds, which was recorded in an account of Lewis Morris's disbursements relating to Esgair Mwyn: 'To Thos. Johnes Abermaide Esq. given by way of gratification for defending our miners, carriers, etc. from the vexations, warrants and commitments by Mr Powell, etc. £21'.[10]

Being unable to hang on to Esgair Mwyn was not the only penalty to be suffered by Herbert Lloyd and William Powell; worse was in store, for Lewis Morris was hell bent on revenge. After his release from Cardigan Gaol, Morris travelled to London to provide evidence for a court case on behalf of the Crown against Herbert Lloyd, William Powell and others. He left behind a Cardiganshire seething

Henblas Abermâd

with unrest as a result of the Esgair Mwyn confrontation, and his Crown underagent was warned in a letter 'not to go near Aberystwyth or in the way of the rioters for that he and other persons that are named are to be destroyed . . .'[11]

Such was the disquiet, that troops were dispatched to Cardiganshire to enforce law and order. Thomas Johnes, as Custos Rotulorum, headed a party of Scot's Greys to protect the mine and its workers from the continued harassment of the mobs incited by Herbert Lloyd and William Powell. Thomas Johnes was assisted by General Campbell with a troop of North British Dragoons and Welch Fusiliers.[12] For the next few months, this motley crowd of soldiers inhabited the peat black hills, their services being used, not only to daunt the rioters but also to 'attend to the shafts and winches for which they were paid labourers' wages'.[13]

Meanwhile, Herbert Lloyd and William Powell, the two magistrates who had been instrumental in unleashing the forces of lawlessness and disorder, were about to be brought to heel for their conduct. A peeved Lewis Morris and a vindictive Thomas Johnes Abermâd were doing all they could to get them removed from the Bench. A letter from Lewis Morris to Gwyn Vaughan on 4 May reveals that: 'Mr

Johnes is wondering why Herbert Lloyd has not been discharged from all offices under the Crown, and desires to know whether anything is intended to be done against the two Justices for their behaviour at Esgair y Mwyn. If not, he hints as if he himself would article against them'.[14]

No immediate action seems to have been taken against them, and Lewis Morris was clearly irritated by the apparent reluctance of the government to move in this matter. In June 1753, Morris wrote to Lord Powis expressing his dismay and sense of frustration: 'It will be of no use to mention a word to Mr Pelham [the Prime Minister] about the affair, further than that the county are surprised that some proceedings are not commenced about the riot made in Cardiganshire'.[15] Morris mordantly concluded: 'These people are not to be dealt with like rational creatures, but a lawless set of wretches'.

For some months it appeared as though Herbert Lloyd and William Powell were not going to be punished for their challenge to the Crown or for maltreating its representative at Esgair Mwyn. Possibly, the government, mindful of votes, did not want to pursue a cause against the Nanteos and Peterwell families. Lewis Morris was, however, persistent in his case against them and was finally vindicated when both Lloyd and Powell were struck out of the Commission of the Peace. On 7 August 1753, Morris triumphantly reported to his brother William: 'Yesterday a sergeant at arms was sent to Cardiganshire by my Lord Chancellor to strike the two rioting Justices out of the Commission of the Peace, which I hope will open the eyes of the county'. Then, in the same letter, in his own inimitable style, he slips into Welsh acknowledging divine help: 'Ond Duw'n unig a wyr y drafferth a gefais i yn cael hyn i ben . . . oni buasai hynny mi fuaswn i yn y gwaelod dros fy mhen a'm clustiau'.*[16]

Although Herbert Lloyd lost his commission in August 1753, he refused to give up his power, for he continued to act in his former capacity as a J.P. Not until 1755 does his name disappear as a magistrate from the Quarter Sessions Records. In spite of this setback, he emerged from the Esgair Mwyn episode with his confidence relatively undiminished and his ambitions burgeoning. Lewis Morris, on the other hand, was left to carry the banner for the Crown with little

*God alone knows of the trouble I had in bringing this to its conclusion . . . were it not for divine help, I'd be in it up to my ears and over my head.

positive encouragement from his masters. The hearing between the Crown and Powell and the others over Esgair Mwyn was held in London in May 1754. Lewis Morris had gone to endless pains in preparing his case meticulously; he had even arranged for the conveyance of seventy four witnesses in wagons from the Esgair Mwyn locality to London, no mean feat in those days; he then had the exhausting task of looking after these country folk in a seething eighteenth century London. But it was all a futile exercise for Morris. The case was settled with the issue being compromised: 'The government agreeing with the claimants for their rights'. The Crown also discontinued its intended prosecution of the ringleaders at Esgair Mwyn for their riotous conduct and assault on the person of Lewis Morris. He was far from happy with this, for he had been given an assurance that an action for false imprisonment against Herbert Lloyd would almost

Dr William Powell, Nanteos

certainly have brought him damages of five hundred pounds. William Powell of Nanteos was also far from happy; according to Lewis Morris, he had been obliged to borrow more than fifteen hundred pounds to cover his costs in the affair. 'Powell', wrote Morris, 'calls for his rents beforehand and curses the hour he ever meddled in this lawsuit'.

Maddened by his losses and the ignominy of the whole affair, Powell now vent his spleen against Lewis Morris. Using all his influence, he instigated an inquiry into the accounts of Esgair Mwyn; the result was that in January 1756 Lewis Morris's Superintendency of the mine was revoked. It was a case of iniquitous character assassination. Morris's name was unfairly blackened, to quote his own words, 'from the malicious and false representations that had been made concerning my conduct'. Lord Powis now took over Esgair Mwyn, whose management he entrusted to his agent, John Paynter, an Englishman recently arrived in Cardiganshire. Paynter's name was to feature prominently in the history of Herbert Lloyd and Cardiganshire, but Lewis Morris's assessment of him, 'If the Treasury wants a tool of destruction, he is the fittest man in the world for it', is a description which could so well have been applied to Herbert Lloyd himself at this time.

NOTES

[1] N.L.W Cards. Q.S./O.B./2.
[2] ibid.
[3] ibid.
[4] ibid.
[5] Bick. Pt. I., p. 10.
[6] *Cymm.*, Vol. 15, pp. 9-43.
[7] *T.C.A.S.*, Vol. 2, p. 41.
[8] *Cymm.*, Vol. 15, p. 15.
[9] *A.M.L.*, Pt. 2, p. 961.
[10] *T.C.A.S.*, Vol. 2, p. 41.
[11] *A.M.L.*, Pt. I, p. 243.
[12] Thomas Rees, p. 414.
[13] Beynon, M.A., Thesis, p. 99.
[14] *A.M.L.*, Pt. I, p. 243.
[15] ibid, p. 245.
[16] ibid, Pt. 2, p. 867.

Chapter Seven

MOURNFUL HOUSES

During these years of Herbert Lloyd's erratic and lawless behaviour, certain events took place at Maesyfelin and Peterwell which were soon to affect the course of his life. The success of John Lloyd had ensured that Peterwell's star glowed in the firmament of Cardiganshire, but dark clouds had hovered over Maesyfelin. The fates were unkind to members of that family, and for those that gave credence to such things it seemed that the curse of Vicar Prichard was stealthily taking effect. To many it appeared that the shadow of Rees Prichard had never left Maesyfelin, for this was an age when the supernatural was taken seriously. All manner of mishaps were attributed to demonic intervention; sickness, crop failure, inclement weather and the loss of animals were often ascribed to the curses of jealous neighbours. Such long held beliefs die hard; even today, the term *rheibio*, to cast a spell, is still in the vocabulary of Ceredigion farmers.

Towards the end of his life Sir Marmaduke Lloyd had written: 'The days of man are few and evil . . . there is nothing more certain than death and nothing more uncertain than the time of dying'.[1] The truth of this dictum was to be reflected in the fate of many of his descendants; leading members of the family fell to untimely deaths, and slowly but inexorably Maesyfelin itself fell into a state of sad decrepitude. Sir Marmaduke Lloyd himself died in 1651 and was buried in the vault at St Peter's Church, Lampeter; in less than a century the illustrious Lloyd family of Maesyfelin was no more.

Disaster had struck even before the seventeenth century was out when the young Lucius Lloyd, Sir Marmaduke's grandson, took his own life. Why a young man of such privileged birth should have wished to end his life remains a mystery and is only one in a catalogue of misfortunes which befell the family. The mansion then passed to his younger brother Charles. There came a brief resurgence in the social fortunes of the family, and royal recognition came their way when Charles was knighted by William III and subsequently made a baronet by Queen Anne on 1 April 1708. But sorrow again crossed their path when three of the daughters born to the mansion died during the first decade of the eighteenth century. With the death of Sir

Charles Lloyd on 28 December 1723, the estate fell to his elder son Sir Charles Cornwallis Lloyd. Once again, misfortune visited the family in the form of an early death; after only six years as the owner of Maesyfelin, Sir Charles Cornwallis Lloyd died in 1729 at the age of twenty four without heirs.

The whole estate now devolved upon his younger brother, Sir Lucius Christianus Lloyd, who was only fourteen years old. To him fell the awesome responsibility of upholding the family tradition, but it was not to be. By 1750 he was dead, and with his death came the end of the family, for he left no son to succeed him. When he had married Anne Lloyd of Peterwell in 1742 it must have been hailed as a promising and auspicious union, for it united the two great ruling houses of Lampeter; she was twenty two years old and he was twenty six. It was, however, to end in tragedy. Their brief life together was blighted by ill health. Within five years Anne had died, and was buried ten months after her father, Walter Lloyd. Her death is recorded thus in the Church Register: 'Buried young Lady Lloyd December the 25th' 1747. It was a bleak Christmas. Sir Lucius Christianus struggled on for another three years before following Anne to the grave. On 20 January 1750, he himself was carried to the family vault. It was the final chapter in the history of Maesyfelin and the whole estate including the Lordship of the Manor of Lampeter now passed to Peterwell.

On 14 January 1746, Sir Lucius Christianus had drawn up his will in which he bequeathed his estate solely to John Lloyd of Peterwell. He had stipulated: 'All singular, my real and personal estate, whatsoever, I give . . . all messuages . . . situated in the several counties of Salop, Somerset . . . Carmarthen and Cardigan . . . unto my brother in law John Lloyd of Peterwell'.[2] It was a strange will, for his wife Anne was still alive when the will was drawn up. He had also excluded other living members of his immediate family such as his mother Dame Frances, and his sisters Emma Ffoy and Elizabeth Sherbourne. This will was described in 1860 by William Edmunds, the local schoolmaster and historian, as having been drawn up in a 'frolicksome humour',[3] and as a bargain between Sir Lucius Christianus and John Lloyd, that the survivor should inherit all the wealth of the first to die. The young Lampeter gentry had devoted much of their time to gambling and games of chance, but in this case it was a wager in the stake of life, the winner to take all. John Lloyd took all. As the sole executor he proved the will on 3 March 1750, and Maesyfelin with its far flung territories and the title of Lord of the Manor was added to Peterwell. It seemed there was no end to the good fortune of John Lloyd.

The youngest sister of John and Herbert Lloyd, Alice, now moved into Maesyfelin with her husband Jeremiah Lloyd; he acted as steward for the estates. Dame Frances Lloyd, Sir Lucius's mother also continued to live at the mansion until her death in 1753, when she was, according to her last wish, 'buried in the chancel of the church at Lampeter near the grave of my dear son Sir Lucius Christianus Lloyd'.[4] Dame Frances had little enough to bequeath, but in her will she left 'to John Lloyd of Peterwell . . . all the large knives and forks . . . being one dozen of each'.

By inheriting Maesyfelin, John Lloyd became one of the greatest landowners in west Wales, but all was not what it seemed. His legacy from Sir Lucius Christianus proved to be heavily encumbered and it was shortly to be nothing but an albatross about his neck. Within three years, the commitments on the estate were such that he was forced to turn to his wife's relatives for financial aid. He negotiated a mortgage with Horatio Walpole, brother to the former Prime Minister, Sir Robert Walpole. Horatio Walpole had been one of the trustees of his wife's marriage settlement and a sum of eight thousand pounds was secured by mortgaging extensive tracts of land in and around Lampeter. This particular mortgage was later destined to haunt his brother, Herbert.

Another problem now beset John Lloyd; his term as an M.P. now was due to end in 1754, but having relished political power he was resolved at all costs to hang on to it. His fellow M.P., Thomas Powell of Nanteos, who had been returned for the Cardigan boroughs seat in 1747, had in the meantime died of an apoplectic fit on a street in London on 16 November 1752. He had subsequently been succeeded by John Symmons of Llanstinan, a leading Tory from Pembrokeshire.

Gogerddan was still the great ruling political power in Cardiganshire. Powerful trustees of the family such as Sir John Philipps, Picton Castle, and Sir Watkin Williams Wynn of Wynnstay maintained a tight control over the county in readiness for the time when the young John Pugh Pryse, the Gogerddan minor, would be old enough to take his seat at Westminster. Accordingly, in 1753, John Lloyd of Peter-

Gogerddan

well wrote to Sir John Philipps to beg the Gogerddan interest in his bid for the county seat at the coming general election. After some deliberation, Sir John Philipps and the other trustees agreed to support John Lloyd on condition that there would be no Whig challenge to John Symmons, who would then retain the Cardigan boroughs seat for John Pugh Pryse when he came of age.

This compromise was threatened by Herbert Lloyd, who had long been restless at Foelallt, and was now flexing his political muscle. Greatly hankering after a seat in Parliament and mad for the power that went with it, Herbert Lloyd wrote to the Reverend John Lloyd of Rug, stepfather to the young John Pugh Pryse and one of the leading Gogerddan trustees, asking 'the Gogerddan interest at the next general election'.[5] It was a brash and audacious move on the part of Herbert Lloyd, and had it been successful would undoubtedly have been injurious to his brother. The bid, however, was contemptuously thrust aside by the trustees, all of whom considered it best to support John Lloyd. The general election of 1754 saw the unopposed return of John Lloyd of Peterwell for the Whigs and John Symmons of Llanstinan for the Tories; they held the County and Cardigan boroughs seats respectively. As a gesture of thanks for being returned, both men donated money to St Mary's Church, Cardigan, where 'all five bells were recast through the generosity of John Lloyd Esq. and John Symmons.'[6] The people of Cardigan would have welcomed the peal of bells once again, for they had been silent since 1705 when the church tower had collapsed. But 'ask not for whom the bell tolls', it was soon to toll for John Lloyd himself.

Only a matter of months after the general election, John Lloyd began to suffer the first signs of failing health. In an effort to obtain a cure, he did what many of the gentry were wont to do and travelled down to the Hot Wells at Bristol for the benefit of the spa water. The first indication of the seriousness of his condition is reflected in a letter which he wrote from Bristol to Lord Hardwicke, the Lord Chancellor, on 18 June 1754 begging to be excused from the duties of Attorney General. 'The situation of my affairs is such', he told Hardwicke, 'that it will be very inconvenient for me to keep this office'.[7]

However, the shedding of the post of Attorney General did not lighten his load sufficiently, and his health continued to deteriorate. Summer brought no improvement; with the onset of autumn, the mists enfolding Peterwell only exacerbated his condition and the family were obliged to resort to the assistance of Dr William Price, the Lampeter physician. He was first called to Peterwell on 16 October 1754, when he prescribed 'Lavender Drops' at a cost of sixpence per bottle.[8] Such simplistic treatment shows how medical science was still in its infancy. We are fortunate that there survives a comprehensive list of all the medicines and treatments which were recommended by Dr Price for Peterwell from October 1754 to June 1755; this provides us with a sharp and fascinating glimpse into the medicaments of the day. The study of medicine was soon to move into a new age of enlightenment but, clearly, Dr William Price of Lampeter was still caught up in the trammels of medieval methods of treatment. Under his care John Lloyd grew steadily worse, dosed with repeated herbal concoctions of mint, rhubarb, gum dragon, oil of almonds, brimstone and sulphur.

The medical treatment prescribed for John Lloyd was harmless but ineffective. Often in the eighteenth century one remedy was as harmful as another; kings and queens drifting into happy unconsciousness were frequently pummelled and thumped back to life only to have all manner of potions thrust down their throats. Queen Caroline, George I and George II all suffered atrociously before dying. John Lloyd seems to have been spared the drastic and brutal extremes often endured by royalty, and as far as we know he was not bled, but his condition continued to deteriorate. In November, Dr Price was again summoned to Peterwell when he prescribed a bottle of hartshorn drops at a cost of sixpence. We shall never know the exact nature of John Lloyd's illness, but the symptoms of a cough and a fever getting progressively worse over a period of one year suggest that it could have been consumption. A very large proportion of the medicines prescribed were for chest ailments, and massive doses of pectoral syrup were supplied. Consumption was at this time widely endemic in Wales, for damp living conditions often predisposed people to this condition.

As time went on, it became increasingly evident that John Lloyd would never again take leave of Peterwell in his own strength. Normally, he would have been preparing for his journey to London for the new session of Parliament. All this was now out of the question. He must have felt crushed by his indisposition, for only recently he had been re-elected as M.P. with another glorious seven year mandate; this was now being slowly and cruelly forced from his grasp.

Christmas of 1754 came and went under the shadow of his sickness and the new year was to usher in six more months of suffering. Throughout it all he was nursed by his wife Elizabeth, who made sure that constant fires were kept alight in his bedroom to offset the cold air made raw by the white mists creeping up from the nearby Teifi. One wonders what her feelings must have been: Peterwell, gripped by bleak weather, was a far cry from the courtly elegance of St James's Palace where she had formerly been a lady in waiting: and there was precious little to assuage the heavy 'ennui' of the grim Cardiganshire winter. Looking out from the mansion windows she would have seen the long grass whipped by icy blasts of sleet, and beyond that the Teifi foaming at every turn. This was her fourth year in this land of Wales, but she must now have seriously been considering what the future would hold for her. While her husband lay helplessly stricken, a few miles away at Foelallt hovered his ambitious brother, keenly awaiting the inevitable outcome.

February saw Dr Price step up his visits to Peterwell and increase his useless doses of cinnamon, mint and linseed. In the midst of John Lloyd's illness we find almost comic relief in amusing references to Madam Letitia, the lunatic aunt, who received large doses of 'tincture of rhubarb' at sixpence a shot. Her presence at Peterwell was a long shadow from the past; she was now the only survivor of the days of Daniel Evans. Possibly, she was fortunate to have been allowed to spend her years within the sanctuary of Peterwell's walled garden, for in the eighteenth century treatment of the mentally ill was clouded with superstition and inhuman cruelty. The mad were mocked and abused and even Howel Harris had paid the fashionable visit to London's Bethlehem (later to be known as Bedlam) Hospital for the mentally sick to stare upon life's less fortunate.

Meanwhile, news of John Lloyd's illness had reverberated far beyond the confines of Peterwell. In March 1755 a premature announcement of his death appeared in the *Gentleman's Magazine,* claiming that he had died on 23 February. At Peterwell, the fight for life continued, but it was a losing battle. April proved John Lloyd's cruellest month and the intensity of his treatment speaks for itself; he now had 'large blisters for the back . . . plasters for the feet . . . large pots of blistering ointment all over . . . saline nervous draughts . . . and repeatedly a pipe and bladder fixed at 6d'.[9] Vomits, purges, sweats and red hot blisters were applied to his person, the only remedies available to Dr Price. The following month saw Dr Price ride to Peterwell almost daily; no less than seventy two different items of medicines and treatments were prescribed for the mansion in May. Madam Letitia was still ailing; but not surprisingly, Elizabeth Lloyd now showed signs of stress and strain and was supplied by Dr Price with 'Anodyne stomach draughts' at a cost of one shilling.

The outside world was still watching this life and death struggle, and no man more closely than Wilmot Vaughan of Trawsgoed, the son of Viscount Lisburne. It was not from any sense of concern or compassion for Lloyd, but simply because he desperately wished to acquire his parliamentary seat. He had tried to contest the 1754 election, but had been frustrated by the Peterwell-Gogerddan pact. The Trawsgoed family had never really approved of Peterwell, which had challenged them for the Whig leadership in the county. Here now was the chance to step into a dead man's shoes; the only trouble was the man was not quite dead! Wilmot Vaughan now devoted all his energies to preparing the way to procure the seat when the time came.

On 5 June, rashly anticipating Lloyd's death, Vaughan wrote to Newcastle, the Prime Minister, offering himself for the seat:[10]

> I received an account this day from Cardiganshire informing me that Mr Lloyd of Peterwell died there on Tuesday last, and as my friends have given me the greatest encouragement to offer my services to the county on the present vacancy, I hope I shall meet with little trouble in securing my election.

Back at Peterwell it was true that John Lloyd hovered on the brink of death, but he still stubbornly remained this side of the grave, making Vaughan's letter smack of indecent haste.

Ten days later, on 15 June, with mounting impatience, Vaughan again wrote to Newcastle, this time scarcely concealing his disgust at the way John Lloyd was clinging so tenaciously to life.[11]

> Mr Lloyd is still alive, it is supposed he cannot live long. It seems a kind of miracle that he exists under so many dreadful symptoms as he is reported to have . . . I am doing everything possible to render myself indisputable whenever the vacancy takes place.

At last, the doomed John Lloyd was to oblige putting an end to Vaughan's suspense. Mrs Lloyd, his wife, sent an account of his last days to London: 'The delerium has left him; he is now in a sort of lethargy. A few days must determine his fate'. Clearly, the storm of his fever had abated, and the calm which so often precedes death had settled over John Lloyd. Dr Price had visited him every day during the last fortnight, but nothing from the limited pharmacopoeia of the eighteenth century could save him. He finally died on 23 June 1755 at the age of thirty seven, exactly one year after he had written to Lord Hardwicke complaining that he was not well. Dr Price's total bill for attendance and medicines over one year was fourteen pounds and ten pence, which was settled by Herbert Lloyd on 2 July 1755.

Surprisingly, John Lloyd had never set about drawing up his will despite ample warning of impending death. His intestacy was to add to the confusion and squabbling after his day. He was survived by his wife Elizabeth, but, as there were no children, John Lloyd's real estate passed to his brother Herbert, who now became the owner of Llechwedd Deri, Peterwell, and Maesyfelin in addition to his own inheritance of Foelallt.

The only tangible memorial to John Lloyd currently in existence is a ring struck to commemorate his death. It was common for the wealthy to instruct relatives to have such rings distributed to perpetuate their memory; John Lloyd's ring is made of gold and enamel and contains his name and date of death. The Peterwell family were partial to such mementoes; Daniel Evans had bequeathed five pounds to his mother-in-law and five pounds to his sister-in-law specifically to buy 'in memoriam' rings.[12] Friends of the Peterwell family also showed regard for such keepsakes; George Whitefield in his last

Memorial Ring of John Lloyd

will and testament desired the Wesley brothers to so remember him: 'I leave', he wrote, 'a mourning ring to my honoured and dear friends . . . the Rev. Messers John and Charles Wesley in token of my indissoluble union with them'.

John Lloyd had had a brief but bright spell as the owner of Peterwell; he had been struck down in the middle of a promising career. The mansion had seen many changes, and it was now left with a nervous widow and a mentally and physically sick old lady; a half an hour's ride away, however, was the predatory brother, awaiting his chance. The preceding years had been a mournful time for both Maesyfelin and Peterwell: but ahead lay total catastrophe.

NOTES

[1] *Lloyd Family Records,* p. 29.
[2] P.R.O. Prob., 11777, f. 84.
[3] *Arch. Camb.,* 1861, p. 20.
[4] *Lloyd Family Records,* p. 61.
[5] Nanteos Mss., Lewis Pryse to Wm. Powell, 12 Apr. 1753.
[6] N.L.W., 13661B.
[7] B.L. Add. Mss. 35592, f. 369.
[8] Gog. Mss. Medical Records of John Lloyd of Peterwell.
[9] ibid.
[10] B.L. Add. Mss. 32855, f. 346.
[11] B.L. Add. Mss. 32856.
[12] P.R.O. Prob., 11435.

Chapter 8

LORD OF THE MANOR

On 25 June 1755 John Lloyd's coffin was laid to rest in the family vault at St Peter's Church, Lampeter, and all the rights and privileges of the Lord of the Manor transferred to his brother Herbert, heir to all his estates. The premature death of his brother had provided him with a God given opportunity of stepping up in the world, and he grasped it with both hands. Throughout his life Herbert Lloyd had been forced to play second fiddle to his brother John who had inherited not only the Peterwell estate, but also a goodly measure of his father's legal skill and political acumen; but now he had a platform from which he could launch his own political and social ambitions. He immediately left Foelallt which, although spectacularly set amid hills of purple heather and yellow gorse was, nevertheless, stark as compared with Peterwell. This mansion, screened by thick leaved oaks and elms, stood in a richness and splendour of its own, and was altogether a more fitting home for an aspiring gentleman. Here at last was the chance to gratify his pride and indulge his arrogance.

At Peterwell itself the freshly bereaved widow, Elizabeth Lloyd was given precious little time to grieve: on the part of Herbert Lloyd himself, there was not even a charade of mourning. Almost before John Lloyd had drawn his last breath, Herbert Lloyd had ridden post haste to claim his inheritance and with callous indifference he seized all the documents and papers relating to the estate and immediately took possession of the keys of the mansion. Very soon an acid atmosphere of hostility replaced the veil of sickness which had hung so heavily and so long over the house and before many weeks had elapsed Elizabeth Lloyd felt compelled to leave and to seek refuge elsewhere.

Elizabeth Lloyd was not the only one who was to feel the new presence at Peterwell, for Herbert Lloyd now held sway over the lives of the inhabitants of Lampeter itself. The town he was to rule with a 'rod of iron'[1] for the next fourteen years was 'small and straggling, consisting of a single cobbled street, with indifferent cottages',[2] and alehouses scattered along the edge of the common. Lampeter at this time was a town of many taverns and such names as The Swan, The Greyhound, The Ship, The Star, The Nag's Head, The Crown, The

Three Horse Shoes, The Green Dragon and The Black Lion are to be found among the records. There was a need for these inns since Lampeter with its weekly markets and many fairs had grown to be a significant centre of commerce, in addition to which it was also used as a droving centre. The taverns also had another function, for they were frequently the meeting places of the Court Leet, the Quarter Sessions and the Parish Vestry, but although justice was dispensed in the convivial atmosphere of a tavern over foaming mugs of ale, it did little to temper the harshness of the judgments and the punishments meted out.

As Lord of the Manor, Herbert Lloyd presided over the Court Leet which controlled the affairs of the town. This Court was an ancient institution with its origins in feudal times and it had powers to deal with all the minor vexations and nuisances which afflicted eighteenth century Lampeter. The chief officer of the Court was the Steward who selected fifteen or more of the inhabitants of the town to act as jurors for the various cases which were brought before them. The Court Leet was convened by the Bailiff who went round the town ringing a hand bell and announcing: 'His majesty's Leet Court of the Lord of the Manor will be held on . . . at the . . . Inn, to which are to be summoned and warned fifteen good and lawful men . . . to be impannelled in a jury'. The Court officials consisted of a Portreeve (Mayor), Town Clerk, Steward, Bailiff and two Constables. These appointments were controlled by the Lord of the Manor and they would be sworn into office in open court after partaking of the 'sacrament before two vouchers'.[3] Defaulters who refused to participate in the work of the Court could be fined six shillings and eight pence. The Court itself dealt in the main with minor misdemeanours and its penalties usually took the form of fines; since these passed into the purse of the Lord of the Manor it is not surprising that the frequency of the meetings increased during Herbert Lloyd's early years at Peterwell.

The Court Leet was also the instrument for creating burgesses who held a key role as voters in the election of the M.P. for Cardigan boroughs. Like his father before him, Herbert Lloyd fully realized its potential in advancing his own political career. On 30 September 1755 he convened the Court and set about the business of swearing in new burgesses favourable to him in readiness for his attempt to secure a seat at Westminster. At this first meeting no less than fifty three burgesses were created. These burgesses were drawn from all strata of society. Members of the gentry frequently made their appearance at Lampeter Court Leet to be sworn in; John Dyer of Aberglasney, Marmaduke Gwynne of Garth, Thomas Johnes of Croft Castle, John Johnes of Dolaucothi, John Pugh Pryse of Gogerddan, Roderick Gwynne of Glanbrân, John Jones of Crynfryn, David Lloyd of Breinog, Edward Vaughan of Greengrove, all rode to Lampeter for this purpose. Among the clerics are to be found the names of Daniel Rowland, Llangeitho and the Reverend John Lloyd of Alltyrodyn. The economic life of the locality is reflected in such entries as Joseph Mathew, Staymaker, William Price, Apothecary, Jenkin Davies, Periwigmaker, Richard Thomas, Harper, Josiah Morgan, Mason, and John Davies, Joiner. The servants at Peterwell provided Herbert Lloyd with many voters; John Hirkman, Coachman, David Thomas, Footman, James Calendar, Gardner and Jenkin Jenkin, Servant, received their voting tickets in October 1755. Lloyd's tenants from many outlying parishes were also drawn in to swell his ranks of supporters; Thomas Richard of Llanfair, David Williams of Cellan, Evan Daniel of Castell Buged and long lists from 'ye parishes of Pencarreg, Llancrwys, and Caio' were presented as 'fit burgesses within ye town and liberty of Lampeter'.[4] At his first Court Leet, Herbert Lloyd ensured its unswerving loyalty by appointing his henchman David Daniel, Blacksmith to the powerful office of Portreeve and his own brother-in-law Jeremiah Lloyd, Maesyfelin to the key post of Steward. The foreman of the jury was Oakley Leigh who was destined to play a crucial part in the administration of the Court Leet and the town for many years to come. Men such as Herbert Lloyd, whose characters are an amalgam of ruthlessness, naked ambition and a lust for wealth and power, prove a magnet to lesser beings eager to serve their powerful masters and to promote their wicked designs. Such a man was Oakley Leigh whose name figures frequently in the records of the Lampeter Court Leet. He seems to have been Lloyd's main instrument in controlling the affairs of the Borough. Tradition ascribes to him the role of an unscrupulous villain ever willing to indulge his master's whims and to carry out his nefarious plans. He was appointed to succeed David Daniel as Portreeve but, unlike his predecessor, he was literate, competent and rose quickly to prominence in the town.

Born in obscurity, the son of 'Oakley and Blanche Leigh of Lampeter', in March 1716, he was four years older than Herbert

Lloyd. His association with the Squire of Peterwell ensured for him wealth and status and the term 'gentleman' was soon to be appended to his name in the records. Key posts fell his way in rapid succession: he was made Bailiff responsible for the collection of fines and rents; his name appears as Churchwarden; and on five occasions he was to hold the office of Portreeve of Lampeter. As such, he could participate in the work of the Quarter Sessions administering justice and fulfilling many of the significant responsibilities undertaken by a Justice of the Peace in the eighteenth century.

Leigh was a notorious philanderer, using the power he gained in the shadow of his master to gratify his own lusts and desires. He fully merits his description as 'Lloyd's infamous agent . . . whose bastards overran the town',[5] for the Parish Register records with astonishing frequency the births of his many 'natural' children. He lived at Brongest, a farmstead on the outskirts of the town and within flooding distance of the Teifi. It is still in existence but the present house is a modern one and little remains of the original dwelling. He survived his mentor, Sir Herbert Lloyd, by nineteen years and continued to

Old Brongest
(Home of Oakley Leigh)

play an active role in the affairs of Lampeter until his death. The records show that he was buried on Christmas Day 1788. In his will he readily acknowledged the existence of eight 'natural' children and to his credit he did make provision for them. There is a certain poignancy in the reference in the will to the youngest son John and the concern for his future education. Four years later, John Leigh's body was discovered on Cellan mountain; he had attempted the journey from Llandovery to Lampeter in mid winter and, overcome by the cold, had frozen to death. A memorial tablet to Oakley Leigh's long suffering wife, Judith, still stands high in the porch of St Peter's Church, Lampeter, but his only epitaph is to be found in the pages of the Parish Register with its many references to his own extra marital exploits.

Assisted by Oakley Leigh, Herbert Lloyd's involvement with the Court Leet brought him into close contact with the inhabitants of Lampeter for the business conducted by the Court had a direct impact upon their everyday lives. Although the Court Leet Records are in a very poor condition, many of the pages are rat chewed, crumbling and scarcely legible in parts, enough survives to give us a clear picture of a small eighteenth century town. Therein is to be found a whole range of eighteenth century experiences; the dirt, filth, disease, crime, cruelty, brutality, punishment, drunkenness and blasphemy which were so characteristic of the age.

One persistent problem in Lampeter was the grossly unhygienic condition of its main street and its general environment. As was the custom of the time, the people of Lampeter merely opened their doors and windows to fling out their waste and rubbish using the street as a repository for all their refuse. There was no sanitary system in the eighteenth century; the magnificent mansions of Peterwell and Maesyfelin would have been served by an open cesspool, but the poor in their one or two roomed hovels had no such facilities. They are described as 'making a public convenience of every nook and cranny'. The situation would become so intolerable that scarcely a Court Leet went by without a threat that 'all persons as lay down dunghills in the street of Lampeter to be fined six shillings and eight pence'.[6] This was indeed a heavy fine, for at this time it could be equivalent to a week's wages for some of the townsfolk, but the need to clean up the town was obviously taken seriously.

On 30 September 1758, the Court Leet, 'before Herbert Lloyd,

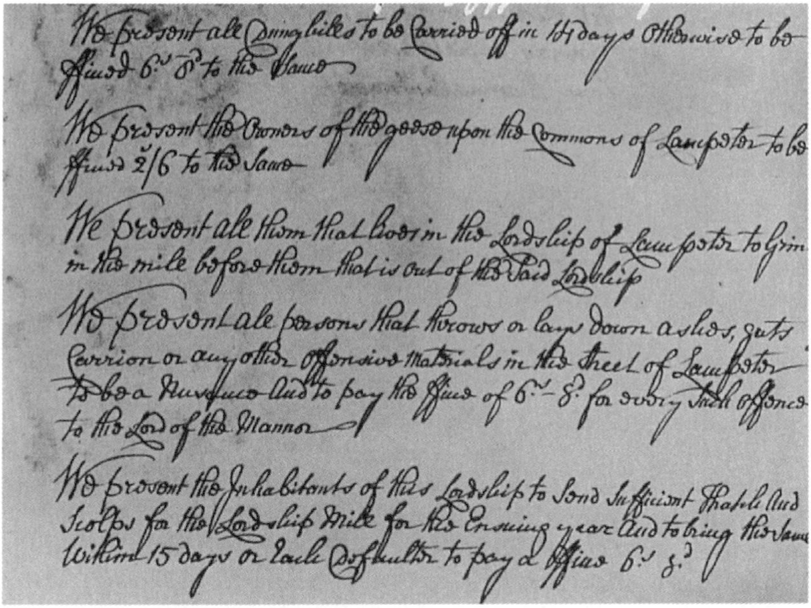

We present all dunghills to be carried off in 14 days otherwise to be fined 6s 8d to the same

We present the owners of the geese upon the commons of Lampeter to be fined 2/6 to the same

We present all them that lives in the Lordship of Lampeter to grind in the mill before them that is out of the said Lordship

We present all persons that throws or lays down ashes, guts carrion or any other offensive materials in the street of Lampeter to be a nuisance and to pay the fine of 6s 8d for every such offence to the Lord of the Manor

We present the inhabitants of this Lordship to send sufficient thatch and scolps for the Lordship mill for the ensuing year and to bring the same within 15 days or each defaulter to pay a fine 6s 8d

Lampeter Court Leet Records

Lord of the Manor, Jeremiah Lloyd as Steward and Oakley Leigh, Portreeve' made the following presentment:

> We present the inhabitants to clean and carry away all the muck with the said street of Lampeter within 14 days or to be fined . . . all dunghills to be carried away or the inhabitants fined.

It was an age of utter indifference to cleanliness and the welfare of their neighbours; the Records refer to mouldering mounds of 'feathers, ashes, guts and carrion' having been cast into the street by butchers and citizens alike. People carried nosegays of herbs and bags of crushed lavender to obtain some relief from the perpetual stench, but the basic problem remained, for every Court Leet admonished inhabitants for their mounting dunghills and not even Herbert Lloyd's threats and fines seemed able to coerce the population into mending its ways.

The hazard to health was obvious; heavy rain could suddenly transform the main street of Lampeter into a river of filth, making it a breeding ground for all kinds of disease. Waterways became contaminated and enteric infections were endemic. The Court, fully aware of the damage to the town's water supply, perpetually ordered the people to 'scour thoroughly their water courses'. On 27 October 1756, 'before Herbert Lloyd', the watercourse leading from the Creuddyn to Maesgoodin was stated to be 'out of repair and must be repaired in three weeks'. Specific instructions were given:[7] 'The course and channel is to be three feet deep and three feet wide. The work is to be done by able workmen at the expense of the said corporation and the money to be levied by way of tax . . . or the inhabitants to be fined £1 19s. 11d.' Standing water posed a problem for the Court: 'The pool hard by Robert Mathews's house leading from the town to the mill . . . and the pool by Widow Lloyd's house' were ordered to be attended to immediately under threat of fines. Each Whitsuntide all the inhabitants of the town were ordered to clear the waterways 'according to the ancient custom': armed with pails, shovels and sticks they were compelled to broaden and deepen channels to free the streams of all the rubbish, rotting vegetation and the debris of the passing year. Most sacred of all was Nantbach, the town's water supply, yet even this was on occasions threatened with pollution and the Court Leet ordered: 'Anybody that shall throw or empty any nuisance into the brook called Nantbach which serves the inhabitants of the town . . . to be fined'.

Another town facility which required continual attention was the mill pond. Herbert Lloyd had a particular interest in this, for as Lord of the Manor he owned the mill. Since the middle ages this had been a focal point in the economic life of the town, but each year the mill pond became choked with weeds and rubbish. The Court charged the inhabitants to 'scour and clean' it thoroughly within fourteen days on pain of fines and punishments. The people of Lampeter were also expected to keep the mill itself in a state of good repair; but they were apparently reluctant to do so for every year the Court Leet Records contain threats to the inhabitants who did not bring their expected quota of 'thatch, wattles and scolps' to maintain the building. One Elizabeth Phillips was fined sixpence for not complying and failing to bring her share of material to repair the building.

Herbert Lloyd kept a keen eye on the condition of the manorial mill for it provided him with a lucrative source of income. His tenants were obliged to bring all their corn to the mill and as Lord of the Manor he was, by custom, entitled to a proportion of all the corn ground. One of his first acts on succeeding to the Lordship was to issue a directive that the mill measure was to be changed thus increasing his share of the grain brought in by his tenants. The court ordered:[8]

> 25 October 1755 . . . the miller should make and divide his measure for the raising of the toll . . . and when he has done so, to destroy the small measure there made use of now.

Persons who tried to evade the toll by grinding their corn elsewhere were subjected to a penalty. Once again Elizabeth Phillips was caught out on this score and suffered 'for grinding corn out of the Lordship Mill' and was fined sixpence.

Lampeter Court Leet jealously guarded the rights and privileges of local tradesmen; sometimes, during fairs and market days, outside bakers would invade the town to sell their wares arousing much hostility among the locals. But these men, referred to as 'foreign bakers', were banished by order of the Court. Traders setting up their stalls were obliged to pay a due known as 'pitching pence' to the Lord of the Manor; each year the Court appointed two persons to collect the fees and also to ensure that law and order was kept in the markets and fairs. In October 1755 'Thomas Jones and David William' were appointed as 'fit persons to raise the pitching pence for the ensuing year'.

These 'vigilantes' were necessary for the eighteenth century was an age quick to quarrel, when men were generally aggressive and feelings were openly and barbarously expressed. Street violence was a feature of London and gangs roamed the city robbing and mutilating their hapless victims; but even in a rural backwater such as Lampeter the peace was frequently shattered by quarrels and fights. Before the Court Leet was brought a constant stream of offenders from both the town itself and the surrounding parishes accused of fighting with such ferocity that they drew blood. Although Herbert Lloyd himself could scarcely be classed as a pacifist, he was quick to see to it that the high animal spirits of his tenants were suppressed and any disruptive behaviour was sharply curbed by Court fines.

In October 1758 at a Single Court Leet before Herbert Lloyd and Oakley Leigh, no less than five cases of assault were considered. Evan David was 'fined 6s. 8d., for abusing Thomas Evan to the effusion of bloodshed'. John Rathan was fined 3s. 4d. for 'assaulting and beating

David Morgan of the Parish of Pencarreg'. John Evan was fined 3s.4d. 'for assaulting and beating James John'. Differences between married couples often flared into open brawling: 'William Evan Jenkin and Gwen his wife' were fined 3s. 4d. for assaulting and drawing blood from John Morgan and Mary his wife'. Possibly Mary Morgan was an aggravating person, for her name appears regularly in the records and Evan Williams of Caio was fined 6s.8d. 'for striking and beating her to the effusion of her blood' in 1760. It would appear that there was inter-parish hostility, for men from Pencarreg, Llanybydder, Cellan and Caio often appeared before the Court accused of 'assaulting and beating' one another. Even the Court Leet officials indulged in violence; on 1 October 1763 George Bishop was sworn in as Portreeve for Lampeter, but lower down on the same page his name is presented for 'assaulting and beating William Jones' for which he was fined the sum of 6s.8d.

The eighteenth century was also a clamorous age: all day long there were curses, oaths, shouting, blaspheming, menaces and threats. Lampeter was no exception; common slanderers, scolds and sowers of discord were punished by the Court Leet. Herbert Lloyd and the other justices had the power to impose an instant fine of 1s. for swearing; this they frequently did, for they themselves were often the victims of the most gross verbal abuse. This was not a feature confined to the ordinary people. Indeed, the language of the Court was coarse. Queen Caroline herself indulged in the most vulgar expressions but Sir Robert Walpole, the Prime Minister was even worse. The Queen was once so shocked by his language to her daughters that she felt obliged to constrain him.

At the centre of Lampeter, as a sober reminder to all offenders, stood the stocks and whipping post. To Herbert Lloyd and Oakley Leigh these instruments of punishment were deemed vital to the running of the town—and when they fell into a state of disrepair in September 1758, immediate instructions were issued to get them repaired. The town blacksmith and carpenter, David Daniel and David Thomas, were threatened with 'each a twenty shilling to be levied on their goods and chattels if they shall neglect to put up the stocks in the street of Lampeter in less than five days time'. The inhabitants were ordered to bring locks to the stocks and whipping post 'at their own charge'.

The unfortunate victims in the stocks would have been pelted with

Stocks and Whipping Post
(Originally stood outside the Town Hall, Lampeter)

rotting fruit, clods, filth and any available missile; there was no question of compassion, the suffering of others was an accepted form of the entertainment of the time. Apart from executions, the whipping of half naked women provided a popular source of amusement; the Lampeter whipping route lay between The Green Dragon (the site of the present Werndriw) and Thomas Daniel's house (unknown). The women were tied to the back of a cart and flogged in the sight of jeering crowds who thronged the route.

We have seen how a certain Ann Morgan was so ordered to be whipped in October 1750 by Herbert Lloyd in his capacity as a J.P. after being found idle in the town. Her punishment would have been fully applauded by the people of Lampeter; such people were suspected of pilfering and greatly feared for the damage they might cause to properties by fire, which was a very real threat at a time when the majority of houses were built of wood and thatch. But above all, Ann Morgan would have been hated on account of the danger of carrying some dread disease such as the plague or smallpox: vagrants were supposed to form one of the most common means by which infection was spread. Women could also be whipped for giving birth to illegitimate children, such was the callousness of the times that many Acts were passed endorsing this form of punishment on persons 'for bringing a child burdensome on the parish'. Theft was commonly punished by whipping and Thomas John of Llanddewibrefi was sentenced to be 'stripped from the waist upwards and whipped by the master of the House of Correction, being first tied to the whipping post in the town of Lampeter, until his body be bloody' for stealing a pair of shoes.

Thieves and vagrants were not the only source of trouble to Herbert Lloyd's Lampeter and its Court Leet: one persistent problem was caused by unkempt and straggling animals which, untethered, roamed from their common grazing strips to foul the street and forage among the decaying refuse of the town. They are referred to as

Eighteenth Century Punishment

'mangy horses, donkeys, geese and unringed pigs', and their owners were subjected to heavy penalties:

> 24 April 1766—We present all mangy horses . . . to be a nuisance and the owners fined. We present all pigs that are not ringed . . . and the owners of such pigs fined 5s.

Unclaimed animals were placed in the town's pound and they ultimately became the possessions of Herbert Lloyd since Peterwell had the 'Right of Estrays'. He therefore had a vested interest in seeing that the pound was kept in good condition and the townsfolk were frequently ordered to 'repair the pound or be fined within fourteen days'.

Another regular source of income for Herbert Lloyd came from the old manorial dues payable on the death, marriage or transfer of property of a freeholder or his children. It fell to the Court Leet to order these dues to be paid. On 1 October 1763 the court recorded:

> We present three daughters of Widow Lloyd, married. Thirty shillings to the Lord of the Manor.

The following week brought more money from Maespwll which was a neighbouring farm of Peterwell:[9]

> 9 October 1763 . . . We present the death of David Davies of Maespwll who was a freeholder of this Lordship, and upon his decease there is due to the Lord of the Manor, 10 shillings. We present Thomas Davies to be a common freeholder upon the death of his father; 10 shillings payable to the Lord of the Manor. We present the daughter of David Davies of Maespwll married, ten shillings payable to the Lord of the Manor.

Any would-be squatters were quickly removed from Peterwell land. In 1767 one Francis Evans sought to build himself a dwelling illegally, but the jurors of the Court Leet threatened him that unless he carried away the stones in seven days time he would suffer a 'fine of £1 19s. 11d. for digging and entering the foundation of a building in the Lord's soil'.

Court Leet fines were greatly increased during Herbert Lloyd's tenure of the Lordship: the fine for unringed pigs and other straggling

Comforts of Bath—feasting

livestock was increased from 3s. 4d. in 1755 to one guinea in 1767; the fine for not grinding at the manorial mill went up from 6d. to 6s. 8d.; and the fine for not bringing thatch, wattles and scolps also went up from 6d. to 6s. 8d. This could have been a sign of the seriousness of the situation or, as is more likely, an indication of the chronic state of Herbert Lloyd's finances and the pressing need to recoup additional funds for political purposes. But most drastic of all was the fine for not repairing the common pound; in 1768 it was increased to a staggering £3 3s. 0d. as compared with the previous sum of 3s. 4d.

Although Herbert Lloyd profited from all these fines, it appears that the town itself also benefited from the rigorous application of its laws and penalties; the frequently flooded commons were drained, fences were repaired, defective gates were replaced, footpaths and roads were cleared, and boundaries were clearly defined. Even the Court Leet officers themselves were made accountable and 'William Evan Jenkins, Constable', was twice brought to heel and 'fined 6s. 8d. for neglect of performing his duties and appearing at the Court'.

But it was a century of extremes: whilst the Court Leet Records echo the clamour, the chaos, the aggression, the savage punishments and perpetual stench of the town, a short distance away at Maesyfelin and Peterwell was reflected the elegance of the time. Portraits of the Lloyd family show the gentry encased in deep velvets, resplendent in fine silks and rich satins; elegantly wrought furniture graced their living rooms; delicate china and silver plate imported from London glistened on their tables; and a magnificent time piece acquired in Holborn ticked away the time of day at Peterwell. For Herbert Lloyd life was good; whenever the urge took him he could order his coachman to take him out of Lampeter with its filthy street, modest inns and mean dwellings to escape to the health giving spas at Tunbridge Wells and Bristol; but, above all, to Bath with its Pump Room and elegant crescents. Here, he found pursuits undreamt of by the Lampeter folk, and here also he squandered the rack rents wrung from their impoverished persons.

NOTES

[1] *Arch. Camb.*, 1861, p. 160.
[2] T. Rees, *Cardiganshire,* p. 9.
[3] Gog. Mss. Parlt. Box. Pet. Bundle.
[4] Falc. Mss., Group I, Nos. 15-18.
[5] Inglis-Jones, p. 30.
[6] Falc. Mss., Group I, Nos. 15-18.
[7] ibid.
[8] ibid.
[9] ibid.

Chapter 9

FACE TO FACE WITH THE POOR

The mid-eighteenth century was an age of great divide, and there was an awesome gulf between the life of the squire and the peasant. As Lord of the Manor, Herbert Lloyd was described as having lived at Peterwell in true baronial style. It is said that when he passed to and fro from London his tenants rushed fresh relays of horses to Llandovery to help his retinue;[1] but the lot of these tenants and others who formed the core of the community was very far removed from the plenty of Peterwell. It is probable that Lloyd's horses in their 'twenty five stalls' were more comfortably accommodated than many of the labouring poor, whose habitations were often little more than mud cabins covered by rafters patched with straw, leaves and clods of earth. Indeed, one visitor to Cardiganshire in the eighteenth century even described the people themselves as 'clods of moving earth scarcely indistinguishable from the soil'. The interior of their homes would have been dark and acrid with peat smoke; the Window Tax

A Cardiganshire Cottage

robbed many of light and the Hearth Tax often meant that there was no proper fireplace; underfoot lay earthen floors covered with rushes. In many instances animals occupied one half of the dwelling so that the whole atmosphere was perpetually impregnated with the stench of sweat and urine making it the ideal breeding ground for fevers and disease.

The occupants of these cottages lived wretchedly, merely subsisting from one harvest to the next: they had no reserves to cushion them against adversity; unemployment, ill health, an accident, or the death of the bread winner pitched them into a state of irretrievable destitution where they foundered at the mercy of the Parish. The records of the Lampeter Parish Vestry Books bring us face to face with such people. Tradition has it that the poor, moved more by fear than esteem, would bow their heads and simulate an attitude of respect for Herbert Lloyd as he rode through the town. Possibly, his great gilded coach emblazoned with the Peterwell coat of arms was one of the few colourful diversions in their drab lives.

An Act during Elizabeth's reign[2] had made it legally obligatory for every Parish to raise a poor rate to deal with the problem of poverty and it was the function of J.P.s such as Herbert Lloyd to adjust the poor rate to meet the demands on Lampeter Parish. Oakley Leigh, as church warden, administered poor relief for many years, so that his involvement with both Peterwell and the Parish brought him into close contact with the two extremes of the Lampeter social scale. The church wardens and overseers of the poor met in the vestry adjoining the church, hence the record of their distributions became known as the Parish Vestry Books. These meetings, however, were usually adjourned to one of the town taverns where ale was consumed at the cost of the Parish. It is these accounts which provide us with sometimes comic, but more often stirring glimpses into the life and death struggle of the ordinary, obscure and uncelebrated paupers of Lampeter.

Before they could qualify for relief the Lampeter poor were required to display a badge bearing the letters P.L. representing 'Pauper Lampeter' in 'an open and visible manner . . . at the end of the left sleeve'. Galling and humiliating as this must have been, if they did not do so they were liable to lose their Parish pay.[3] This device of badging the poor was to distinguish the legitimate Lampeter paupers from vagrants or illegal claimants who might have attempted to procure assistance from an already overburdened Parish. An Act of 1697 had ordered that all persons in receipt of Parish pay should wear a poor badge 'made of red or blue cloth'. The Lampeter Overseers insisted on this law and the Parish Vestry Books stipulate that 'All Paupers receiving relief are to wear the customary letters upon their

The Paupers that are Supported by this Parish are to Wear the Customary Letters upon their Outward apparel
Present W. Williams Clk

A copy of the record as entered by the Vicar in the Parish Vestry Book

outward apparel'. The problem of maintaining paupers placed a heavy drain on the Parish and each year the Poor Rate was increased to meet the demands of providing weekly sums of money, food, clothes and housing for the needy. Lampeter had special cottages for the use of the destitute, but it is clear that these humble dwellings ill withstood the vagaries of the Welsh weather for the Parish Vestry was constantly called upon to replace storm damaged walls and rotting straw which was repaired by allowing 'thraves of thatch at one shilling and six pence a thrave' to make habitable their ruinous hovels.

'The poor die very fast here', wrote William Bulkeley for Anglesey in 1741, and the same was true of Lampeter. The heaviest costs incurred by the Parish poor were for shrouds, coffins and the need to replace tools for digging graves; the Lampeter Parish Vestry Books refer to the necessity for new 'picks and shovels', and poignantly, 'the need to replace the bier for the burying of children'. We have seen how illness raged even amid the affluence of Peterwell and Maesyfelin, but it struck the poor with a merciless ferocity. Ill health was an ever present concomitant of life: fevers burned with an intensity which reduced entire families to lie dying on the dank straw of their gloom filled cottages; various plagues and distempers came and went in waves bearing many to St Peter's churchyard before their time. The Parish did what it could to alleviate such distress: 'David Hugh, Tynrithin was allowed one quarter of barley for his children who were very sick: Jane, Tynffynon being blind and very ill of a fever' was 'ordered a Peck of Barley and 5/6'. Thomas David William, a poor and sick cobbler's apprentice, was given two shillings to enable him 'to go to Aberaeron to procure sea water for his health'. But the

Likewise allow'd to Thomas David William two Shillings in order to go to the sea side for the sake of his bad State of Health

A copy of the record as entered by the Vicar in the Parish Vestry Book

Parish, ever keen to cut costs, only 'agreed with Mr Thomas the Surgeon, to treat the strange and disagreeable malady of Margaret David on a basis of 'no cure, no pay'![4]

The great scourge, however, was smallpox. Sporadic outbreaks struck Lampeter with tragic effect, and those it did not kill, it disfigured or maimed for life. It was perilously infectious, often wiping out whole families: the Sexton transmitted it to his wife and daughter who both died of it. The great mansions were no less vulnerable. When Thomas, Herbert Lloyd's brother died of it in 1725, there perished with him many of the Peterwell servants. It was with good reason that Edward Lluyd had called smallpox 'Death's trustiest servant'. Some of the gentry refused to employ servants who had not already contracted the disease: to be left with a pock marked face might have been disconcerting, but at least it meant that one had survived and was free from further ravages. It is interesting to note that Thomas Johnes was sufficiently enlightened to have had his children vaccinated against smallpox: in his letters he encouraged his brother John to follow his example. However, vaccination was as yet only a new-fangled defence pioneered by Lady Mary Wortley Montague and exclusive to the rich. Later, it was to become widespread after being successfully pursued by Dr Jenner in 1798. Meanwhile, the Lampeter poor had no such access to these prophylactics and they were obliged to seek relief from suffering in the only way open to them, by wrapping their infected sores in cool dock leaves.

Those who survived smallpox were at risk to other chronic afflictions such as crippling rheumatism, to which the damp earthen floors

The Parish Vestry

of their cabins, insulated only by dried grass or rushes, made the poor particularly vulnerable. Even as late as 1902 a surveyor's report described Cardiganshire cottages as having waterlogged floors 'with big holes enough to bury a dog in them'.[5] Lewis Morris often referred to the ill health of Cardiganshire people. A letter of his written in 1760 gives us a sharp, well nigh audible impression of a form of pleurisy which afflicted his entire household, man and beast alike. From it we can almost hear the cacaphony of coughing which racked them all:[6]

> Wel dyma fy nhylwyth yn ddyn ac yn anifail. Myfi a'm gwraig yn pesychu am y mwyaf; Jenny my little girl in a chin cough; Sion y Defaid (y bugail) in a violent cough and a swelled head, bled this

morning; Sion y Gwartheg . . . in an intermitting fever . . . coughs much; Arthur yr amaeth yn cyfarth fel llew; y forwyn fach clowyn yn nhepil ei morddwyd; y ddwy gaseg fawr, a'r gaseg las bach, a'r eboles, a'r ceffyl Wmffre, a'r gaseg Charlton yn pesychu (clefyd Lloegr) am yr uchaf, a minnau yn rhoi pesygwriaeth iddynt.*

If the Morris family, housed as they were in the comparatively salubrious and comfortable surroundings of their residence at Penbryn, Aberystwyth, succumbed to such a state of illness, how much more susceptible were the poor in their crowded and cramped conditions. Lewis Morris also commented on the inferior quality and scarcity of food in the county, and the diet of the poor did nothing to fortify them against sickness. Whilst the tables of Peterwell were laden with salmon, venison, brawns and such plenty, the labouring poor existed mainly on semi-liquid dishes of *uwd* and *llymru*, with barley bread, rye and oats. Ironically, although they would have seen the drovers drive out herds of beef on the hoof from Lampeter to be sold for the tables of the rich, they themselves scarcely knew the taste of meat. Occasionally, when there was a glut of herrings on the coast, those who could afford it bought fish, and the *Morris Letters* record that herrings were sold for ten a penny. One agricultural report describes a hill farmer as having only 'half a salt herring for supper, with potatoes and butter milk . . . and after he had finished, the youngsters would scramble for the bones to suck as a treat'.

The lives of the poor were very uncertain. Many lived and died in the open, sometimes within sight of Peterwell. In October 1762, while Herbert Lloyd was in attendance at St James's Palace, one of his tenants was discovered, stricken, on his land. The Quarter Sessions Records for 26 October contains the following almost lyrical account:[7]

Late in the dusk of the evening, David Richard William John was found speechless, lying under a small furze bush in a field called

*Behold this is the condition of my family, man and beast. My wife and I cough like mad; Jenny my little girl in a chin cough; Sion the sheep (the shepherd) in a violent cough and a swelled head, bled this morning; Sion the Cowman . . . in an intermitting fever . . . coughs much; Arthur the ploughman barks like a lion; the little maidservant has a lump in the fleshy part of her thigh; the two big mares, and the little grey mare, and the filly foal, and the horse Humphrey, and the mare Charlton are coughing (English disease) for the most, and I have to give them medicine.

> Caegarreg on the demesne of Peterwell . . . he did languish and did live till about 4 o'clock the following morning and then departed of this life through the inclemency of the weather.

Not all deaths were so natural: murders or fatalities as a result of brawls or violence were fairly frequent. One such unfortunate victim was Catherine Evans, wife of Thomas John, Shoemaker, who on 15 August 1763 was found in the Teifi, near Llanfair bridge, 'having come to her death by strangling with a certain linen handkerchief of no value about the neck . . . some person or persons unknown did fix, tie and fasten it, and she was killed against the peace of our Lord the King'.[8] Herbert Lloyd as a J.P. and his brother-in-law Jeremiah Lloyd, the coroner, examined the circumstances of the woman's death. Peterwell mansion was often used as a seat of justice where persons apprehended on a murder charge were taken prior to being made to appear at the Great Sessions. One such person was Margaret Lettice, who was taken to Peterwell on 14 August 1762 to be examined by Herbert Lloyd, 'charged with larceny and murder'.[9]

Unwanted babies seem to have been at risk; the records refer to infants found drowned in the Teifi and other streams from time to time. Very often, young girls gave birth in the most abominable circumstances, clandestinely in filth and on straw in outhouses, and they were frequently unable to fend for themselves, let alone provide for a dependant infant. Child murder was sufficiently prevalent for the government to warrant at least one witness at a still birth to confirm the circumstances of death. All too often pregnant girls were driven out of Lampeter Parish if they came originally from another parish. Each parish was anxious to avoid the cost of bringing up an illegitimate child and for this reason the Lampeter Overseers ruthlessly expelled Mary James of Berthlwyd and Mary Jenkin 'big with child'—who were both sent back to their respective parish of Llanwnnen because they were in a state of pregnancy. When the coroner decided that an adult had committed suicide, that person was 'buried without benefit of clergy'. Life was cheap and death familiar. To perish on the open road was almost common: on 19 October 1740, Richard Welshman, a wandering beggar died on the Peterwell road near Pontfaen; on 23 June 1743 Richard Hugh, a straggling beggar died near Brongest; and on 18 August 1753, 'William Glandynin, a Scottish fiddler died near Peterwell'.[10]

Driven from the Parish
(Illegal claimants were sent to their native parishes to reduce the costs of poor relief)

Some were obliged to spend a lifetime at the mercy of the Parish. One such person was 'Evan the Idiot' who survived only by being boarded out to local farms at a cost of between four and six pounds a year. His essential needs were met by being given 'britches, old coats, clogs, stockings, smocks and flannel vests' as and when the church wardens deemed them necessary.[11] When he died, Oakley Leigh arranged for the distribution of free beer to the bearers, to be paid for by the Parish.

Lampeter Parish Vestry gave such aid as was in its power to the sick and dying; cartloads of turf and peat for extra warmth were sometimes allowed, and a little extra money was given to ease the last days of poor people. But when the Parish paid for a nurse to 'watch over' the patient, it meant that the end was nigh. A typical account of the final weeks of a Lampeter pauper reads as follows:[12]

Ann Davies, Bola Haul, Cost of nurse at 1s6d. a week for 6 weeks	9s. 0d.
Cost of medicines	1s. 3d.
Allow'd for firing	1s. 6d.
Allow'd 2/- extra for 4 wks.	8s. 0d.
Paid to Old Sarah David for washing her corpse	1s. 0d.
To Sexton for digging her grave	1s. 0d.
To Carpenter for coffin	8s. 0d.

Tregaron practised greater economy than Lampeter in relation to pauper burials; they had a common coffin known as *arch bawb*, which was used to convey the body of a poor person to the grave, and then returned to the church to await its next fleeting tenant.

Sometimes, when misfortune struck, the old Welsh spirit of camaraderie found expression in the collection of *Cymhortha* which was given at the church door. Occasionally, people were given official Begging Briefs. One such person was Thomas John Rowlands of Llangrannog, who in August 1730 was given permission to beg by the Quarter Sessions when he lost his entire possessions in a:[13]

> . . . lamentable and terrible fire . . . at dead of night . . . which reduced the poor petitioner to such mean circumstances as to be unable to support himself, wife and five small children and servants . . . In consideration, therefore, he had the liberty to pass and travel through this county to collect the benevolence of such, whose hearts Almighty God shall incline to relieve his miserable condition.

This was signed 'at the Quarter Sessions held at Lampeter', and the petitioner would have been allowed to beg at St Peter's Church door.

In a county which whirred with pheasants and was alive with game such as partridges, black cocks, hares and rabbits, one might have expected the poor to subsidise their meagre fare by helping themselves to the God given plenty of the countryside. But what God gave, the gentry took; the fowl of the air, the beast of the field and the fish of the streams were not for the poor. An Act of 1619 prohibited all people from hunting except the owners of land worth one hundred pounds or more, or the eldest sons of the Lord of the Manor. Ordinary people

The Medieval Church, Lampeter
(This church was demolished in 1821)

caught poaching a rabbit were fined five pounds or sent to prison for three months or, occasionally, even transported. Poachers within the vicinity of Herbert Lloyd did so at great peril; Thomas William Jerry, a mason, 'was obliged to leave the country and for many years dared not return' because he shot an animal of Herbert Lloyd's while hunting a hare.[14] Alice M. Harford of Falcondale records in a letter that 'Sir H. Lloyd was held in such awe . . . that any poacher . . . he sent to gaol, walked the thirty miles alone [to Cardigan] and delivered himself up'.[15]

A letter of Thomas Johnes the Custos written in 1759 shows clearly the inflexible attitude of the Cardiganshire gentry towards the offence of poaching. During the summer of 1759 John Paynter of Hafod and Thomas Johnes had witnessed the son—who was not named—of Thomas David Lewis, a keeper at Hafod, walking at Trawsgoed accompanied by some dogs and carrying a dead hare. Thomas Johnes recalled the occasion for his brother:[16]

> Paynter asked him how he came to kill the hare. He told him—because the dogs happened to run faster than the hare. I took little notice of him then . . . but when John Paynter was present, it was thought advisable to proceed against him by information before a magistrate to [make him] pay five pounds. I wrote to Jack Jones, [the Aberystwyth attorney] to desire he would find a person that saw him course and kill the hare . . . you will send for him to meet you at Lampeter or Peterwell . . . He is a most impudent rascal to deserve no quarter.

If, as suggested, this man was made to appear at Peterwell before Herbert Lloyd, the likelihood was that he got 'no quarter'! It was an age of great inequality, when the squire reigned supreme. As such, Herbert Lloyd even extended his own demesne by encroaching upon common land. The Court Leet Records show that in 1760, 'A slang and part of Lampeter common [was to be] . . . for the use of Herbert Lloyd, Esquire, and his heirs for ever'.[17] He was empowered to do this by an Act of 1710 which gave the gentry the right to enclose land: by 1760 no less than 334,974 acres had been enclosed in England and Wales; but the following century really saw the rapacity of the landowners when 7,000,000 acres were enclosed causing untold deprivation and suffering.

As for the poor, they were trapped in a tide of poverty which never ebbed. Peterwell and the other mansions stood as oases of plenty where people vied for employment such as scullery maids, dairy maids, gardeners, footmen and butlers. In the mansion, there was always an adequate supply of food and living in the shadow of the genteel also brought many other perquisites. Faithful servants were bequeathed money or other gifts: Herbert Lloyd left his five guinea piece, his gold watch and £300 to a servant named Elizabeth Dasper;[18] Dame Frances Lloyd of Maesyfelin left her clothes to her 'faithful woman servant'. Local artisans such as carpenters, builders and glaziers got a large proportion of their employment from the existence of the mansions. Herbert Lloyd was constantly engaged in renovating and improving Peterwell, but he paid his men only a

An eighteenth century vagrant

niggardly wage. We learn from the Morris brothers that 'Sir Herbert Lloyd built his fine seat at Peterwell at a charge of 6d. a day only, without diet'.[19] Some of the more resourceful of the town increased their income by trapping foxes, killing crows and rooting out deadly nightshade. Lampeter Parish Vestry paid David Thomas of Olwen 2s. 6d. for each fox, 5s. for a 'she fox' and one penny for each crow caught.

But one may well ask what was left for the poor who derived no benefits from the mansions? Yet, it was by no means all gloom. While Herbert Lloyd sought the refinements and comforts of Bath, the ordinary folk of Lampeter found enjoyment in the rough and boisterous activities of the time. Young men fought, wrestled and hurled themselves into mass football matches which raged like warfare across miles of territory; summer interludes were performed; at Lampeter churchyard people danced and played fives against the church wall and

Cockfighting

Medieval Font
(This originally stood in the medieval church, Lampeter, but is now in Maestir Church)

even sharpened their knives and scythes against the ancient medieval font, which still bears the scars and can today be seen at Maestir Church.[20] Like the gentry, the poor crowded round to watch the sport of cockfighting. One cockfighting pit was located on the road between Llanfair and Lampeter in a small field near the Teifi. This was the half way house for the Peterwell and Llanfair mansions and it is likely that Thomas Johnes, Herbert Lloyd and others turned up occasionally to join in the excitement of the scene. The cock pit was said to be the great leveller in the world of gaming, 'where prince and peasant frequently rubbed shoulders in their obsession for the sport'.

Also in common with the gentry, when they could afford it, people of the lower orders turned to drink as a release from the toils and tensions of life. Ale was a penny a quart and it was a cheap anodyne to combat the misery and deprivation of their lives. Wakes, fairs and saint days provided plenty of occasions for overindulgence; very often, however, as we have seen, their excesses in this direction caused them to be hauled before Herbert Lloyd at the Court Leet where they were punished on a charge of being 'drunk and disorderly'.[21]

Soon, there was to be a transformation resulting from the influence of the Methodist preachers inveighing against sensual pleasures and lax living. By the end of the century, for many people, sobriety leading to total abstinence would replace the drunken wakes and uninhibited pleasures, and men would become soaked in a doctrine which made them obsessed with death and sin. But during Herbert Lloyd's reign over Lampeter, the poor still snatched enjoyment where they could. In their tumbledown cottages clustered around the fringes of the common, they struggled to meet the level of each day's needs, being resigned to their lot in this life which for many meant queueing at the Parish Vestry for just enough to keep the wolf from the door.

NOTES

[1] *Arch. Camb.,* 1861, p. 160.
[2] 43, Eliz., C.2.
[3] L.P.V.B.
[4] ibid.
[5] Nanteos Mss., Box 4, James Hughes to Sylvanus Lewis, 4 May 1902.
[6] Davies, ed., *Morris Letters,* Vol. 2, p. 178.
[7] N.L.W., Wales, 8/859.

[8] ibid.
[9] ibid.
[10] L.P.R.
[11] L.P.V.B.
[12] ibid.
[13] Parish Register, Llanbadarn Fach.
[14] Rowlands, *Hist. Notes,* p. 177.
[15] N.L.W. 13485, C. Alice Harford to G. E. Evans, 17 July 1904.
[16] D.C. Mss., T.J. to J.J., 2 Oct. 1759.
[17] Falc. Mss., Group I, Nos. 15-19.
[18] Pet. Mss., No. 65.
[19] Davies, ed., *Morris Letters,* Vol. 2, p. 404.
[20] See illustration of font, p. 110.
[21] Falc. Mss., Group I, Nos. 15-19.

Chapter Ten

AN UNEASY INHERITANCE

While disease and hardship haunted the poor, spectres of a different kind stalked Peterwell. From the start, Herbert Lloyd's inheritance brought with it many thorny problems which were never to be resolved during his lifetime. They sprang primarily from various claims against the Peterwell and Maesyfelin estates and a perpetual shortage of ready money to fund his lavish and expensive life style. Herbert Lloyd's wealth, like that of most of the landed gentry of the eighteenth century, was tied up in land, presenting him with the ever present problem of having to transform his acres into cash. To this end, bit by bit, the great domain of Peterwell was steadily whittled away by mortgages. His difficulties were compounded by the fact that much of the income from his estate was often paid in kind. A typical Cardiganshire tenancy agreement was: 'Rent £4 4s. 0d. plus 2 hens, 40 eggs, 6 chickens, a teal of oats and a load of lime per annum'.

As early as 1753, with his eye on Parliament, he had taken a loan of fifteen thousand pounds on lands pertaining to Foelallt. By 1754, he was in such dire straits that he even attempted to sell Foelallt by placing an alluring advertisement in the London newspapers. On 30 April 1754 the *Gloucester Journal* described Foelallt as 'A Capital Mansion . . . in good sporting country . . . where there is plenty of grouse, and all sorts of game, with a new commodious garden having a basin of water in the centre of it, walled in and planted with fruit trees, with a barn . . . good stables, kennels, oathouses . . . with a trout river . . . and a large Sheep Walk'. Despite the offer of post paid replies, no deal was ever concluded due either to lack of interest or, as is more likely, because Herbert Lloyd placed too high a price on the property. Attempts to sell Foelallt were abandoned when in 1755 he inherited Peterwell.

Here at last his troubles should have ended; but it was not to be. On the death of his brother John, intestate, the Peterwell mansion and all the real estate fell to Herbert Lloyd as the younger son and heir in law. John Lloyd's personal estate, consisting of his, 'Plates, jewels, china, linen, household furniture . . . coaches, chariots, horses, stock of cattle . . . implements and diverse large sums of money in his house at the time of his death', were to be divided between his widow Elizabeth and his next of kin. Half was to go to the widow, the other half was to be divided equally between Herbert Lloyd and his two sisters Alice and Elizabeth.[1]

But events were to show that a grasping and avaricious Herbert Lloyd had no intention of honouring his legal obligations either to his own family or his sister-in-law. Back at the mansion after John Lloyd's funeral, Elizabeth Lloyd was obliged to draw her widow's weeds tightly around her and begin a long drawn out legal battle for what should have been rightfully hers. But from the start her position was made virtually impossible by Herbert Lloyd's conduct; he selfishly took possession of the whole mansion and appropriated its effects, refusing to enter into any negotiation concerning a rightful share out and even forbidding her lawyers access to legal papers.[2] Elizabeth Lloyd, alone and far from the custodial influence of her family at Gunthorpe Manor, stood in a desperately vulnerable position. In no time at all, the former leafy paradise turned into a nightmare abode and, unable to endure it, she soon moved away from Peterwell to continue her fight against Herbert Lloyd in the Law Courts. Lloyd was no more charitable to his own sisters, he refused to pay out their share and they were obliged to turn to the Courts for help with their claims. In addition, he was also challenged in his inheritance by members of the Maesyfelin family, who claimed that Sir Lucius Christianus Lloyd had not been within his rights to bequeath the Maesyfelin estate to John Lloyd in 1750. Embattled on all sides by such litigation, it is not surprising to find that Herbert Lloyd attempted to let Peterwell and in 1756 the following advertisement appeared in a London newspaper: 'To be let . . . the Demesne of Peterwell . . . consisting of 130 acres of meadow besides pasture land with convenient outhouses all in good repair . . .'[3] Two months later the mansion itself was advertised: 'The House of Peterwell . . . being a very handsome house with a good walled garden with . . . warren, fishponds, coach houses, pigeon house . . . all in good repair'.[4] Once again, there is no evidence that any deal was struck in respect of the letting or the selling Peterwell.

Meanwhile, Lloyd's financial affairs deteriorated; large areas of his eastate were mortgaged and in 1757 he sold off 'woods and groves' to Robert Morgan, the ironmaster of Carmarthen. In 1758 he borrowed £260 from John Jones of Crynfryn, the Aberystwyth attorney. But it was still not enough; he was obliged to borrow from kinsmen and the following letter sent to John Johnes, Dolaucothi gives an indication of his sense of desperation:[5]

Dear Sir.

I Have not Heard from Bowen yet which surprize me much. ——
Mr Skyrme Has been Here & Has used me very Ill so yt I am Determined to Have nothing to say to such a villain, therefore beg to see you Here to morrow on Business of Great Consequence to me & you. ——
I beg to know whether you did talk with yr Brother abt Lewis of Llanerchaeron money for I must Have 'em more of it to morrow when I see you, which I beg you will not faill Doing, & you will Ever oblige Dr. Cozen

yrs most affectly
Herbt Lloyd.

Peterwell
7ber 16th 1757.

Letter from Sir Herbert Lloyd to John Johnes, Dolaucothi

Dear Sir,

. . . I beg to know whether you did talk with your brother about Lewis of Llanerchaeron's money, for I must have them. More of it to-morrow when I see you, which I beg you will not fail of doing, and you will ever oblige dear cousin,

Yours effectionately,
Herbt. Lloyd.
16 Sept. 1757.

The Johnes brothers were only too well aware of Herbert Lloyd's financial embarrassment, and there is even a suggestion that they hoped to exploit it. In October 1757 Thomas Johnes the Custos informed his brother John, 'He (Herbert Lloyd) seems much distressed for cash, and we may come in for a good bargain'.

To add to his worries there now came a claim from a totally unexpected quarter. A certain Francis Llwyd of Doctors Commons laid claim to the Maesyfelin estate alleging that he was the true heir to Sir Lucius Christianus Lloyd. This Francis Llwyd was a cousin to Sir Lucius and his brother Sir Charles Cornwallis Lloyd who had died in 1729. Francis Llwyd's claim was based on the contents of the will of Sir Charles, drawn up 'on or about 20 January 1728'. Under the terms of the will the estate was devised 'to the use of his younger brother Sir Lucius only, thereafter, to be devised to the use of the first sons of his body successively in tail male'; in default of such issue the estate was to go to the 'testator's cousin Francis Llwyd of Doctors Commons for life'.[6] As we have seen, Sir Lucius died without issue in 1750 and bequeathed the estate to John Lloyd; this, claimed Francis Llwyd, was invalid, and the estate of Maesyfelin was rightfully his.

Llwyd filed a Bill of Complaint in the Court of Chancery stating that he had been cheated by John Lloyd as to the extent of the debts and incumbrances on the Maesyfelin estate. In a further Bill of Complaint drawn up on 26 May 1758, Francis Llwyd made serious allegations concerning the conduct of John Lloyd; he complained to the Lord Chancellor that he had been coerced by John Lloyd into accepting a settlement on the Maesyfelin estate. Thus, on 12 March 1750, he had covenanted with John Lloyd not to remarry, he being a widower, and not to have a legitimate son, in return for payment of one hundred pounds to each of his daughters on his death, and in return for an annuity of fifty pounds. He now wished this agreement set aside on

Sir Charles Lloyd of Maesyfelin

the grounds that it had been obtained by deceit and as a result of duress.[7] The Court of Chancery had an unenviable reputation for long delay and matters were sometimes resolved by a process of attrition rather than as a result of the dispensation of equity. The affair dragged on for years, but Herbert Lloyd was saved by the intervention of fate in 1764, when Francis Llwyd died and nothing came of the litigation.

This was just as well, for throughout the 1760s Herbert Lloyd faced another battle in the courts brought about by his sister-in-law Elizabeth Lloyd. On her marriage to John Lloyd on 24 March 1750, she had brought with her a dowry consisting of freehold estates in Norfolk and the city of Norwich reputedly valued at eighty thousand pounds. After his marriage, John Lloyd sold part of this estate and eight thousand pounds of this was vested by the trustees in a mortgage on the Maesyfelin estate to pay off debts after the death of Sir Lucius Lloyd; another six thousand pounds from Elizabeth Lloyd's fortune had been settled on the Peterwell estate and the trustees of her marriage settlement were now pressing Herbert Lloyd for the repayment of this sum. Elizabeth Lloyd was also entitled under the law to one half of her late husband's personal estate, but neither money nor goods were forthcoming from Herbert Lloyd. He similarly continued to withhold the fair share of the personal estate owing to his two sisters Alice and Elizabeth. Actions were accordingly commenced against Herbert Lloyd by all parties, and once again Chancery attempted to decide the issues between them.[8] The dispute festered on for years, and Elizabeth Lloyd was to die before a settlement was reached, but her beneficiaries carried on the fight.

Throughout his life Herbert Lloyd was not only reluctant to settle debts but he was always seeking to beg or borrow money from others; not always with success. Evidently John Johnes of Dolaucothi had tired of his requests and was rebuked by Thomas his brother for not assisting him in 1764: 'Your neighbours have behaved very uncivilly to the Bart.', wrote the Custos, 'a person of his figure and fashion to be refused cash when his creditors are pressing is really monstrous'.[9] Lloyd's financial affairs grew steadily worse. In both 1765 and 1766 he again attempted to let the house and demesne of Peterwell, placing advertisements in the *Gloucester Journal.* By 1768 his predicament was such that his contemporaries regarded the sale of Peterwell as inevitable; on 24 November 1768 Lord Lisburne wrote to James Lloyd of Mabws stating that the mansion 'must come soon to market'. Lisburne by this time felt nothing but contempt for Herbert Lloyd and feared only that 'some other Herod might purchase Peterwell and start up with commanding influence amidst our mountains'.[10]

Although by fair means or foul Herbert Lloyd had managed to withstand the claims of his creditors for most of his life, he failed to stem the tide of the law beyond 1769. In the spring of that year, the trustees and relatives of his sister-in-law at last were able to obtain an order to distrain upon the Peterwell estate, 'to take, lead, drive, carry away and impound stock' to settle debts. It was not until two years after his death that the trustees eventually managed to obtain a judgment on the eight thousand pounds owed to them; a decree of the High Court of Chancery dated 6 July 1771 declared that they were entitled to that sum from the estate 'of the late Sir Herbert Lloyd'.

Peterwell had indeed proved an uneasy inheritance for Herbert Lloyd. Ostensibly, it had provided him with a lavish stage on which to play out his political and social ambitions. But in reality, the props were too fragile to support his grand designs and this, coupled with his own profligacy, eventually brought crashing down this distinctive seat so assiduously built up by his ancestors.

NOTES

[1] D.R.O., (Aber.), Pet. Box, DX/3/3.
[2] ibid.
[3] *Gloucester Journal,* 7 Sept. 1756.
[4] ibid., Nov. 1756.
[5] D.C. Mss., T.J. to J.J., 16 Sept. 1758.
[6] D.R.O., (Aber.), Pet. Box, DX/3/3.
[7] ibid.
[8] D.R.O., (Aber.), Pet. Box, DX/3/II.
[9] D.C. Mss., T.J. to J.J., 17 Feb. 1764.
[10] N.L.W., 14215 C., Lisburne to Mabws, n.d.

Chapter Eleven

THE ROAD TO WESTMINSTER

Ownership of Peterwell and control of the Court Leet were considered by Herbert Lloyd as mere stepping stones toward a far higher goal; from the start his real ambition was to gain a seat at Westminster. Cardiganshire at this time returned two M.P.s, one for the county and one for Cardigan boroughs. It was not for nothing that the leading families struggled for seats in Parliament; the role of M.P. conferred not only status and a social eminence, but also very real practical benefits. Election to Parliament opened the door to influence at both local and national levels: M.P.s were conceded a say in local patronage and might expect honours and offices for themselves. Sensible of all this, Herbert Lloyd had made his first bid for Parliament as early as 1753 when he had tried to wheedle the support of the Gogerddan trustees to back his candidature for the Whig nomination.[1] He was, however, unanimously rejected, Sir John Philipps and the others being somewhat surprised at his impertinence.

In the eighteenth century, although the party divisions between Tory and Whig existed, in reality the differences in principle between them were few. Alliances and allegiances could be forged across party lines as the county families sought to consolidate or increase their influence. Very often in Cardiganshire an agreement was reached whereby the two seats were shared to avoid the expense of a contested election. We saw how John Lloyd of Peterwell was returned unopposed in both 1747 and 1754 as the Whig member for the county seat, which left the Cardigan boroughs seat clear for the Tories. John Lloyd had gained the support of Gogerddan, without which it was well nigh impossible to achieve anything, for they remained the dominant political force in Cardiganshire because of their control over the Cardigan and Aberystwyth boroughs. The leading Tories in the county were the Pryses of Gogerddan and the Powells of Nanteos: the leading Whigs were the Vaughans of Trawsgoed and, more recently arrived on the political scene, the Lloyds of Peterwell and the Johnes of Llanfair and Dolaucothi.

The death of John Lloyd in 1755 had left a vacant county seat and

Trawsgoed

Herbert Lloyd had attempted for a second time to gain the nomination to follow his brother to Westminster; in this he was supported by Thomas Johnes the Custos. This time, however, Wilmot Vaughan of Trawsgoed had placed himself firmly in line for the seat and we saw how he assiduously canvassed government support with his repeated letters to the Duke of Newcastle during John Lloyd's long illness. As a result, Newcastle had prevailed upon Thomas Johnes and Herbert Lloyd to stand down in favour of Wilmot Vaughan, who was returned unopposed to Parliament on 3 December 1755. Growing political rivalry had developed between Peterwell and Trawsgoed, as Peterwell had attempted to set themselves up as the leading Whigs in the county. In the 1754 election, John Lloyd of Peterwell had been supported by the Gogerddan trustees at the expense of Wilmot Vaughan, who was consequently cast into the political wilderness and greatly peeved by the whole situation. However, the premature death of John Lloyd had given Vaughan another chance to contest the seat, and this time he made his success absolutely sure by securing the support of the Prime Minister, the Duke of Newcastle.

A deep feeling of discord and social jealousy had also developed between Thomas Johnes the Custos and Wilmot Vaughan of Trawsgoed. Normally, the offices of Custos Rotulorum and the Lord Lieutenancy of the county were vested in the same family, but in Cardiganshire, the Lord Lisburne, Wilmot Vaughan's father, was the Lord Lieutenant of the county whereas Thomas Johnes held the office of Custos Rotulorum. For many years to come Thomas Johnes was to support Herbert Lloyd against Wilmot Vaughan in all his political aims, thereby fuelling the Peterwell-Trawsgoed rivalry which was to last throughout the sixties.

Herbert Lloyd, the new owner of Peterwell, did not have the same respect and standing as his brother John. His conduct as a J.P. and his generally wayward behaviour gave him little credibility as a political figure and Wilmot Vaughan of Trawsgoed made no secret of his feelings of contempt and disgust for this dubious squire of Peterwell. In October 1755 he sent the following barbed account of Lloyd to Newcastle:[2]

> The views of the present Mr Lloyd of Peterwell are so very extensive, his principles so little fixed and his whole character so unstable that I must be a politican of a very sanguine complexion to promise myself any aid from that quarter.

Wilmot Vaughan of Trawsgoed

Vaughan's assessment of Lloyd was highly uncomplimentary but true. His instability and lawless escapade at Esgair Mwyn had already cost him his commission of the peace, and such a loss had seriously undermined his authority, but resilience and audacity were prominent traits in his character. He now sought to get himself reinstated as a J.P. and thereby regain some of his former standing in the county.

At this time it was possible for any influential figure in the county to submit names of persons suitable to be made J.P.s to the Lord Chancellor for consideration. In 1756, Herbert Lloyd, with the aid of Thomas Johnes, submitted a new list of persons to be appointed magistrates with his own name heading the list. Wilmot Vaughan was staggered by the sheer effrontery of this move and he expressed his amazement to William Powell of Nanteos: 'I have learned', he wrote, 'to wonder at nothing that comes from that hand, yet I must own this last production struck me with some degree of surprise and indignation'.[3] Apart from his own name, Herbert Lloyd had also included the name of Lewis Morris to be made a J.P.; evidently he had made his peace with Morris since the Esgair Mwyn fracas. William Powell, still consumed with hatred against Morris, even feared that Lewis Morris would somehow influence the Lord Chancellor to accept the new list, but his fears were allayed when Newcastle wrote to Vaughan stating that, 'No regard is paid to Lewis Morris, he having proved himself to be a very base and dishonest fellow'. Clearly, poor Lewis Morris had suffered most unfairly as a result of William Powell's vendetta against him.

This latest attempt by Herbert Lloyd to manoeuvre himself back into a position of J.P. once again unnerved Wilmot Vaughan who looked upon Peterwell with perpetual suspicion and contempt. Fearing that the new names had been chosen to undermine the power of Trawsgoed, he complained to the Duke of Newcastle:[4]

> This list was obnoxious to me and disreputable to the county . . . and was framed to gratify the particular views and spleen of these two gentlemen. Every gentleman who is suspected of having the least attachment to me . . . is omitted. The whole of this great work has been the joint labour of Mr Johnes and Mr Lloyd . . . calculated to initiate their interest and popularity.

The animosity between Vaughan and the other two intensified when it seemed that Lord Hardwicke, the Lord Chancellor, was prepared to approve Lloyd's new list. It was all too much for Vaughan who turned to his father, Lord Lisburne, for assistance to check Lloyd and Thomas Johnes. Lisburne responded by promptly using all his authority against them. He informed William Powell: 'I suppose you have had the famous list which Mr Herbert Lloyd presented to the Lord Chancellor in his own hand . . . To destroy this modest project . . . I would move in conjunction with you . . . I think the sooner the better to defeat this scheme'.[5]

Trawsgoed now countered Herbert Lloyd by submitting their own list of persons to be recommended as J.P.s. 'Far from imitating their narrow and ungenerous spirit', wrote Wilmot Vaughan, 'I included in mine every person who had pretensions either by fortune or character'.

A tense struggle ensued with each of the opposing factions attempting to promote their own nominees to the Bench. After some eighteen months of intrigue and wrangle, Wilmot Vaughan and Lord Lisburne won the day by finally persuading Lord Hardwicke that it was in the best interest of everyone to reject Herbert Lloyd's list. It was a triumph for Vaughan and a slap in the face for Lloyd. The latter's reaction to it was summed up in a letter written by Thomas Johnes the Custos to his mother in 1758 describing the incident: 'Vaughan has taken out a Commission of the Peace for Cardiganshire. Herbert is left out and you may be sure not a little enraged'.[6] His anger at being rejected can only be imagined. Once again he had failed in his design to strengthen his position within the county, and his name as a magistrate was not to reappear until 1761.

Whilst attempting to get himself restored as a magistrate, Herbert Lloyd became involved in another remarkable affair which erupted in Cardiganshire in 1757. Unrest frequently flared up in the county, and landlords turned overnight into war lords, using their own armed mobs to settle petty differences and generally pervert the course of the justice they were supposed to uphold. The autumn of 1757 saw Cardiganshire gripped by a particularly sharp spasm of lawlessness which became sufficiently serious for Lewis Morris to describe it as being tantamount to 'Civil War'. One of the main perpetrators was Herbert Lloyd of Peterwell.

The whole affair revolved around the fortunes of Thomas Johnes of Abermâd, whose ancient family seat was described by Meyrick as 'standing beautifully on an arm of the river Ystwyth'. This Thomas

Johnes was the magistrate who had given possession of Esgair Mwyn mine to Lewis Morris on behalf of the Crown in 1753. Thomas Johnes of Abermâd was an unpleasant and extremely violent person, who constantly misused his authority according to his own whims. His behaviour was such that Wilmot Vaughan had complained to the Lord Chancellor that, 'Mr Johnes of Abermâd had been guilty of several misbehaviours in his office of a Justice of the Peace by supporting an armed mob in order to prevent the execution of a process against himself, and also by irregularly superseding the warrants of the other Justices of the Peace issued against offenders'.[7] The *Morris Letters* refer to Abermâd as a thoroughly unsavoury character, who had a large number of illegitimate children in the county.

Thomas Johnes, Abermâd, was a cousin to Thomas Johnes the Custos and John Johnes of Dolaucothi. In 1757, however, an altercation occurred between Abermâd and the Johnes brothers over a mortgage in Carmarthenshire; this led to the issuing of an Exchequer Writ against the Custos. But Abermâd owed money to both the Johnes brothers and Herbert Lloyd. Maddened by his imperious behaviour, they determined to avenge themselves on Abermâd; to assist them in this purpose they hired a lawyer named Francis Skyrme of Llawhaden. He was instructed to retaliate by drawing up a writ against Abermâd for money owed to the Johnes brothers, and for the sum of one thousand pounds owed to Herbert Lloyd. However, drawing up a writ was one thing; its execution against such a defiant character as Abermâd, quite another. For years he had ridden in the face of the law, and he was not likely to submit passively to any writ from the Custos. Skyrme, therefore, decided to act with guile; surprise and force were to be the tactics against Abermâd. The plan is revealed in a letter from Skyrme to John Johnes, Dolaucothi, and we get an outline of the carefully drawn up scheme to arrest Abermâd:[8]

> I think our best way will be to get the under Sheriff to your house . . . fix for meeting the defendant at Tregaron . . . I think twenty resolute fellows sufficient for our purpose, but they must be in secret. Please consult Mr Herbert Lloyd to fix the day.

But this meticulous plan was never given the chance of being put into operation, for Herbert Lloyd precipitated the whole action by taking matters into his own hands. He sent word to Abermâd 'pretending to be his bosom friend' and lured him to Llanybydder on the pretext of discussing some business with him. There, he suddenly assaulted him and carried him off to Cardigan Gaol assisted by a mob of one hundred men. According to Lewis Morris, Herbert Lloyd 'attacked Abermâd before he had taken his foot out of the stirrup . . . caught him by the shoulder . . . bound his hands behind his back . . . placed him on a blind horse . . . and away with him to Cardigan . . . and fifty of Johnes of Llanfair's tenants to defend him [Abermâd] from his own people'.[9]

John Owen, another epistolary gossip of the Morris circle, gives a detailed account of the mortifications endured by Abermâd at the hands of Herbert Lloyd. He states that he was viciously manhandled by Lloyd at Llanybydder, 'he was then dragged to Bronwydd. The following morning he was taken to Cardigan where he was kept on display opposite the hall, bound on the back of a horse for everybody to stare at him. He was then placed in a beer house for two to three days . . . with armed men as sentries, and when his son, came looking for him, he was really hammered . . . he was then carried to gaol . . . He threatened to call his mob to release him, but they were too cowardly and remained at home being afraid of the blunderbusses. At last he was taken out of gaol on a writ of *habeas corpus*, and sent to Llansawel with one hundred armed men. From there, five men took him to London to see him secure in the King's Bench'. Owen concluded his lengthy account with the description of Abermâd in the unpleasant confines of the Fleet prison for debtors:[10]

> I went to see him recently and there is a great difference between his lodging now and Abermâd. He is in some old dirty stinking loft with little room to turn and without a messenger or the convenience to go out and see anyone; nor to do anything else. He is in the midst of a crowd of people, the same kind as himself, listening to their wicked talk, but possibly not too wicked for a man of his kind . . . I do not see any possibility of freedom . . . because he is in great debt to Herbert Lloyd . . . What a hell of a thing to be doing, cutting each other's throats like this.

John Owen never spoke a truer word. In Cardiganshire itself the whole region had been pitched into a new state of lawlessness. The violence spread like a forest fire, with most of the prominent families committing themselves to one side or another. Lewis Morris, acting almost like a foreign correspondent, once again gives us a picture of events in a letter written to his brother William on 8 October 1757:[11]

> It is civil war in Cardiganshire between Abermâd and Llanfair . . . with 140 men of a side or more. Abermâd hath several allies, Nanteos, Trawsgoed, Aberllolwyn and Llandudoch. Llanfair has strong allies, colliers from Pembrokeshire, miners from Esgair Mwyn . . . Lewis Llanychairon etc . . . All are under arms. You never heard of such madness. Thank God you are in a country where all the people are not mad or wicked.

Lewis Morris was never very partial to Cardiganshire, but it seems that this time his disgust of the county was justified. It is clear from the letter that Wilmot Vaughan had now thrown in his lot with Thomas Johnes of Abermâd; much as he had previously disapproved of Abermâd's lawless behaviour, such was his hatred of Herbert Lloyd and Thomas Johnes the Custos, that on this occasion he had decided to support Abermâd. Within a short time this affair had developed into a great county quarrel drawing into its vortex anyone who had any influence: Lewis Morris pithily and aptly referred to the fracas as 'a case of dog eat dog'. The year came to its close with Abermâd still languishing in the chronic conditions of the Fleet prison, but fortunate to have survived the disease and stench which killed off so many of the prison population at this time. He still had not been formally tried for his debts and Francis Skyrme, the lawyer, was still seeking to obtain a judgment against him.

The new year, 1758, brought with it a change of heart in Herbert Lloyd towards Johnes of Abermâd. Incredibly, after the vicious assault upon his person at Llanybydder he now sought to make his peace with Abermâd, but without consulting Thomas Johnes the Custos. The Custos, however, was privy to the whole affair: 'I am credibly informed', he told his brother, 'but it is a great secret, that Herbert sent Gwyn the Glazier to Tom Johnes Abermâd, to tell him that he was about raising a large sum of money, if he would be reconciled to him and forgive him what was past'.[12] Clearly (after all the aggravation of the past months) it was a dramatic turn about on the part of Herbert Lloyd. Francis Skyrme was infuriated by Lloyd's vacillation, and he regarded him as a highly dangerous double agent.

He then wrote to John Johnes warning him of Herbert Lloyd's deceit. 'I hear the traitor who first deceived, is endeavouring to deceive us . . . you know my meaning', Skyrme wrily remarked to John Johnes.

Back at the Fleet prison, Abermâd, understandably, became obsessed with thoughts of revenge, and was using his allies to try and get John Johnes of Dolaucothi removed from the Bench. Francis Skyrme warned Johnes on 23 March: 'I find Abermâd intends pushing you out of the Commission of the Peace, which I believe you may despise; however, I think it will be adviseable for you to take all proper caution, and to be armed against such an infernal villain'.[13] This threat alarmed Johnes of Dolaucothi, and their correspondence reveals that both the Custos and his brother were becoming increasingly concerned that Abermâd's release from gaol was imminent. Skyrme had warned that the case against Abermâd was so tenuous that the rules of Court would not allow him to be detained for very much longer, unless an action for 'debts and costs' was brought against him. The backlash of Abermâd's anger constituted a very real threat, for he was a particularly powerful and vicious squire who commanded a significant following in the north of the county.

The fears of the Johnes brothers were finally allayed when Skyrme managed to nail down Abermâd; he resorted to the invidious trick of bribing some of Abermâd's own men to testify against him in Court. On 2 May 1758 Skyrme requested Johnes of Dolaucothi 'to get three or four of the Abermâd mob . . . to make an affidavit of his behaviour . . . it will be of service. The Court I believe is fully advertised of his behaviour'. Skyrme's tactics against Abermâd proved successful. On 2 August 1758 he was sued for the repayment of a mortgage debt, and in an affidavit it was maintained that, 'he had lived in open and public defiance of the law for many years'.[14] The hapless Thomas Johnes of Abermâd was, therefore, destined to be detained within the stinking confines of the Fleet prison for another two years.

But blood is thicker than water and the passage of time took the heat out of the situation on both sides. By 1760 even Thomas Johnes the Custos was expressing concern about his condition in gaol and attempting to negotiate his release. Abermâd himself, mellowed by the three years incarceration, was glad to compromise and clutch at any opportunity to get out. Herbert Lloyd and Thomas Johnes the Custos now did their utmost to get him out of the Fleet. The motive was not entirely philanthropic; the year 1760 was the year of the run

Dolaucothi

up to the general election of 1761, and the continued detention of Abermâd, who commanded a strong political following in the north of the county, was an embarrassment which Herbert Lloyd and the Custos could ill afford at such a sensitive time. Therefore, after months of negotiation, Abermâd finally stepped out of the Fleet prison in the first week of June 1760. The Custos, with great relief, described his release:[15]

> Johnes of Abermâd is at liberty, his discharges all signed on Saturday last, and the next morning he marched out in great triumph. I hope it will not be long before he makes his appearance in the county.

After all the provocation, there was a grand reconciliation and Abermâd even honoured his debts. 'He has settled everything with regard to us',[16] wrote the Custos to his brother. Herbert Lloyd, in particular, welcomed an end to all the rancour; he was now trying to put forth a new image of respectability and amity on all fronts, and a spirit of concord best suited his purposes. The reason was the approaching general election; henceforth all his efforts became concentrated on this issue, and he was determined for the third time to present himself for Parliament. In all this he was cleverly assisted by Thomas Johnes the Custos who became his election agent.

Having alienated Wilmot Vaughan of Trawsgoed and William Powell of Nanteos, Lloyd had to cultivate the support of Gogerddan who still held the political hegemony of the county. The year 1760 saw an artful Herbert Lloyd and Thomas Johnes enter into a new era of intrigue and political stratagem. They were well aware of the need to win over the confidence of Sir John Philipps, Picton Castle, the most powerful of the Gogerddan trustees, and they did this by ingratiating themselves with John Pugh Pryse, the Gogerddan heir. He had been just seven years old when his father Thomas Pryse, M.P. had died in 1745. During the intervening years the trustees had safeguarded his interests; he had by now come of age and the time was ripe for him to claim his political inheritance.

Wholly sensible of all this, Herbert Lloyd and Thomas Johnes took a special interest in the welfare of the young John Pugh Pryse. As a young boy he had been sent away to school in London, but he showed a deep attachment to Cardiganshire, which was now being exploited by Herbert Lloyd. Lewis Morris became involved and was even attempting to teach John Pugh Pryse some Welsh. They entertained him at their London clubs and enthusiastically supported his candidature for the county seat at the coming general election. This was only a ruse to strengthen their own standing: John Pugh Pryse really had no need of their backing, but the truth was that they had need of the great Gogerddan influence in order for Herbert Lloyd to gain the nomination for the Cardigan boroughs seat.

In their apparent eagerness to support John Pugh Pryse for his seat, Herbert Lloyd and Thomas Johnes even went so far as to offer to pay all his election expenses. This was a staggering commitment on the part of Herbert Lloyd, considering his own financial situation was little short of desperate. Nevertheless, their tactics won the confidence of the ageing Sir John Philipps who welcomed their generous and seemingly sincere support for John Pugh Pryse.

Meanwhile, Wilmot Vaughan, the sitting member for the county, took a less sanguine view of these activities of Herbert Lloyd and Thomas Johnes. As usual, he was becoming thoroughly alarmed. Once again Thomas Johnes and Herbert Lloyd had touched upon the raw political nerve of Trawsgoed. He knew that he had no chance of being re-elected for the county seat at the coming election, for this would now revert to Gogerddan in the person of John Pugh Pryse, but the prominent presence of Herbert Lloyd threatened any hopes he might have had of contesting the Cardigan boroughs seat.

Wilmot Vaughan now resorted to the old tactic of writing to the Prime Minister reminding him of Herbert Lloyd's outrageous past deeds; he pointed out to Newcastle that Lloyd and Vaughan only supported Pryse from 'motives of jealousy and envy'. Even Wilmot Vaughan's uncle, Thomas Watson, M.P. for Berwick-on-Tweed showed concern about Herbert Lloyd's intentions. Thomas Watson also wrote to Newcastle to remind him of Herbert Lloyd's indecorous conduct: 'It's alleged', he coldly commented, 'that one Mr Lloyd, now of Peterwell is to be a candidate against Mr Vaughan. Your Grace, I believe, remembers this gentleman was lately struck out of the Commission of the Peace for some very illegal acts'.[17] It was a devastating letter, but Herbert Lloyd's new image of respectability was hard to dent.

Gripped by panic, Wilmot Vaughan again wrote to Newcastle making a blistering attack on both Herbert Lloyd and Thomas Johnes the Custos; he even suggested that Thomas Johnes be removed from his office of Custos Rotulorum, 'to show the country by that act, that the government disapproves of his conduct'.[18] This last personal attack upon the status of the Custos was too much. Johnes retaliated by writing to Newcastle himself, thoroughly disparaging Vaughan. He reminded Newcastle how the Trawsgoed family had acted against the Crown in the Esgair Mwyn affair in 1753, and how he himself had withdrawn his opposition to Vaughan in 1755, at the request of Newcastle himself, thereby enabling Vaughan to acquire John Lloyd's seat without a contest. This outburst seemed to have the desired effect, for Newcastle cooled somewhat in his support of Vaughan after the Custos had explained his tactics in a letter:[19]

> Mr Pryse the present candidate for the county of Cardigan has absolute command of the town, and nothing but an immoderate expense can ever give the least uneasiness for the Borough; by our present connections with him, we have a certainty of one Whig for the town and a good chance of his becoming another himself for the county.

During the coming months leading up to the election, Lloyd and the Custos continued to court the favours of the Gogerddan camp to promote their own interests. They held election dinners where they had the ideal opportunity of furthering their claims. On 9 February 1760 Richard Morris, informed his brother Lewis of an invitation which he had received to a dinner to be held at the Prince of Orange in Jermyn Street; present there were all the important Cardiganshire gentry, including John Pugh Pryse and Thomas Johnes. Herbert Lloyd spent the evening strategically placed at Pryse's right hand. From a letter by Richard Morris written in the quaint macaronic style so often favoured by the Morris brothers, we get an intimate glimpse of the scenario:[20]

> Gŵr ieuanc mwyn naturiol y Brys Gogerddan, e fu ef a'r Sions a'r Harbard efo'r Duc Newcastle, met a gracious reception. Yn ddigon siwr o ynill y Maes. No gentleman of note against us but Pwel.*

*Pryse Gogerddan is a gentle natural young man; he and Johnes and Herbert had been with the Duke of Newcastle; met a gracious reception. Certain to win the field. No gentleman of note against us except Powell (of Nanteos).

The following month, March 1760, we get an account of the big election feast—*Gwledd y Lecsiwn*—which was attended by Richard Morris. Once again he described the occasion to his brother. At this feast Herbert Lloyd, possibly under the influence of drink, reminisced about the Esgair Mwyn affair when he had held a pistol to the head of Lewis Morris, but claimed now he was genuinely fond of Lewis Morris: '. . . a'r Harbard yn tyngu fod yn dda gantho'r Llew yn ei galon, er rhoi pystol wrth ei Lechwedd yn Esgair y Mwyn gynt a'i anfon i garchar Aberteifi'.[21] *

Clearly, these were halcyon days but, beneath the *bonhomie,* Herbert Lloyd and Thomas Johnes pursued their aim with deadly seriousness showing themselves to be masters in the art of political manoeuvre. The outcome of all this socialising and canvassing was that Sir John Philipps entered into an agreement with them whereby John Pugh Pryse would stand unopposed for the county, and John Symmons for the borough. But when the time of the election arrived, it was Herbert Lloyd's name which went forward for Cardigan boroughs and not that of Symmons. How Lloyd and Johnes finally contrived to arrange this is not clear, but they had evidently outwitted Sir John Philipps and the local Tories. This tactical success was referred to by Wilmot Vaughan writing some years after the event:[22]

> At the last election, Sir John Philipps closed with Sir Herbert Lloyd and Mr Johnes, thinking to secure Mr Pryse an easy seat for the county . . . But this scheme though deeply conceived, Sir Herbert soon turned to his own purpose, and in the result defeated the original intention with some dexterity and address. Had Sir John thought Sir Herbert would have represented the Town, he would never have separated Mr Pryse and me.

This observation by Vaughan was probably true, for Sir John Philipps of Picton Castle would not normally have approved of Herbert Lloyd to the extent of helping him to get a seat in Parliament. It had been a piece of brilliant political strategy, triumphant for Herbert Lloyd but disastrous for Wilmot Vaughan.

As it was, Vaughan's political doom was sealed for the present.

*. . . and Herbert swearing that he loved Lewis Morris in his heart, despite the fact that he had previously placed a pistol to his forehead at Esgair Mwyn and transported him to Cardigan gaol.

An Election Entertainment
(Hogarth)

Chairing of the Member
(Hogarth)

Although Newcastle had promised to support him, he did not even manage to secure his own nominee as mayor of Cardigan, without which his cause was virtually lost. Thomas Johnes, on the other hand, gained the sheriff of his choice and was delighted that he had at last vanquished his old antagonist Wilmot Vaughan. With great joy he wrote to John Johnes:[23]

> I desire you will congratulate me upon our Cardiganshire sheriff; it has given me infinite satisfaction. We had a very hard struggle, it must have mortified and hurt Vaughan beyond expression.

It had indeed injured Vaughan, who now withdrew in a fit of pique, surrendering the field to his opponents. Johnes described Vaughan as '. . . fallen from the great man to a pitiful figure', and he was reduced to pleading the support of Newcastle for an alternative seat. Eventually, Vaughan succeeded his uncle, Thomas Watson, as M.P. for Berwick-on-Tweed at the end of 1765, and he held that seat until the general election of 1768 when he was again returned for Cardiganshire.

As for Herbert Lloyd, it was now 'roses, roses all the way'; at last he had achieved the ambition he had so ruthlessly pursued. After his election on 20 April 1761, he placed a notice in the *London Evening Post* expressing his gratitude to the burgesses of the contributory boroughs of Aberystwyth, Lampeter, Cardigan and Adpar: 'Your steady and spirited behaviour . . . I have the deepest sense of and can never forget'. Nor, as it turned out, were they to forget it! The Morris brothers, as usual, reported on the event, and William wrote to Richard on 9 May 1761 stating that: 'John Pugh Pryse and Herbert Lloyd were carried on chairs through crowds of people shouting loud enough to deafen gentle people'.[24]

The year 1761 belonged to Peterwell; a combination of astuteness and naked cunning had propelled Herbert Lloyd from the comparatively modest Court Leet at Lampeter to the fount of all power at the Palace of Westminster.

NOTES

[1] B.C.R.O. Pryse Mss., John Lloyd to Thos. Lloyd, 16 Mar. 1753.
[2] B.L.Add.Mss. 32856, f.612.
[3] Nanteos Mss., W.V. to Wm.P., 24 Feb. 1756.

[4] B.L.Add.Mss. 3560.
[5] Nanteos Mss., Lisburne to Wm.P., 30 Feb. 1756.
[6] D.C.Mss., T.J. to Mrs Johnes, 16 Sept. 1758.
[7] Nanteos Mss., W.V. to Hardwicke, 20 Sept., 1756.
[8] D.C.Mss., F. Skyrme to J.J., 12 Sept. 1757.
[9] *A.M.L.,* Pt. 2, p. 919.
[10] ibid., pp. 922-24.
[11] Davies, ed., *Morris Letters,* Vol. 2, p. 28.
[12] D.C.Mss., T.J. to J.J., 20 Jan. 1758.
[13] D.C.Mss., F. Skyrme to J.J., 23 Mar. 1758.
[14] Cwrtmawr Mss. 717 B, p. 57.
[15] D.C.Mss., T.J. to J.J., 13 June 1760.
[16] D.C.Mss., T.J. to J.J., 17 Nov. 1761.
[17] B.L.Add.Mss., 32857.
[18] B.L.Add.Mss. 32894, f.513.
[19] B.L.Add.Mss. 32901.
[20] Davies, ed., *Morris Letters,* Vol. 2, p. 174.
[21] *A.M.L.,* Pt. 2, p. 961.
[22] N.L.W.14, 215, C.
[23] D.C.Mss., T.J. to J.J., 21 Dec. 1761.
[24] Davies, ed., *Morris Letters,* Vol. 2, p. 347.

Chapter Twelve

THE VULTURE KNIGHT

The year 1761 saw Herbert Lloyd's political fortunes at their zenith, but it was to prove a watershed; over the next seven years they were to plummet. His personal fortunes, which had always been in a precarious state, were to deteriorate even further during the next few years, dissipated by personal extravagance, election expenses and the continuing litigation over his inheritance.

Now, however, as the new member for Cardigan boroughs he had within his grasp the power he had craved and he wasted no time in exploiting it to his own advantage. The fact that he was still without his commission of the peace sorely rankled, but he was now in a position to rectify this. Furthermore, this time there would be no Wilmot Vaughan or Lord Lisburne to block him; the power now lay with him as M.P. In the spring of 1761 a new list of Justices headed by Herbert Lloyd himself appeared for Cardiganshire.[1] All were Lloyd's friends and supporters; they included Lewis Morris, henceforth his staunch ally, and many others of dubious reputation such as Thomas Johnes of Abermâd, John Paynter of Hafod, John Ball of Grogwynion and John Jones of Crynfryn, the Aberystwyth attorney; all these were generally hostile to Trawsgoed and all were later to throw the county into ferment by promoting anarchy in the north of the county.

Never the most modest of men, Herbert Lloyd himself soon became puffed up with an inordinate vanity. His portrait at this time shows him to have been a man of striking appearance, with cold eyes, elongated features and an aquiline nose; a contemptuous curl to his lips conveys an impression of the superciliousness and ruthlessness which characterised his life. The Custos described him as a 'figure of fashion and elegance', and he was very much a man about town being accompanied on most occasions by his personal valet, John Baker.

Soon after becoming M.P., we find Herbert Lloyd attempting to become an officer in the Carmarthenshire Militia. There was no financial gain in this, but it would give him the opportunity of decking himself out in military finery and allow him to parade like a peacock at Bath or, suitably epauletted, 'cut a dash' in London as was the wont of public figures of the eighteenth century. To this end, Herbert Lloyd now persuaded his brother-in-law, John Adams, to resign his commission in the Carmarthenshire Militia so that he himself could take his place. The outcome of his application said nothing for his reputation. At a meeting of the officers specially convened to discuss his case, they crushingly rejected him. The incident is recorded in a letter from Illtyd Evans to the Vaughan family of Golden Grove:[2]

> Mr Herbert Lloyd came down the latter end of last week with . . . Adams from London, in order to be made a captain in the Carmarthenshire Militia in Mr Adams's stead, who was to resign in his favour. He applied to Mr Rice who, it seems did not approve of it; but offered him to the rest of the officers of the Militia. They one and all declared against him. Last Sunday, they set out for London but on different roads, Mr Lloyd greatly dissatisfied, as said.

Clearly, Herbert Lloyd's new found status as an M.P. made little impression on the Rice family of Dinefwr and the men of Carmarthen.

But Herbert Lloyd was in no way deflated by this setback; if anything, it acted as a spur to higher goals, for we now find him attempting a significant leap up the social ladder by applying for a baronetcy. It might have seemed ludicrous to many, but Lloyd was no fool and he meticulously prepared the ground.

On 9 September 1761, George III had married Princess Charlotte of Mecklenberg and the following month found Herbert Lloyd at St James's Palace 'kissing the King's hand' and presenting to him the congratulations of the Borough of Cardigan.[3] It was an astute move and Herbert Lloyd henceforth contrived to force his presence on his Majesty as often as occasion allowed. The following year the birth of a royal son gave him another opportunity of waiting upon the King. This time he presented a congratulatory message from Cardigan on the birth of the Prince of Wales, the text of which appeared in the *London Gazette* for 26-30 October 1762. This address was couched in extremely sycophantic language even by eighteenth century standards, and read in part: 'As natives of this remote part . . . we are particularly interested in this pleasing event . . . a Prince who is to enjoy that ancient and glorious title derived from this country'.

It was not a case of flattery gets you nowhere, for, to the astonishment of all, he received an order from the Earl of Bute to present himself at St James's Palace on 6 December to receive a baronetcy.

He was ecstatic, and in a hand trembling with triumph he wrote the following unctious reply to Bute's request:[4]

> I beg leave to return your Lordship's my most sincere grateful acknowledgement for the honours you have done me. I shall certainly attend at St James's on Monday next—I hope your Lordship will always command me on all occasions, either in private or in public.

A Bill was prepared granting 'our trusty and well loved Herbert Lloyd of Peterwell . . . the dignity of a baronet'.[5] Thus, after much ruthless clawing at the rungs of the social ladder, Lloyd had achieved a meteoric leap upwards and the *London Chronicle* for 7 December 1762 announced that 'Herbert Lloyd Esq. Member for the Borough of Cardigan' once again '. . . kissed the King's hand'.

But the whole affair of the granting of the baronetcy was not as smooth as it would appear, and there is an indication of a slight hiccup behind the scenes. Despite allowing Herbert Lloyd to kiss his hand on 6 December, the signs are that George III was seized with a fit of regret regarding the appointment. Although the warrant creating him a baronet had been signed by His Majesty and countersigned by Lord Halifax, Secretary of State, the actual Bill together with this warrant was sent to the King for his signature and final approval on 10 January 1763.[6] But the following day Mr Weston, Under Secretary of State, informed a Mr Grubb, possibly one of the law officers, that George III had ordered this warrant to be destroyed.[7] It is not clear why George III should have adopted this attitude; possibly he had had some information relayed to him concerning Herbert Lloyd's character, for the King was known on occasions to take a firm moral stand. However, his Majesty evidently reconsidered the matter and the difficulty was resolved, for the *Annual Register* officially reported that on 18 January, Herbert Lloyd of Peterwell had been created a baronet. The title cost him one thousand pounds.[8]

Lloyd's triumphant return to Cardiganshire as a baronet caused amazement and stupefaction. Even Thomas Johnes the Custos was flabbergasted. '. . . Herbert's title', he told John Johnes, 'I dare say surprised you very much, I am sure it did me . . . He is exceedingly pleased'.[9] But John Johnes of Dolaucothi was not impressed by this sudden social exaltation of Lloyd and was in no mood to welcome him; he even had to be urged by the Custos '. . . to compliment him and wish him joy'. Certainly, not everyone in Cardiganshire felt inclined to celebrate, and the attitude of others was not as sanguine as that of Thomas Johnes the Custos. The Reverend John Lloyd of Alltyrodyn was stung into composing a number of satirical verses which must have reflected the views of many others in the county:[10]

A would-be member brought of late,
From borough little known,
In an address of early date,
His incense to the throne.

Soon tidings came when Tivy flows
Through tyrant-harassed land,
That Lloyd to envied honours rose,
And kissed the royal hand.

O! had our gracious sovereign's touch
But cured him of his evil,
I'd own St. George ne'er boasted such
A triumph o'er the devil.

Lloyd of Alltyrodyn represented that cultured element of Cardiganshire society who obviously regarded the Baronet with disapproval, if not downright contempt.

Sir Herbert Lloyd returned to Peterwell by Christmas 1762, where he found that all his old problems stubbornly remained; elevation to the baronetcy had done nothing to absolve him from his financial problems. To ease his situation we now find him doing what most prominent persons in the eighteenth century did, to forage round for a sinecure. He wrote to Bute soliciting his support for '. . . a place now vacant in the custom';[11] but there is no evidence to show that he acquired it. A few years later, and in even more desperate straits, he turned to Newcastle in his quest for a sinecure. In an overtly obsequious letter he begged Newcastle for a place '. . . in the Green Cloth', which was particularly lucrative. 'I would not presume to fix on any particular situation', he grovelled, 'but confide entirely on your Grace whether you will grant me a position in the Green Cloth Trade, but should like a place that I may still continue in Parliament'.[12] The Duke of Newcastle took no notice of his appeal; but Lloyd sent a second letter to the Duke, this time even offering to procure a parliamentary seat for a nominee of his. 'Any person', he proposed, 'your Grace may recommend to that borough [Cardigan] cannot fail of success, as one of the contributory boroughs is my own, and are the majority of the electors of the town of Cardigan'.[13] This offer shows how blind Sir Herbert Lloyd was to the actualities of his situation. Once again, the Duke chose to ignore Lloyd's letter, possibly because he had been informed of his sliding reputation and declining fortunes.

Just as Lloyd turned to his superiors for favours and advancement, so in the stratified society of the eighteenth century others looked in similar fashion to the Baronet. It was an age riddled with patronage at all levels, and one of the most assiduous canvassers for posts was the indefatigable Lewis Morris. He already owed his Commission of the Peace to Sir Herbert Lloyd, but we find that he also frequently solicited his help to acquire situations for various members of his family. '. . . Sir Herbert Lloyd', he wrote in 1764, 'is a particular friend of mine . . . he'll do for my sake any service in his power'. When in 1764 a relative of Lewis Morris wanted to get '. . . some little post . . . in the Stamp Office', Morris complied by contacting Sir Herbert: 'When he [Sir Herbert] comes to town in January on the meeting of Parliament, I'll give you a letter to him as he will be on the spot', Morris promised the applicant.[14] Ironically, of all the wonderfully illuminating letters of Lewis Morris, one of the last he wrote, dated 18 January 1765, also contains a reference to both job seeking and Sir Herbert Lloyd; in it he described the Baronet as being 'a good back on occasion'.[15] Sadly, however, Lewis Morris himself was also in need of help, but beyond the assistance of Sir Herbert. Worn out by his punishing schedule of travel and hard work, and racked by ill health, he died on 11 April 1765. He lies buried beneath the chancel of Llanbadarn Church alongside John Pugh Pryse of Gogerddan whom he had befriended as a young man during his lifetime.

The web of patronage enmeshed all aspects of the eighteenth century, and it was particularly prevalent in the ecclesiastical sphere. Lloyd often interfered in church appointments for which purpose he kept on friendly terms with Bishop Squire of St David's. Clearly there was collusion between the two over Cardiganshire livings; in July 1763 Lloyd wrote to the Bishop thanking him for the 'many favours he had received', and sent him 'some of the produce of the county of Cardigan' as a token of his gratitude.[16] The conspiracy between

Lloyd and the Bishop aggravated many persons within the county, and particularly so when the Baronet secured the living of Llanarth for John Lloyd of Alltyrodyn,[17] who had now been forgiven for composing his satirical verses on the granting of the baronetcy. The irony of the situation was suitably noted by an anonymous poet who referred to Bishop Squire as a 'scoundrel', John Lloyd, Alltyrodyn as a 'vile wasp', and Sir Herbert Lloyd as a 'Vulture Knight' in the following verses:[18]

Hail thrifty bard! Well has thou sung
And well thy end attained,
The *Vulture Knight* by satire stung,
Thy muse hath wisely chained.

Chain'd the muse! Suppress the thought
The Knight misunderstood;
The streams that once preferment brought,
Must again be pursued.

Proceed *vile wasp;* and scribble on,
To greater things aspire,
Scoundrels, 'ere now have mitres won
For instance, Dr Sq--re.

The anonymous poet had named him well, especially as far as his treatment of Evan Evans, the distinguished poet and cleric known as Ieuan Brydydd Hir was concerned. The previous decade, Evans had been rash enough to offend Lloyd by satirizing his betrayal of Thomas Johnes, Abermâd, in 1757. It was to prove a costly piece of verse. Sir Herbert's wrath and thirst for vengeance knew no bounds; Evans was hounded out of the county and such was his terror of Lloyd that he was once seen by Lewis Morris at Ystrad Meurig 'with a ghastly look on his face', fearing that the 'formidable Sir Herbert was at his heels'.[19] Despite attempts by Lewis Morris and others to intercede on his behalf, the continuing spleen of Sir Herbert Lloyd ensured that Evan Evans was never able to procure a living in his beloved Cardiganshire.

Not only was Lloyd vindictive, but his actions invariably succeeded in reducing everything to chaos. By 1763 the situation in the north of the county was close to anarchy, caused by Sir Herbert Lloyd's acolytes whose names he had submitted in 1761 for appointment as Justices of the Peace. Law and order had ground to a standstill and even Sir Herbert showed concern at the situation. John Paynter, writing to Lord Powis, gives us an impression of the disorder:[20]

> Sir Herbert Lloyd convicted a third time John Ball for impudently keeping an ale house—no magistrate can stop the career of that lawless fellow . . . Sir Herbert is bent on asking the war office for military force to assist the magistrate—Without that aid, nothing can protect this country from the rage of Johnes and Ball.

The Johnes referred to is the irrepressible Thomas Johnes of Abermâd. John Ball was a violent unruly character, formerly a friend of Sir Herbert Lloyd. He used the law entirely for his own ends and kept an inn near Tregaron; he had at his disposal a mob of armed miners which ultimately even Sir Herbert could not control.

But for one reason or another the most disruptive magistrate of all seems to have been Sir Herbert Lloyd himself. Wherever he had dealings, trouble of one form or another usually ensued. February 1763 saw a fresh furore break out between the J.P.s when Sir Herbert interfered in the choice of John Paynter's officers when he was High Sheriff. Paynter promised the office of deputy sheriff to John Jones the lawyer, but Sir Herbert prevailed on him to give the office to his own friend and supporter, David Lloyd of Breinog. The consequences were calamitous. John Jones was so maddened by this decision that he ran amok; both he and John Ball attacked John Paynter's home in revenge for Sir Herbert's choice, and so alarmed was Paynter that he sent the following account to Lord Powis:[21]

> Last Friday Jones of Aberystwyth and six ruffians came furiously to Havod. Their language was hellish and they frightened Mrs Paynter. They determined to ruin the pretty places of Havod. I am in danger every moment . . .

John Paynter blamed this attack on Sir Herbert Lloyd, concluding that John Jones threatened to drive away five hundred of his sheep and twelve of his oxen to be sold. This disturbance in the north of the county was noted with anxiety by Thomas Johnes the Custos. As Custos Rotulorum he was naturally perturbed; but he also laid the blame at Sir Herbert's feet and wrote to John Johnes stating that the trouble was caused by the Baronet 'improperly interposing in the choice of the High Sheriff's officers'. Sir Herbert had also attempted to appoint his own Peterwell agent Evan Jenkins to the office of Recorder but, such was the fear engendered by Johnes of Abermâd, John Ball's mob and John Jones, that Jenkins absolutely refused to accept the post stating that he should be murdered if he ever 'kept court at Aberystwyth'.

The name of John Paynter features prominently in the history of Cardiganshire at this time and is closely connected with that of Sir Herbert Lloyd. In many ways they were parallel personalities. Paynter was a rapacious adventurer who had left his houses in London and Surrey to seek his fortune in Wales. He acted originally as agent to Lord Powis, but when Lewis Morris was shabbily dismissed from his management of the Esgair Mwyn mine in 1757, it was John Paynter who succeeded him. But he was neither as honest nor as capable as the Anglesey bard. In 1758 Paynter took a great liking to Hafod which was owned by Thomas Johnes the Custos. After negotiation, the Custos, who resided at Croft Castle, agreed to let Hafod to John Paynter at an annual rental of one hundred pounds; within a year, Paynter had cheated Thomas Johnes by felling timber at Hafod in excess of the value of one hundred pounds without permission.

Herbert Lloyd, however, was one of Paynter's closest acquaintances and he even helped him stock Hafod by supplying him with ninety pounds worth of sheep and cattle. Lloyd and Paynter were very much birds of a feather. To their social superiors such as Lord Powis and others they were a couple of sycophants, servile and ingratiating; but to the less highly connected persons of Cardiganshire they were brutally oppressive. The Hafod Church Records show that Paynter, like Sir Herbert, aroused the antipathy of the ordinary people and one Cornelius Griffith, an unfortunate juror was fined ten guineas for using abusive language towards him.[22]

Neither Lloyd nor Paynter liked to settle their debts and any bailiff who ventured to approach either Hafod or Peterwell risked harsh treatment. When John Charlton, who was owed money from the Esgair Mwyn mine, called at Hafod for payment, he had to flee for his life. His account of the episode gives a sharp impression of the violent life style of both Mr and Mrs Paynter at Hafod:[23]

> Instead of settling, his servant threw the stool in my face, and, hearing of a noise, Mr Paynter asked what was there? His servant answered, 'That rogue Charlton'. With that, Mr P. came out with a stick, and began to beat me as hard as ever he could, instead of settling accounts. Then his lady came with a stick and began to beat me, then they saw that there was John Ball . . . and John Jones . . . they set on throwing stones as hard as ever they could, and told me they should murder me. To which I made answer—it was a fine way to pay a debt.

Callers at Peterwell faced an equally hazardous reception; any person bearing a writ to the mansion was forced to cram it into his mouth, swallow it, and was then unceremoniously horsewhipped down the Portland marble steps, glad to flee for his life.

It was to Paynter that Sir Herbert Lloyd turned for help whilst engaged on rebuilding and extending Peterwell; possibly he considered that Paynter, as a product of London, was sufficiently suave and urbane to advise him on this matter. The Baronet was at this time engulfed in debt, yet he proceeded to improve and enhance his mansion. This was a feature of the age; the passion for elegance and the mania to show style in all things drove the country squires into often crippling competitive extravagance. Money or no money, Sir Herbert was not going to suffer Peterwell to lag behind in its manifestation of grandeur. Possibly, he sought to emulate Croft Castle with its four towers and imposing architecture but, more probably, his envy was stirred by Nanteos which, recently completed after some twenty years of rebuilding, now represented one of the finest examples of Georgian architecture in the whole of west Wales.

In the years following his baronetcy, Lloyd devoted much of his energy into making Peterwell a place of arresting splendour; an army of carpenters, masons and glaziers chipped and hammered away in an effort to transform it into a noble shrine for perpetuity; surveyors were constantly consulted and furnishings were ordered from London. Time and again Paynter was summoned down from Hafod to advise on the work; he was not always willing to come and once blamed his stay at Peterwell for a severe cold he had caught. But Lloyd continued to plague him for assistance: 'Help me with some alteration in and about my house', pleaded Lloyd, 'I trust you will not refuse me one day's visit'.[24]

In 1763 John Paynter was appointed High Sheriff and an even closer relationship developed between the two men. Thomas Johnes the Custos wrote to Paynter congratulating him upon his appointment but he expressed a different sentiment to his brother, to whom he wrote: 'Paynter certainly does not want means of expending his money. He must have some dark design of his own, which he alone can discover'.[25] The perfidious Paynter himself pretended to Lord Powis that he was not in any way elated by this honour, claiming that he '. . . preferred to be rooting among the dismal caverns of Esgair Mwyn rather than heading a mock pageantry'.[26] In reality of course, John Paynter revelled in this mock pageantry, for the office of High Sheriff provided him with the opportunity to indulge his social pretensions, and it furnished him with that extra kudos and recognition which he sought after taking over the tenancy of Hafod.

One of the most significant functions of the High Sheriff was to be in attendance at the Great Sessions which were held at Cardigan. In the spring of 1763 the arrival of these proceedings gave Sir Herbert Lloyd and John Paynter the ideal platform for their arrogance and vanity. Here, they could parade through the town with the full panoply of the law behind them since it fell to John Paynter as High Sheriff to receive the judge and escort him to the Guild Hall accompanied by all the magistrates of the county. It was a colourful and spectacular occasion which attracted vast crowds. Much of the preparation for the ceremony was the responsibility of Paynter who consulted closely with Sir Herbert. As the date of the Sessions grew nearer, Paynter grew increasingly anxious and on 5 March 1763 he wrote to Sir Herbert Lloyd, who was in London, expressing his concern.[27]

> My Dear Herbert,
>
> Your last and only letter since you went to London is dated 5 February . . . I think 30 days a long time to be without hearing from you especially at this important juncture when I wish to receive all my instructions from you . . . But would you believe it that this very day the King's Patent was brought to me by a poor woman who happened to be at Rhydfendigaid Mill where she found it; And she told us that a poor cobbler carried it there from one of the Alehouses at Tregaron. It was tied with a piece of pack thread without any direction but that which you put upon it in London. The great seal is broken all to pieces and such a dirty packet I do believe you never saw.

The 'King's Patent' was the document stamped with the Royal Seal officially conferring upon him the office of High Sheriff: evidently John Paynter was upset by the precarious, almost fortuitous manner in which he had received his great honour.

In a postscript to this letter, Paynter set out the preparations he intended making for the Great Sessions. From these we get an interesting glimpse of the pageantry involved in the administration of justice in the eighteenth century, which had something of a carnival atmosphere. It was John Paynter's privilege to greet the judge and escort him to court, flanked by a bodyguard of men dressed in handsome liveries and carrying javelins. 'I send you a list of the Javelin men for your approbation', he informed Sir Herbert, 'The livery are blue cloth with yellow waistcoats and breeches, all exceedingly good'.

For John Paynter the proper presentation of these Javelin men was important for his image as High Sheriff; for Cardigan town they provided excitement and colour which drew spectators from far and near, thronging its streets to be deafened by the noise of bells and trumpets which heralded the grand procession. Through the town marched the magistrates, many of them pompous but inapt, such as Abermâd and John Ball, yet it was a high social occasion which was followed by a dance and grand dinner given by John Paynter as High Sheriff. Paynter had already mentioned the dinner to Sir Herbert Lloyd in a letter, 'I hope to do nothing that shall be disgraceful in my office', he confided, 'the High Sheriff shall give a handsome dinner'. Clearly, John Paynter was anxious to impress.

However, there attaches to the Court of Great Sessions at Cardigan in the spring of 1763 a far deeper significance than mere ceremonial. We learn from Paynter's letter that Sir Herbert Lloyd had 'decided to act as foreman of the Jury'. Then follow lines of sinister consequence in the light of what was to emerge in the folk history of Cardiganshire, for Paynter invited Lloyd to choose his own jury: 'Name the Gentlemen which shall be most agreeable to you', he wrote, '. . . they have got it here that the Grand Jury is to be of the name of Lloyd and no other. Be it so if you please'.[28] Evidently, Sir Herbert Lloyd had sent his instructions and John Paynter was prepared to comply, but such collusion on the choice of Jury in April 1763 is startling when we consider that this was the exact time when the trial of Siôn Philip is alleged to have taken place. Of all the infamous incidents attributed to Sir Herbert Lloyd, none was more damaging to him than this.

NOTES

[1] N.L.W.Wales, 4/897/5.
[2] P.R.O.Chancery, 202/149/2.
[3] D.R.O. Cawdor/Vaughan Mss. 17/507.
[4] B.L.Add.Mss. 5276.
[5] B.L.Add.Mss. 36132, f.196.
[6] P.R.O. Home Office papers 49/1.
[7] ibid.
[8] D.C.Mss., T.J. to J.J., 20 Dec. 1762.
[9] ibid.
[10] *Lloyd Family Records,* p. 83.
[11] B.L.Add.Mss. 5726, f.209.
[12] B.L.Add.Mss. 32968, f.23.
[13] B.L.Add.Mss. 32973, f.21.
[14] *A.M.L.,* Pt. 2, p. 647.
[15] *Cymm.,* Vol. 15, p. 73.
[16] Lucas Mss. 2876.
[17] Meyrick, p. 361.
[18] Rowlands, Hist. Notes, p. 78.
[19] *A.M.L.,* Pt. 2, p. 587.
[20] P.C.Mss. 3416.
[21] P.C.Mss. 3910.
[22] *Cymm.,* Vol. 15, p. 81.
[23] ibid., p. 79.
[24] P.C.Mss. 5189.
[25] P.C.Mss. 3983.
[26] D.C.Mss. T.J. to J.J., 4 Mar. 1763.
[27] P.C.Mss. 3246.
[28] ibid.

Chapter Thirteen

THE BLACK RAM

Nid câr da ond acer o dîr. (*Siôn Tudur,* C.16)

A world away from the gaping crowds and pomp at Cardigan Assizes and some two hundred yards from Sir Herbert's great mansion stretched an eighteen acre field bordered by the river Teifi. Nothing distinguished it from the surrounding meadows except for the humble cottage built upon it. This did not form part of the Peterwell demesne for it still remained in the ownership of a freeholder named Siôn Philip. This field was to be associated with a deed so heinous that its name has over the years been inscribed in the folk annals of Cardiganshire.

The nearness of the field to Peterwell and the sight of the rude cottage was a source of intense annoyance to the haughty Baronet. It served as a constant reminder that his lust for power and his appetite for wordly possessions had not been entirely fulfilled. What rankled him even more was the realisation that he was being thwarted by one who was in the social order of that time very much his inferior. He had on many occasions sought to acquire the field by purchase, but Siôn Philip had consistently refused his offers of money and resisted all his blandishments. The freeholder's stubborness arose from a mixture of courage, pride, and an affection for a piece of land which had been cultivated by his forebears over many generations. Yet it was the type of stubborness which must inevitably lead to tragedy, for it was to clash with the ruthless obsession of a man who could not tolerate anything that hindered his own desires and ambitions.

Sir Herbert's tactics had ranged from flattery to outright threats and on one occasion he had even entertained his lowly neighbour at Peterwell in a vain attempt to weaken his resistance by making him drunk. The magnificence of Peterwell and the liberal quantities of the finest wines did not prove a snare for the wily Siôn Philip, for he still remained unwilling to part with his beloved field. To him, that special feeling which came from owning the earth beneath his feet was more satisfying, more fulfilling, infinitely more rewarding than any wealth which the Baronet might proffer. He and his wife continued with their unpretentious way of life, but sensing that the shadow cast by the great mansion over the field had become more menacing as Sir Herbert Lloyd, in desperation, sought to hatch a scheme which would secure for him possession of the field. But not even Siôn Philip could have foreseen the extent to which the Baronet was prepared to go to realise his petty ambition of becoming the owner of the field. Arrogant and ruthless, he did not hesitate to resort to foul means when fair methods had failed. Against his predatory neighbour, Siôn Philip stood no chance and his own steadfastness would only lead to the most tragic of consequences.

Tradition has it that Sir Herbert was accustomed to take himself up to his magnificent rooftop garden from where he could survey his many acres extending as far as the eye could see. His horizons were marred only by the sight of Siôn Philip's cottage standing in the corner of the field. One afternoon, as he glowered obsessively in its direction watching the peat smoke drifting up from the wide chimney, his tortured mind conceived of a plan to trap his neighbour into parting with his land. The plan was as simple as it was diabolical, for he

Siôn Philip's Cottage
(An artist's impression)

intended to incriminate Siôn Philip on a false charge of sheep stealing which, in the eighteenth century, was a felony punishable by hanging. Having failed to persuade the freeholder by all other means, he now felt confident that the threat of the hangman's rope would soon change his mind.

The following day, he cunningly circulated a rumour in Lampeter that a black ram, the pride of the Peterwell flock had been stolen. In the meantime, he had ordered two of his most trusted servants to hide the ram in one of the outbuildings. The whole neighbourhood was alerted, mock searches were organised and a general feeling of unease filled the town. To Siôn Philip and his wife there must have been a heightened feeling of tension, for they were never free of the threatening proximity of their powerful neighbour. They scoured their hedgerows and field to ensure that the ram was not lodged in a ditch or caught in some hawthorn bush, desperately hoping that the animal would show itself somewhere, soon. But the black ram was to turn up in the last place on earth where they would have wished it to be found.

A few days after its disappearance, Sir Herbert Lloyd ordered the same two servants to take the ram under cover of darkness to Siôn's cottage and lower the animal down the gaping chimney which led to a cavernous inglenook fireplace. This was known locally as a *simne lwfe* and many a night Siôn Philip and his wife must have sat around their fire able to see the stars as they peered through the wide chimney. To-night, however, it was to have a much more sinister purpose, for as soon as the servants had left Peterwell on their mission, Sir Herbert Lloyd sent for Thomas Evans, the Lampeter Constable, and ordered him to proceed post haste to Siôn Philip's cottage. It was a strange request at such an unearthly hour, but no one disobeyed the Baronet.

As the Constable, accompanied by Sir Herbert and his trusted acolyte Oakley Leigh, hurried through the heavy night frost to the mean cottage, he must have wondered at the purpose of this strange excursion for he knew that Siôn Philip was an honest man. Nearing the cottage, they must have noticed the Peterwell servants skulking away having carried out their master's command. Inside the dwelling, the scuffling of the ram had already awoken Siôn Philip and his wife, and before the dreadful realisation of what had happened had penetrated, there was a loud knocking at the door and in burst Sir Herbert and his companions. In the presence of the Baronet, the constable and the black ram, any protestations of innocence on the part of Siôn Philip would have been totally useless. The ruse must have been obvious to anyone who knew the dubious reputation of the master of Peterwell, but who would have the temerity to dispute the evidence that the ram had been discovered on the cottager's hearth? His denials of guilt would have been lost in the river mist as he was led protesting back through the cold night air towards the menacing outline of Peterwell with its four great towers, stark against a starlit sky.

Siôn Philip was roughly pushed up the white marble steps and through the oaken doors into what must have seemed the intimidating vastness of Peterwell after the one small room of his own cottage. He was taken into Sir Herbert's own study and there in front of a blazing log fire he was confronted by the Baronet. After turning out all the others, Sir Herbert gave the freeholder a last opportunity of parting

An Eighteenth Century Constable

with his field, but he had not bargained for the intransigence of Siôn Philip and the sense of outrage which was to overcome the terror which must have overwhelmed him. He refused to compromise and his resoluteness only served to fuel the fury of his accuser. Realizing that even he had failed to browbeat the freeholder into accepting his terms, Sir Herbert ordered that Siôn Philip be now confined in the Lampeter stocks, hoping, no doubt, that this ordeal would make him more amenable and to accept the hopelessness of his predicament. Constable Thomas Evans, staff in hand, stood guard while he was secured by his feet and left to suffer his humiliating ordeal exposed to the gaze and at the mercy of all and sundry. Possibly, the populace of Lampeter, sensing that a grave injustice was being perpetrated, did not add to his suffering by pelting him with stones, clods and filth as was the punishment for ordinary offenders.

Hoping that his time in the stocks had broken Siôn Philip's will to resist, Sir Herbert had him released and returned to Peterwell. But still he refused to submit to the Baronet's demands. Infuriated and insulted, he now decided to expose his recalcitrant neighbour to the full rigours of the law. He grimly ordered that Siôn Philip be marched forthwith and under heavy escort to Cardigan gaol, there to be confined until his appearance at the Court of Great Sessions in spring 1763 on a charge of stealing the black ram. Torn from the arms of his distraught wife, he was forced to walk the thirty miles to Cardigan. To prevent the possibility of sympathetic intervention by the local populace, six special constables were sworn in by Sir Herbert and, for added security, a large number of Peterwell henchmen formed a mounted bodyguard. These were said to have 'continually yelled and hooted at the prisoner all through the snow covered roads until Cardigan was reached . . . by which time Siôn was looked upon as a criminal of the very blackest and deepest dye'.[1] Even in fine weather the journey would have been a difficult ordeal, but the records tell us that at the time the whole countryside was gripped by severe, icy weather.

At Cardigan he was promptly clapped in irons and thrown into the town gaol to spend his time in a dark cell awaiting his fate. He knew that the prospect of securing justice was remote. The thought of facing the full force of the law was terrifying, and he was aware that his very survival depended on the awesome task of convincing a jury hand picked by Sir Herbert Lloyd that their master was lying and that the

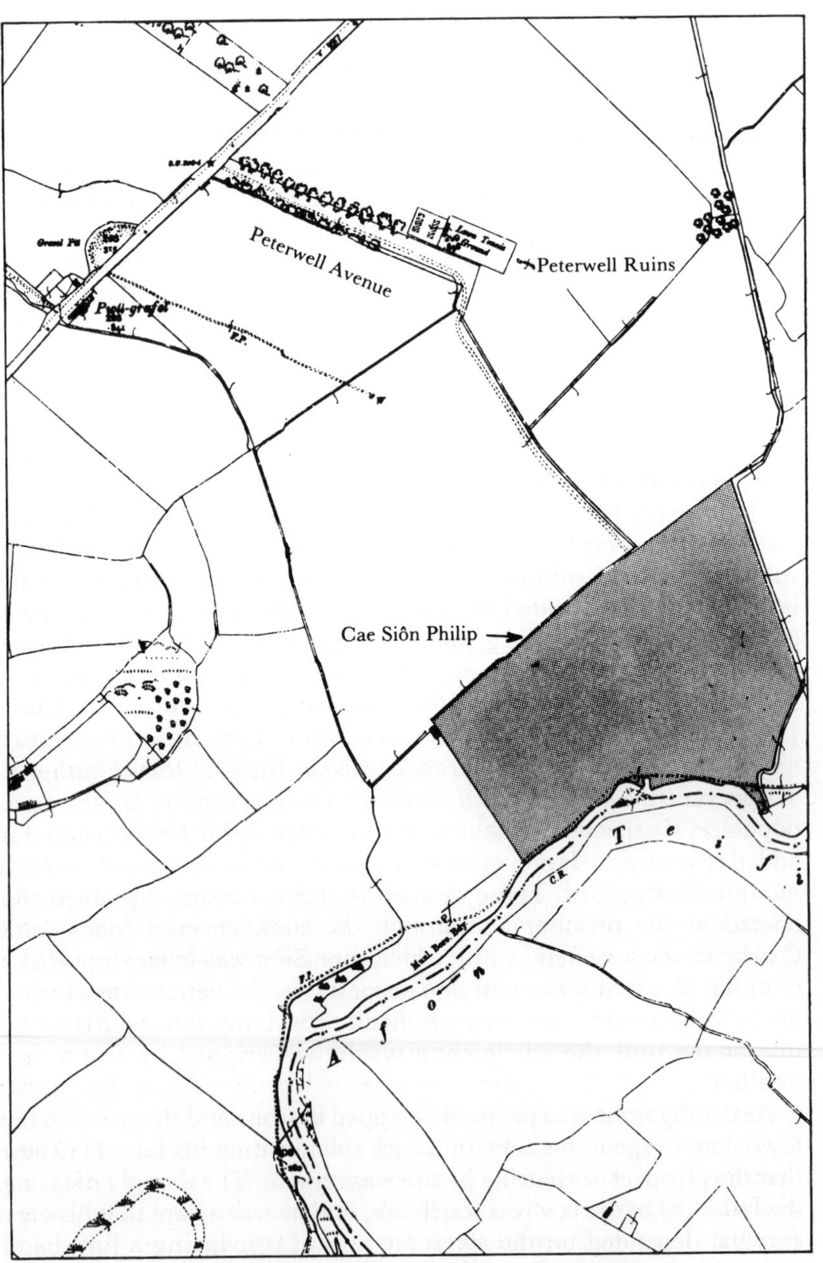

Map showing the location of Cae Siôn Philip

witnesses were themselves guilty of perjury. He could have had no illusions about his ultimate fate.

In another part of Cardigan town, a far different mood prevailed as preparations for the Assizes were being made. It was a time of spectacle and entertainment and John Paynter as High Sheriff had prepared meticulously for the occasion. He and Sir Herbert were ready to welcome the assize judge with all the traditional pomp normally accorded to him. The complement of Javelin men, all carefully selected and attired in blue and yellow livery escorted the judge and his retainers to the Guild Hall. Into Cardigan had poured the gentry of the county in all their sartorial elegance, accompanied by their ladies vying with each other in all their finery as they prepared for the Assize Ball. It was one of the most eagerly anticipated convivial events in the Ceredigion social calendar and Cardigan became the display centre for all the wealth and fashion of the county. A French observer described the ceremony which accompanied the holding of the Assizes: 'The judges, upon their approach, are received by the sheriff . . . they enter the town with bells ringing and trumpets playing, preceeded by the sheriff's men to the number of twelve or twenty, in full dress armed with javelins'.[2] For the rural squires it was the highlight of the year; for the multitudes, a spectacle to brighten their humdrum lives, but for the wretches in Cardigan gaol awaiting their doom, the sound of the revelry must have filled their hearts with fear and trepidation.

April 1763 saw a Cardigan unusually crammed, for the Assizes had attracted crowds of country folk surging in anxious to witness the fate of Siôn Philip. Their sympathy lay with the accused, but it was the silent inarticulate support of an uneducated rural people intimidated by the presence of Sir Herbert Lloyd's retainers inside and outside the Guild Hall. He never went to Cardigan unguarded but was flanked by a band of men carrying long oaken staves so that his entourage resembled a forest, 'being like a moving grove'. It was such a sight which beset Siôn Philip as he was dragged, dishevelled and pale after weeks of incarceration in a dark cell, to appear at the court.

The trial itself was a grotesquely unequal contest. The man torn from his humble cottage faced a bewigged judge of stern countenance and scant sympathy, and he heard the Attorney General bring against him the charge of sheep stealing. He had not the advantage of a lawyer to cross examine his accusers, for at this time it was the invidious practice not to allow a counsel for the defence of persons accused of a felony. Instead, Siôn Philip was allowed to call a dozen or so witnesses to testify as to his good character. Although the men of Lampeter knew him to be a person of integrity, not one had the courage to step forward for fear of Sir Herbert's wrath.

Thus Siôn Philip had to conduct his own defence, a task made more difficult by the fact that the whole proceedings were in English. Indeed, one eighteenth century writer was so shocked by the prejudice of the Courts in Wales against monoglot Welshmen that he proclaimed: 'If ever my life or property should be subject under law to the decision of a Jury . . . O! May it be a Jury impannelled to the East of the Severn'.[3] As he listened to the pedantic intonations of the lawyers in a language he could scarce understand, Siôn Philip must have longed for the cry of the curlew and the ripple of the river Teifi flowing past his cottage. Listening to Thomas Evans the Constable and John Woodward, the Peterwell servant who testified against him, giving their false evidence would have aroused in him a deep but impotent anger at the injustice of it all. He must have realised that in spite of his courageous stand, his land would be irretrievably lost and that the victory would go to Sir Herbert Lloyd. Alone against all the powers of the court, he made a noble if halting stand, but the inevitable verdict of guilty was reached by the jury.

The court became hushed as they now awaited the final climactic act in the drama. The Court Crier was ordered to call out: 'O yes, O yes, O yes. My Lords, the King's Justices strictly charge and command all manner of persons to keep silence while the sentence of death is passing on the prisoner at the bar on pain of imprisonment'. The judge, holding his nosegay of herbs and flowers to sweeten the air fouled by the stench of the prisoners who had been confined in conditions of filth and squalor pending their trial, donned the black cap. This, symbolic of the powers of darkness, was placed on his full bottomed wig, and evoked shudders of horror from the onlookers. The judge issued a customary warning of damnation for all similar wrongdoers and then pronounced the awful sentence of death. His dreaded words echoed around the silent court:[4]

> The law is that thou shalt return from hence to the place whence thou camest, and from thence to the place of execution where thou shalt hang by the neck till the body be dead! dead! dead!—and may the Lord have mercy on thy soul.

The Bench
(Hogarth)

As the words 'dead, dead, dead' reverberated throughout the chamber, all eyes must have been fixed on Siôn Philip standing mute and passive in the dock. But what of Sir Herbert Lloyd, the architect of his downfall? Did he permit himself a grim smile of satisfaction knowing that the field for which he was prepared to sell his soul would now be his?

Executions could be carried out as quickly as three days after the sentence unless petitions for clemency were lodged. Although such pardons were common, they required the support of an influential personage if they were to stand any chance of success. But there was no one to intercede on behalf of Siôn Philip and his last days were to be spent languishing on his bed of mouldy straw deep in the bowels of Cardigan gaol. The place of execution was Banc-y-Warren, a hill situated a short distance outside Cardigan town where the crowds surged in anticipation to view the final suffering.

In Cardiganshire a hangman was normally employed from outside the county and this was especially necessary if the condemned was a popular local hero, as was sometimes the case. On such occasions the executioner himself might be attacked by the crowd and a hangman named John Acton, sent for from Shrewsbury in 1780, stipulated certain conditions before he agreed to work in Cardiganshire. He insisted that a fast chaise should be made available so that he could beat a hasty retreat. He charged a fee of five guineas and demanded that he should be fully compensated if he suffered any injury to his property or his person. He had apparently suffered badly at the hands of a mob when he officiated at a previous hanging. To use his own words he had 'been used ill in Wales some time ago'.[5] At Banc-y-Warren the crowds must have been unusually subdued, aware that they were witnessing an act of great injustice, but poor Siôn Philip was not cast in the mould of the dashing hero.

As the procession approached Banc-y-Warren, the tension would have been heightened by the sombre sound of the bells of St Mary's tolling bleakly across the hill. Ironically, these bells had been recast and installed mainly through the generosity of John Lloyd of Peterwell, Sir Herbert's brother. Siôn Philip, closely guarded and bound, would have been carried in a cart, probably seated on his own coffin, and accompanied by a clergyman praying constantly for his soul. It is likely that the gentry present sat in their carriages looking upon the scene as a fitting end to their week of revels. We do not know if Sir Herbert Lloyd remained to witness Siôn Philip's end, or whether he had ridden post haste to Lampeter to claim his prize. Tradition holds that Siôn Philip died bravely and with dignity, maintaining his innocence to the end. It was customary for the condemned to make a full confession exhorting the assembled multitude to foresake the paths that led to the gallows. Such confessions would sometimes be printed and sold, serving as a warning to all men of the terrible consequences of a dissolute life. Siôn Philip had nothing to confess and his death only served to remind his fellow men of the foolishness of seeking to resist the greed of the Squire of Peterwell.

Such then is the story of the Black Ram as recorded in the folk annals of Cardiganshire. The first person to relate the story in print was William Edmunds, Headmaster of Lampeter Grammar School.

Hanging of Siôn Philip
(An artist's impression)

In an account written in 1860 he held that in the locality of Lampeter the story was 'on every hearth . . . in every mouth'. Therefore, less than a century after the date of the supposed happening, the story was very much alive in the neighbourhood. Yet, it remains one of those tantalising tales still eluding positive historical proof. The Cardigan Gaol Files for this period are incomplete and no reference to Siôn Philip's confinement or execution is to be found. No reference was made in any of the surviving letters of Sir Herbert nor in those of his contemporaries. Sheep stealing was not an uncommon offence at this time and the execution of a felon would not have caused much of a stir. Even if some suspicion had existed concerning Sir Herbert's part in the affair, it is doubtful whether any of the squires, who were themselves justices, would have been prepared to suggest that the judicial system could have erred to the extent of hanging an innocent man.

Yet a person by the name of Siôn Philip did exist in Lampeter. A perusal of the Lampeter Parish Register reveals that on 8 January 1716, 'John, ye son of Philip Jenkin' was baptised. According to Welsh practice at the time he would be known as Siôn ap Philip or Siôn Philip. In the list of marriages for 1748 there is an entry recording the marriage of John Philip to Mary Rees on 6 June. If this was the Siôn Philip of the story, then he would have been forty seven years old at the time of his death.

The existence of the field in question is indisputable and to this day it is known as Cae Siôn Philip and forms part of the Pont Faen Farm on the outskirts of Lampeter. J. H. Davies, Principal of the University College of Wales, Aberystwyth, maintained that: 'The witness of old documents in London bears testimony to the truth of the transaction', whereby Siôn Philip's field became the property of Sir Herbert Lloyd. No further light can be shed on this, but most certainly the law in the eighteenth century would have allowed for the transfer of the land, for the estate of a convicted felon would have been subject to forfeiture. Normally, it would have reverted to the Crown but Earl Jowitt, the legal commentator, held that it could revert to the Lord of the Manor who would in this case have been the Baronet. In a sale catalogue of the *Estate of the Manor and Lordship of Lampeter* dated 28 August 1807, the field is referred to as 'Cae Siôn Philip' and valued at thirty pounds.[6] Therefore, thirty eight years after Sir Herbert's death, it was still part of his former estate.

That Sir Herbert Lloyd was capable of misappropriating the

property of others is beyond question; in the same year as the Siôn Philip incident, Thomas Johnes complained that he had stolen the stock of one of his Llanfair tenants 'without the least colour of Law or Equity'.[7] Is it a coincidence that John Paynter, the High Sheriff, in choosing the jury which would have tried Siôn Philip, wrote to Sir Herbert entreating him 'to name the gentlemen which shall be most agreeable to you'?[8] Is it a further coincidence that Howel Harris, two months afterwards should have despaired of his salvation and written in his diary: 'Cried for Sir Herbert'.[9]

The author was informed by the present owner of the field, Mr Lloyd Davies, that the remains of a dwelling existed in the corner of Cae Siôn Philip and evidence of occupation such as fragments of crockery have been unearthed after ploughing. Recently, the bowl of a clay pipe, was discovered near where the cottage reputedly stood.[10]

Although it is not possible to produce positive documentary proof, the circumstantial evidence suggests that the folk tradition could have a basis of truth. That it was very much alive less than a hundred years after Sir Herbert's death, a time span of less than two generations,

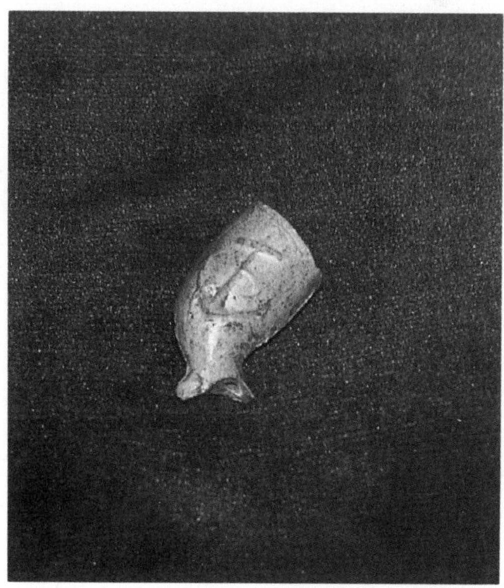

Clay pipe unearthed in Cae Siôn Philip

means that the story as recounted at that time could have been based on contemporary accounts of the incident. Of all the tales about Peterwell, none has seared itself more deeply into the folk lore of the locality than the affair of the Black Ram.

The eighteen acre field is there for all to see, serene and peaceful, revealing nothing of its past, but the pitiful remains of Peterwell no longer cast a baleful shadow over it. Even so, its very existence ensures that Sir Herbert Lloyd will be remembered as the infamous squire who hanged Siôn Philip for his field.

NOTES

[1] Evans, *Lampeter,* p. 209.
[2] Cottu, p. 43.
[3] J. Evans, *Letters.*
[4] Hay . . . p. 58.
[5] N.L.W., 13664 C.
[6] In the possession of Major Herbert Lloyd-Johnes.
[7] D.C.Mss., T.J. to J.J., 25 Nov. 1763.
[8] P.C.Mss. 3246.
[9] *C.C.H.M.C.,* Vol. 32, p. 38.
[10] The clay pipe and other objects were found by Mr. Roy Heath of Pontfaen Cottage.

An opera based on the Black Ram incident was composed by Professor Ian Parrott. He completed the work in 1951; a concert version for radio was performed in 1957; the overture was subsequently performed by the Hallé Orchestra at the Albert Hall, and it was successfully staged at the King's Hall, Aberystwyth in 1966.

Chapter Fourteen

'A MOST SICKLY AND IRRITABLE TIME'

Many suffered at the hands of Sir Herbert and much of his life was spent in breathing fire and fury upon others, but he himself was no stranger to pain and discomfort. An ever recurring theme in the letters of the Baronet and his contemporaries was the question of his health. Much of his life was overshadowed by illness, and in particular the gout which was the scourge of the eighteenth century. This condition was generally exacerbated by an excess of alcohol, to which Sir Herbert Lloyd, like most of his fellow gentry, was especially partial. Eliza Lewes of Llanerchaeron once sent a servant post haste to Dolaucothi to procure 'two dozen bottles of wine' for Sir Herbert Lloyd's visit, 'lest I be put to the blush', she added, 'as my stock is very low'.[1] Nor was he alone in this respect; John Johnes of Dolaucothi spent much of his time 'pushing the glass as freely as ever', and was ever being urged by the Custos to 'use more exercise out of doors and less over the bottle'. The cellars of Peterwell were famed for their contents; Sir Herbert had his own personal wine bottles impressed with his name and the year of vintage, many of which have been unearthed in the vicinity of the mansion.

Wine bottles bearing the name of Sir Herbert Lloyd
(Unearthed at Peterwell)

The state of his health caused Sir Herbert Lloyd to spend many months away from Peterwell taking the waters at Tunbridge Wells or Bath, which for the gentry was the panacea for all ills. Certainly, Sir Herbert seemed impressed by the efficacy of the Tunbridge Wells spa water: 'I have been here one month for the benefit of my health', he wrote in 1761, '. . . where I have received more benefit than I can by words express . . . I am now in better health than I have been these ten years past'.[2] This improvement however was short lived; the following winter so reduced his condition that the Johnes brothers looked towards Peterwell anticipating the very worst, 'Tis impossible', wrote the Custos bleakly, 'but that the little Gentleman in black must have him soon'.[3]

Despite this gloomy prediction, Sir Herbert Lloyd not only survived, but 1762 proved to be his *annus mirabilis*, and he returned to Peterwell flaunting his amazingly acquired baronetcy. But gout was no respecter of titles and during the early months of 1763 we again find him trapped by ill health in rural Cardiganshire when he would, no doubt, have preferred to have launched himself, flushed with success, upon the London scene. On 17 January 1763, John Paynter remarked to Lord Powis, 'Sir Herbert is gone for Peterwell so extremely ill that I fear he will be laid up for some time'.[4]

The cold played havoc with his condition; throughout the whole of February he was confined to the mansion and he could not even summon enough strength to canvass Bute personally for the sinecure which he desperately needed. Instead, he wrote to him apologising '. . . being long confined with gout prevents my personal waiting of you'.[5] By March, however, he was sufficiently recovered to spend the entire month in London, much to the annoyance of John Paynter who wished to consult him about the preparations for the Great Sessions. His health, like his moods, swung from one extreme to another. By July 1763, he was once again totally debilitated and grumbled to John Paynter, 'I have just returned from Llandilo Quarter Sessions, where I have been very much fatigued with business of various sorts and so tired I am not able to step as far as Havod to see you and Mrs Paynter'.[6]

The admission of fatigue is a telling reminder of the physical strain imposed upon Sir Herbert Lloyd and the other squires in the performance of their judicial and other duties in the eighteenth century. Life was not only a round of drinking, gambling and hunting; the gentry also carried out without remuneration the general task of administering the county, which could prove an exacting task. They were often compelled to undertake arduous journeys between places thirty to forty miles apart on atrocious roads which, according to Defoe, 'after heavy rain . . . were often times most dangerous to travellers . . . making constant sloughs sometimes able to bury both man and horse'.[7] Arthur Young, in 1768 described Welsh roads as 'mere rocky lanes full of hugeous stones as big as one's horse'. Along such highways Sir Herbert was obliged to travel to London.

Thomas Johnes the Custos also felt the strain of eighteenth century travel and recounted the hazards of journeys which necessitated having to ride through water up to the horse's saddle. In June 1763 he complained to his brother John Johnes, 'It was with some difficulty that I got home as I suffered much in the flesh by my ride to Cardigan'.[8] The constant soakings he got often made his feet swell and on one occasion he could not get his boot back on for many days, but was obliged to wear a 'big shoe'. No less did Lewis Morris feel the pain of travel; after an excruciating journey from Cardigan to Peterwell in 1764 he described himself as being 'scarce alive . . . being obliged to ride in a wheel carriage which shook me almost to atoms'.[9]

As a magistrate, one of Sir Herbert's duties involved the supervision of the upkeep of these roads, and whatever other shortcomings he had, the records show that he diligently applied himself to the maintenance and improvement of the highways of Cardiganshire. It is likely that he did this because he had a vested interest in the condition of the roads; he travelled extensively and no-one could have been more painfully conscious of the ruts and jolts than he was. If only for his own comfort he showed particular interest in the condition of the road from Lampeter to Cardigan, and on 24 September 1762 at the Quarter Sessions he and Oakley Leigh emphasised the fact that it was 'out of repair'. They made similar efforts concerning the road at Llanbadarn which, on 19 April 1764 was, to quote their own words, 'ruinously out of repair'.[10]

Such conditions, when travelling by coach meant quartering endlessly from one side to another to avoid the huge pools of water and ruts deep enough to break a horse's leg. As late as 1792, Thomas Johnes of Hafod, the son of the Custos, expressed trepidation regarding the west Wales highways: 'Heaven send me a safe return without broken bones', he prayed, 'for going to Cardigan at this time of year is a real work of danger'. Not until the beginning of the nineteenth century did the genius of Telford and Macadam transform the character of the highways.

Even when he lay in bed unable to move on account of gout, Sir Herbert Lloyd's thoughts were obsessed with the condition of the roads. In 1765 urgent letters went out from Peterwell irritably reproving John Paynter and John Ball as magistrates for their 'horrid neglect of duty of the several surveyors near them in repairing the road near Pontrhydygroes'.[11] As justices, it fell to them to organise road improvements, but clearly they had omitted to carry out their responsibilities in this field. Local inhabitants were obliged to devote a certain number of days each year to repairing the roads, but unless the surveyors appointed by the justices ordered them to get on with it, the work remained undone. Nothing annoyed Sir Herbert Lloyd more; he was particularly infuriated by the access to his own residence which he referred to as '. . . that damned lane near Peterwell'.

But what really angered him was the chronic condition of the road to Rhaeadr connecting with the route to London. We learn that he had even gone to the trouble of signing a writ at Hafod giving John Paynter money to be used specifically for the purpose of improving this highway: 'To employ workmen for the repairing of that particular road', he wrote. He further warned Paynter: 'The road from Rhos Fair to Rhandir must not be forgot . . . it is rocky, stony and narrow, but may be mended any time of the year and must be done, for I intend for London in my carriage that way as soon as I am able to stir'. No doubt, the prospect of the tortuous three or four day journey to London, being tossed and thrown in his lurching unsprung coach, made Sir Herbert Lloyd one of the most conscientious of Cardiganshire squires as far as the condition of the roads was in question.

One long journey which Sir Herbert Lloyd consistently braved was that to Bath, where to take the waters was as much part of his social calendar as a medical necessity. Bath, much popularised by Queen Anne and made splendid by Richard Nash, had become the venue for high society and fashion, and was particularly popular with the Welsh gentry. They swarmed there to catch up on their sense of fashion and gossip; in 1764 Thomas Johnes the Custos remarked: 'The place was never so full of company before . . . Rice of Dynevor is here . . . his mother and sister have been here one month . . . and lodgings are extremely scarce'.[12] The same letter informs us that Sir Herbert

Comforts of Bath—Suffering from Gout

Comforts of Bath—A Card Party

Lloyd, anxious as ever to present himself at Bath had been in the city 'for some time'.

To the Baronet, who fancied himself as a sophisticate, this city offered the opportunity of mingling with persons of rank and fortune; the concerts, balls, gaming rooms, coffee houses and social whirl of the famous Pump Room provided him with amenities not to be matched anywhere in Cardiganshire. Healthy or otherwise, Bath was a must in his social diary. Wild horses would not drag John Johnes of Dolaucothi to Bath; his brother the Custos repeatedly implored him to try the waters for his very indifferent health: 'Would you but go to Bath, I am satisfied it would do you infinite service', he begged. Time and again he pleaded with him: 'Should your bowels complaint continue you must go to Bath, that will be sure to remove it as it is most efficacious for that complaint'. But John Johnes remained solidly entrenched at Dolaucothi, brooding over his indisposition and clinging to his inevitable bottle for comfort. Bath, however, was not the answer to everybody's problems: the city did nothing for David Lloyd of Breinog who dropped dead there! But for Sir Herbert it seemed to be a lifeline. His long stay there during 1764 might have been extended because of the climate, for, according to the Custos, it was a most harrowing time for both man and beast. 'The weather', he wrote, 'is vile . . . we have not had one dry day above three months . . . [it is] a most sickly time . . . very few having escaped disorder'. When ultimately Sir Herbert did return to Cardiganshire in June, within two months he was again struck down with another bout of gout. The ever observant Lewis Morris saw him suffering this attack and wrily noted to Evan Evans: 'Met Sir Herbert in the Gout near Cardigan'.[13] Not that Evans, Ieuan Brydydd Hir, would have been disposed to shed tears over his condition; indeed, the information could only have been a source of satisfaction to Evans who was still in exile and unable to procure a living in Cardiganshire because of the continued opposition of the Baronet and his powerful influence over church appointments.

With the turning of the year Lloyd's health became even more grim; the picture we get of him in January 1765 is of a man utterly exhausted and totally immobilised. Wallowing in self pity, he complained to John Paynter that he was 'overwhelmed with gout since last Tuesday night, owing to a cold I took at Leet Court on Monday; I have but one hand and an aching head and no legs and have not been out of doors since Tuesday last'. It seems that he was not exaggerating; by the following month his health had so deteriorated that once again there was cause for alarm and onlookers believed his death was imminent. His critical condition triggered off another scramble for the Peterwell parliamentary seat, but this time it was Thomas Johnes who waited in the wings. Believing the 'Great Man of Peterwell' to be in the terminal stages of his illness, Thomas Johnes even wrote to Lord Powis to beg his support for the borough seat which would fall vacant on Sir Herbert's death. Lord Powis responded immediately to the Custos's request by writing to George Grenville, the Prime Minister, to canvass the seat on his behalf:[14]

> Albermarle Street
> Febr'y 16, 1765
>
> Dear Sir,
>
> The enclosed paper is laid before you at the request of Mr Johnes who is Custos Rotulorum for the county of Cardigan, and whose character, power and large property give him very great weight there and in other places. Sir Herbert Lloyd's life is very precarious. I know it to be so, knowing particularly the bad state his health has long been in. And to succeed him for the borough of Cardigan [in case of a vacancy] no man is so likely as Mr Johnes.

But Thomas Johnes was building political castles in the air. Within a matter of weeks Sir Herbert Lloyd had bounced back from the brink of death to shatter any dreams being entertained by the Custos. One month later he was even back again in his beloved Bath from where, on 23 March, he perkily wrote to John Johnes, Dolaucothi saying: 'Had you enquired at Lampeter you would have found that my residence has been here near one month for the benefit of these waters which have been of great service to me'.[15] Once again the Baronet had proved his resilience and confounded his acquaintances. His health was subject to such remarkable extremes that two years later Thomas Johnes the Custos wrote: 'If anything relating to Sir Herbert would surprise me, it would be his health, which certainly is most extraordinary'.[16]

In addition to his health, the behaviour of the Baronet could also be classed as most extraordinary. He was, as we have seen, a man of a particularly querulous disposition; his whole career was littered with broken friendships and deceitful tricks. Most of the gentlemen of the

Comforts of Bath—A Concert

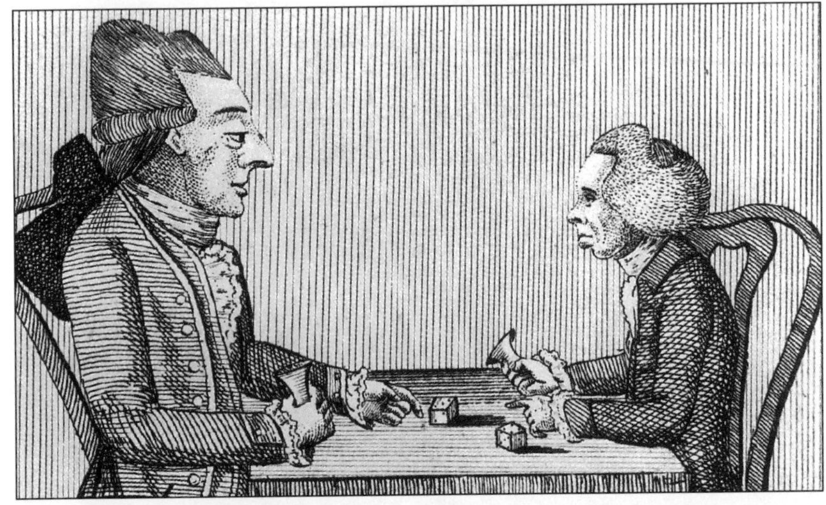

Bath Gamblers

county had felt the lash of his unbridled temper. Even in London men commented on his reputation; Richard, Lewis Morris's brother, wrote from the city saying: 'Mae gair drwg iddo'.* Francis Skyrme, his former lawyer put it more strongly and said: 'He deserves to be kicked'.[17] Although Thomas Johnes supported him politically, he was well aware of how base a personality Lloyd really was, and called him a man 'capable of any villainy' warning his brother John, 'I would on no account trust with him, considering whom you have to deal with'.

This caution was well founded when we consider Sir Herbert Lloyd's activities in the field of droving. In 1762, in his everlasting quest for cash, he attempted to exploit the cattle trade. In no time at all, he had stooped to the despicable conduct of stealing cattle from neighbouring farmers, one of the victims being a tenant of Thomas Johnes at Llanfair. The Custos was quick to react: 'If we suffer it', warned Johnes, 'I dare say he will carry off the stock of any other farm'.[18] With Lloyd looking for cattle to swell his droves, there was need for a constant state of alert among the farmers, for there was no redress once the animals had disappeared.

*He has a bad reputation.

It was natural for Sir Herbert to have had dealings with the drovers, since Lampeter at that time was an important droving centre. Old names in the town such as Drovers Road and Drovers Arms recall the days when the place would have been black with cattle waiting to be shod ready for the great trek to England. For hundreds of years the movement of the drovers and their herds had been part of the shifting autumn kaleidoscope of Cardiganshire; with the falling of the leaves came also the draining away of the cattle from the hillsides whose winter herbage was too sparse to support them. Defoe had been amazed by the sea of swaying and jostling steers which flowed through Cardiganshire: 'The whole county', he said, 'is so full of cattle that 'tis said to be the nursery or breeding place for the whole kingdom'.

During the early 1760s droving had become a highly profitable business. The Custos marvelled at the profits to be reaped: 'I'm not surprised that the Drovers have made so much money', he told his brother, 'there was never such a demand for cattle'. Sir Herbert had also seen his friend and neighbour David Jones of Derry Ormond grow rich quickly by selling cattle and, no doubt, he was filled with plans for emulating him. But after only a few seasons of meddling in droving his ways proved so dishonest that the whole venture ended in ignominy. Thomas Johnes the Custos had unwisely supplied him with cattle but, as usual, experienced difficulties in getting paid by the Baronet. In 1766, he became so nervous about debts for stock that he ordered Evan Jenkins, the Peterwell agent, '. . . to go to Sir Herbert for the balance of the cattle due . . . and be sure to do this before the Baronet leaves the country'. Lloyd's conduct as a drover placed him in that dishonest category satirized by Twm o'r Nant* and the line, 'Thoughout his life he cheated', would have been eminently applicable to him.

But it would be unfair to leave the impression that all drovers were as Sir Herbert Lloyd; many were men of integrity and culture playing an important role in the social and economic life of the time. They opened up for the people of Lampeter and elsewhere a new window on the world, bringing to the quiet backwaters a whiff of the fascination and excitement of life byond the parish. They brought the latest news, fashions and attitudes; they told of robberies, murders and sang the latest ballads; and they acted as messengers and bankers.

*Thomas Edwards, (1739-1810). Poet and writer of interludes.

Sir Herbert Lloyd, of course, was never a true drover in that sense; although Thomas Johnes had described Lloyd as 'having turned drover' in 1762, his association with this trade seems to have ended by 1765.

In many ways Sir Herbert Lloyd was his own worst enemy, he was dishonest, intolerant and petty, and his foul temper proved a short cut to ruin. He clashed bitterly with John Jones of Crynfryn, the Aberystwyth lawyer, and in a letter seething with hatred called him a 'Peevish, illtempered haughty . . . conceited attorney'. It was a classic case of the pot calling the kettle black! He functioned at such a petty level, that he even worked himself into a frenzy over a minor matter like the choice of one of the Javelin men for the procession of the Great Sessions. Paynter had chosen a man called Oliver, but Sir Herbert disliked him and wrote strenuously expressing his disapproval: 'Strike him out', he ordered Paynter, 'and give the livery to the Bearer Thomas Edwards who shall honourably attend you and be of infinite service to us at our many Leets'. He raged on, 'I am superseding that villain at Abermâd . . . *for Oliver's Insolence I will not forgive nor forget*'. These were ominous threats coming from a man like Sir Herbert; the wild scrawl and reckless underlining of the sentences make this particular letter flash with the anger and hatred which obviously gripped him as he wrote.

This savage side to his nature ultimately cost him all his allies; one after another of his early friends were buffeted by squalls emanating from Peterwell, and one after another they went in the other direction to join the steadily increasing cabal against him. One of his greatest losses was David Lloyd of Breinog, his powerful neighbour, whom he very foolishly alienated when he most needed support. 'The Baronet', threatened David Lloyd, '. . . uses me exceeding ill. I shall be glad to have some sort of justice'.[20] As it turned out, retribution was on the way and David Lloyd of Breinog was to exact the sweetest of revenges when he directed his burgesses to cast their votes against Sir Herbert Lloyd at the 1769 by-election, thereby contributing substantially to his downfall.

It is difficult to understand why Sir Herbert treated his much needed friends so atrociously; by 1765 such schizophrenic outbursts and acts of duplicity had put him at variance with most of the influential persons of Cardiganshire. Even John Paynter, his long standing accomplice, had by October 1765 lost all patience and coldly informed Lord Powis: 'He has no reason to expect any favour of me'. Most seriously of all, his outrageous behaviour by now had alienated that triumvirate of power which virtually controlled the county: John Pugh Pryse had grown to abominate him since 1761; Wilmot Vaughan's life-long hatred and mistrust of him had been totally vindicated over the years; and William Powell of Nanteos had come to abhor his brashness and chicanery, not to mention his callous treatment of Anne Lloyd, his sister. All who counted, Whig and Tory alike, became united by the one common bond, detestation of the 'Bart.', and the desire to topple him appeared to have become an all consuming obsession among the gentry.

An incident in 1765 must have afforded grim satisfaction to many of Sir Herbert's enemies, for in May of that year Peterwell was robbed of many of its valuables.[21] The thief was a man by the name of John Collins who had served as a groom at the mansion. The Baronet immediately placed a notice in the *Gloucester Journal* offering a reward of £20 for the apprehension of the thief who had stolen '. . . cash, plate, linen and many other things of great value . . . especially a diamond ring'. The announcement concluded with the request that all information concerning the theft was to be conveyed to Sir Herbert at Bath or to Sir John Fielding in London, who was the blind half brother of the celebrated author, Sir Henry Fielding, and a notable Westminster magistrate.

Evidently the notice had its effect, for the records inform us that John Collins was later apprehended and convicted of 'stealing with force and arms' a long list of sundry items from Peterwell. After his capture, Collins was conveyed to Cardigan gaol to stand trial at the Great Sessions of Summer 1765, when he was found guilty of robbing Sir Herbert Lloyd and was sentenced to death. During the month of August, Collins sought to have the penalty commuted to one of transportation for life, and his sentence was temporarily respited. On 22 August the Secretary of State required the justices of the Great Sessions to report on his case and a further 'respite during pleasure' was granted. Collins, still languishing in Cardigan gaol, now decided to appeal directly for clemency to Sir Herbert Lloyd; on 20 August he sent the following letter:[22]

> At the last sessions at Cardigan I was convicted . . . for a very heinous crime committed against your Honour. I now lie condemned for the same, and I shall suffer death except your Honour

takes pity upon me; having no-one to intercede for me except your Honour. I lay myself at your mercy now, my life is entirely in your hands. Though I am sensible I deserve nothing from you but death. O let my deplorable case move you to take compassion on me. I am apt to believe that you can get my sentence mitigated to transportation for life by your application. So I have nothing to beg but your mercy. From your most undeserving humble and obedient servant in Cardigan gaol.

John Collins.

20 August 1765.

Although Sir Herbert passed this letter on to the Secretary of State there is no record that he actively promoted Collins's cause. The judges concluded on 3 October 1765 that Collins was not 'a proper object of mercy' on the grounds that, 'Crimes of this sort are too frequent in families where servants are kept, and call for exemplary punishment'.[23] A fortnight later, on 17 October the Secretary of State directed that the sentence on John Collins was to be carried out. For some reason, he was not immediately hanged but continued a prisoner in Cardigan gaol until April 1766, when the Gaol Files inform us that he effected an escape. According to the Quarter Sessions Records he escaped not, 'through the wilful neglect of the gaolers', but because the gaol itself was in a 'very bad state of repair'.[24] No further reference to Collins is to be found in the Home Office papers from 1766 to 1769 and the incomplete Gaol Files do not reveal his eventual fate.

As for Sir Herbert Lloyd himself, his fate was already sealed; conspiracies were being hatched and alliances forged to ensure that at the next election he would not be returned to Westminster.

NOTES

[1] D.C. Mss., Eliza Lewis to J.J. (n.d.)
[2] D.C.Mss., S.H.L. to J.J., 23 Mar. 1761.
[3] D.C.Mss., T.J. to J.J., 1 Mar. 1762.
[4] P.C.Mss. 3416.
[5] B.L.Add.Mss. 5726.
[6] P.C.Mss. 3141.
[7] Defoe, *Tour,* Vol. 2, p. 127.
[8] D.C.Mss., T.J. to J.J., 24 June 1763.

[9] *A.M.L.*, Pt. 2, p. 644.
[10] N.L.W. Wales, 4/897/5.
[11] P.C.Mss. 2996.
[12] D.C.Mss., T.J. to J.J., 7 Feb. 1764.
[13] *A.M.L.*, Pt. 2, p. 633.
[14] B.L.Add.Mss. 54321, f.1.
[15] D.C.Mss., S.H.L. to J.J., 23 Mar. 1765.
[16] P.C.Mss. 3874.
[17] D.C.Mss., F. Skyrme to J.J., 17 Oct. 1757.
[18] D.C.Mss., T.J. to J.J., 20 Nov. 1763.
[19] P.C.Mss. 9551.
[20] N.L.W. 13486.
[21] N.L.W. 13664C.
[22] P.R.O., State Papers, 37/4.
[23] Home Office Papers, 1760-65, p. 662.
[24] N.L.W. Cards, Q.S./O.B./2.

Chapter Fifteen

'THERE IS NOTHING HE WILL NOT ATTEMPT'

The years had fled by quickly since his euphoric victory in 1761, and by 1768 Sir Herbert Lloyd's seven year term as an M.P. was coming to an end, which meant that he was faced with the prospect of a general election.

His parliamentary career typified that of the majority of country squires at that time; there is no record of him having spoken in Parliament and his role as an M.P. was totally undistinguished. Those members of the squirearchy who represented rural areas were rarely men of high political ambition or ministerial potential; they attended Parliament courting the favours of the powerful, but what really interested them was influence at a local level. Such was Sir Herbert Lloyd; he liked the power to manipulate affairs in Cardiganshire, but at the end of each session at Westminster he was anxious to escape, being eager to catch the fishing or the hunting season at Peterwell and the other Cardiganshire estates.

His period in Parliament (1761-1768) was a turbulent time in the political life of the kingdom. In 1761 the nation was still involved in the Seven Years War, but differences of opinion over the conflict were emerging among various factions at Westminster. George III was anxious to end 'this bloody and expensive war'. In May 1762, the Duke of Newcastle was replaced as Prime Minister by Lord Bute. Peace terms were agreed with France and we find Sir Herbert Lloyd's name in a list of members who favoured the preliminaries to end the Seven Years War. The Bute administration was short-lived and was followed by that of Grenville. Sir Herbert refused to support this government's efforts to increase taxation following the war. In 1764, however, he did support the expulsion from Parliament of John Wilkes, who had taken a courageous stand on such issues as the freedom of the press and the illegality of general warrants. When the Rockingham administration took over in 1765, Sir Herbert was classed as 'doubtful' and refused to support the repeal of the Stamp Act. When this administration fell and was replaced by Pitt's, Sir Herbert appears to have loyally supported the government for the remainder of his term at Westminster.

Unremarkable as might have been his performance at Parliament, no-one was more anxious to be returned than he. The reasons were two-fold; one was the obvious factor of power and status, the other was the immunity from prosecution for debt which was at this time afforded to an M.P. To a man of his financial liabilities, the latter was a godsend; moneywise, he had been on shifting sand for most of his life, but by 1768 the tide of reckoning was fast approaching. Writs from all quarters were pouring into Peterwell; but, buttressed as he was by his M.P.'s status, he generally chose to ignore them. This protection afforded to an M.P. was farcical; Lady Mary Wortly Montague had actually found it cheaper to buy her spendthrift son a seat in Parliament rather than settle his gargantuan debts.

For Sir Herbert, a debtor's prison seemed the inevitable alternative to being re-elected, and memories of the days when he had seen Thomas Johnes, Abermâd, sweating it out in gaol, breathing air thick with stench and fibrous with disease, must surely have crossed his mind. How sweet was the Peterwell air, and how precious the freedom of Cardiganshire at the thought of the foul and foetid Fleet, and he determined to hang on to them.

But this was going to prove more difficult than Sir Herbert Lloyd imagined. The years between had done nothing for his reputation; age had not brought with it one jot of wisdom; he appeared to be quite purblind to the actualities of his situation. The gulf between himself and the other gentry had widened by the year; gone was the camaraderie which had existed between himself and John Pugh Pryse; gone was the support of Nanteos; gone was Lewis Morris; and greatly deepened was the hatred of Trawsgoed; in fact, even by as early as 1766, his two only allies seem to have been Thomas Johnes the Custos and Griffith Philipps, Cwmgwili. So corroding did they regard his influence that all the other squires became hell bent on jettisoning him not only from the political scene but, if possible, from the face of Cardiganshire.

Although the next general election was not due to be held until 1768, preparations always began at least a year in advance. But so determined was John Pugh Pryse, Gogerddan, to block any attempt by Sir Herbert at re-election, that as early as December 1766 he launched into the mass creation of burgesses so that he could command sufficient voters to swamp Lloyd. In Aberystwyth alone, as many as three hundred and three burgesses were admitted at the

Michaelmas Court Leet. Naturally, such activity by the opposite camp alarmed Lloyd, who contacted his ally Griffith Philipps to express his concern: 'Mr Pryse of Gogerddan, by the advice of his friends . . . has made one thousand burgesses between Cardigan and Aberystwyth'.[1] Not to be outdone, Sir Herbert Lloyd himself commenced a massive campaign of burgess making and, claiming that he had 'stamps for that purpose', he made over twelve hundred burgesses during the next six months. Lampeter Court Leet became a hub of frenetic activity, with Oakley Leigh pressing into the Court all the manpower he could muster for the cause of Peterwell; even Leigh's poor manservant, Evan John, was deemed 'to be a fit person to serve the office of burgess'.[2]

John Pugh Pryse and the other gentry decided to adopt another line of attack against Lloyd. A sum of money amounting to five hundred pounds was collected amongst them in order to launch a legal attack upon the status of Lampeter as a parliamentary borough. If successful, this would prevent Lloyd from creating any more burgesses and thereby cripple him politically. Lampeter was in the position of having no official charter; and since its neighbour, Tregaron, had earlier been disenfranchised for this very reason, Lampeter seemed similarly vulnerable. Lloyd was aware of the threat against him and informed Philipps of Cwmgwili: '. . . they intended attacking my borough of Lampeter next term, as I am informed £500 being already subscribed for that purpose'.[3] To carry into execution this plan, John Pugh Pryse and the others had secured the services of a prominent lawyer named Sir Fletcher Norton, Grenville's Solicitor General and later Speaker of the House of Commons. He was an attorney with a dubious reputation for accepting briefs and payment from opposing parties; on account of this he became known as 'Sir Bull Faced Double Fee'.

He was well named, for Sir Herbert Lloyd also hired Sir Fletcher Norton to carry out an identical legal attack upon the Borough of Cardigan to retaliate against John Pugh Pryse. It was a typically petulant reaction on the part of Lloyd, who wrote to Griffith Philipps: 'Mr Pryse has privately drawn out his case and sent it for Sir Fletcher Norton's opinion . . . I have had likewise Sir Fletcher's opinion on my case . . . and if I can, I will attack their borough and Charter'.[4] Despite, or because, of the involvement of this avaricious lawyer, nothing came of these attempts to disenfranchise either Lampeter or Cardigan boroughs.

Nevertheless, within Cardiganshire, Sir Herbert Lloyd's political power was steadily being eroded by John Pugh Pryse's campaign against him; even the support of his lawyer Albany Wallis was in question: 'Mr Wallis I believe is concerned for both of us', confided Lloyd to Philipps, Cwmgwili, '. . . But I trust he will not quit me for Pryse'. A clearly nervous Sir Herbert was now reaping the whirlwind of his earlier outbursts and indiscretions, for even Thomas Johnes the Custos had cooled in his support. His only solid remaining ally was Philipps, Cwmgwili, Carmarthenshire, and he clung tenaciously to this lifeline: 'I flatter myself with your friendship and countenances', he toadied to Philipps, '. . . though I may not have the pleasure of your personal appearance at the meeting [to decide the nomination of a candidate for Parliament], yet I may have the honour of naming you and your interest in my support'.[5] Obviously, Sir Herbert Lloyd had no-one left of influence to support his nomination in Cardiganshire, and even Philipps had no intention of making a personal appearance at the meeting to endorse Lloyd's bid. Nevertheless, undeterred by all this, Sir Herbert Lloyd boasted: 'I shall, at the next meeting make no small appearance for the county'.

This open rupture between Peterwell and all the other powerful families had succeeded in pushing up the political barometer in Cardiganshire, so that the whole county had become, to quote Lloyd's own words, 'much inflamed . . . and a general meeting must soon be held before we are quieted'. Even the weather proved inclement and compounded his difficulties—a severe blizzard had gripped Cardiganshire and confined him to Peterwell: 'I would have been in London last week', he grumbled, 'had not the very deep snow prevented me and still does and is likely to continue I fear'.

The intention of his trip to London was to wheedle the support of Wilmot Vaughan for his attempt to gain the county seat. Considering the life long antipathy which had smouldered between Peterwell and Trawsgoed over the years, this was an amazing move. Yet, we learn from James Lloyd of Mabws that Sir Herbert Lloyd was now attempting to procure a reconciliation with Wilmot Vaughan at the expense of John Pugh Pryse, and was in fact proposing toasts to Vaughan to that effect. Thick skinned and insensitive as ever, the Baronet actually travelled up to London to present himself to Wilmot Vaughan claiming that he wanted 'no connection with Pryse—desiring to act with [Vaughan] in everything'.[6] The whole expedition was too preposterous for Vaughan who, thin skinned, and still smarting from previous defeat recalled how Sir Herbert Lloyd and the Custos had foiled his political ambitions in 1761. His reception of these overtures of friendship by Sir Herbert Lloyd is summed up in a letter which he wrote to Lloyd of Mabws. 'Knowing the nature of the man', said Vaughan drily, 'I replied with a civil bow. He can take no measures from which to indulge the least glimpse of hope'.

Sir Herbert Lloyd, as usual, had completely misjudged the situation, for not only was Vaughan unwilling to support him, he had even taken steps to prepare a case against him to the Lord Chancellor to have him removed once again from the Commission of the Peace. For this purpose, Vaughan had requested the Cardiganshire gentry to fortify him with every evidence of the facts of his [Lloyd's] injustice'. Wilmot Vaughan grimly concluded his assessment of Sir Herbert to James Lloyd of Mabws: 'I am fully persuaded, till he ceases to exist, he will never cease to persecute. It is become second nature to him'.[7]

Meanwhile, tension was mounting regarding the choice of candidates for the coming election, and John Pugh Pryse, 'finding how uneasy the gentlemen of the county were' over this matter, advertised a public meeting to be held at Cardigan on 22 August 1767. Pryse himself had declared his intention to relinquish the county seat for Cardiganshire and opt for Merioneth instead. At the meeting, John Pugh Pryse proposed that Thomas Powell, the son of Dr William Powell, Nanteos, should be adopted for the county seat, but he refused to stand. The way was therefore clear for Wilmot Vaughan to present himself; although he now held the seat for Berwick-on-Tweed, he wished to return to Cardiganshire. He had already expressed the sentiment to James Lloyd of Mabws that he would, 'with pleasure embrace any opportunity that may be given of offering my service to the County'.[8] It therefore transpired that Wilmot Vaughan, now the fourth Viscount Lisburne, his father having died a year previously, was unanimously adopted as the candidate for the county and in the *Gloucester Journal* on 31 August 1767, he begged leave 'to express my warmest acknowledgements for so distinguished a mark of your esteem'.

Thus, despite all his wheeling and dealing, Sir Herbert Lloyd had been totally excluded from standing for the county; he had no hope

Wilmot Vaughan of Trawsgoed
The Fourth Viscount Lisburne

against Lord Lisburne and the general reaction to his defeat was one of widespread jubilation. Up at Hafod, his former friend, John Paynter, remarked to Lord Powis: 'There is a matter of great triumph in my neighbourhood—having defeated the Baronet, and he has nobody to blame but himself'.[9] In the same letter we learn that Thomas Johnes the Custos was still loyal to Sir Herbert, although in Paynter's estimation he would have succeeded against Lord Lisburne had he been prepared to stand for the county: 'My landlord [the Custos], acted his part with great firmness, and was steady and uniformed to the last. I think he might have carried it against Lord Lisburne in his own person'.

The first round in this political contest had gone to John Pugh Pryse, but the nomination for the borough seat remained. Sir Herbert Lloyd, unabashed, now decided to switch his candidature to this seat, currently held by him. In an attempt to whip up support for his cause, he decided to submit a long list of persons to be made magistrates for Cardiganshire, who would act as a new band of supporters. In collusion with Thomas Johnes the Custos, he now schemed to get this new list accepted, even sneaking up to London to visit the Duke of Grafton and the Lord Chancellor in an attempt to get his new list quickly approved. But his old adversary Wilmot Vaughan, as the new Lord Lisburne, was now Lord Lieutenant for the county, and as such, his signature was required for a new list of Justices. Lisburne, of course, had no intention of approving any list by Lloyd, and he informed Dr William Powell, Nanteos, 'a new Commission of the Peace . . . lodged with the Chancellor where it waited my approbation. I was weak enough to imagine that this was intended as a compliment to me, but when I saw the Duke of Grafton, and the Lord Chancellor, I found from them that the Baronet had been with them at his first coming to town, pressing to have the Commission immediately passed'.[10]

Sir Herbert Lloyd had clearly tried to outwit Lord Lisburne, but in this instance he was 'hoist with his own petard', for we learn from Lisburne that: 'The Chancellor, to use his very words, cut him very short, telling him he would do nothing in it without the full approbation of the Lord Lieutenant'. On 6 December 1767, Lisburne effectively crushed this application of Lloyd's by reporting that there was 'no want of justices' in the county.

The next hurdle for Sir Herbert in his struggle for political survival was the election of the mayor of Cardigan. We have seen in previous elections how crucial an office this was for any aspiring candidate, for the mayor could manipulate the result of an election by arbitrarily allowing or disallowing votes at the hustings. To have any hope of retaining his borough seat, it was vital that Sir Herbert secured the appointment of a mayor sympathetic to his cause.

But John Pugh Pryse was also prepared for this encounter and had chosen as his candidate John Lewes of Carmarthen, a member of the Llanllŷr family. Sir Herbert Lloyd's choice was Ben Davies of Glancuch. There followed on 5 and 6 October 1767 a bitterly contested election for the office of mayor of Cardigan. The affair cost John Pugh Pryse £102-13s.-5d. and John Lewes was eventually elected with a large majority. Sir Herbert, however, with incredible contumacy, refused to accept the decision and insisted on having Ben Davies also sworn in as mayor, which placed Cardigan in the absurd position of having two mayors.

There now followed a legal dispute over this election which was referred to the Court of the King's Bench at Hereford, and early in 1768, the verdict was given in favour of John Pugh Pryse's candidate, John Lewes. Lord Lisburne reported to Dr William Powell that a 'peremptory mandamus' had been issued and sent to Cardigan to swear in Lewes as the legal mayor. But Lisburne, in the same letter sounded a dire warning regarding Sir Herbert Lloyd: 'There is nothing he will not attempt'.[11]

The truth of this dictum was soon to be attested in a theatrical fashion. Meanwhile, one by one, these vital pre-election skirmishes were being won by John Pugh Pryse, and it was a disconsolate Sir Herbert who tried to rally his shrinking forces in order to get himself nominated so that he could hang on to his borough seat. This aspiration, however, was to be finally and completely scuttled by John Pugh Pryse in late January 1768 when he found the ideal candidate to oppose the Baronet.

That person was Pryse Campbell of Stackpole Court, Pembrokeshire, to whom the nomination for the borough seat was now awarded. Campbell was delighted to accept, stating: 'I was told that Sir Herbert was afraid of my being candidate, . . . but I think we may bid him defiance'.[13] He could indeed! For Lloyd, this was a sledgehammer blow. His worst fears had been realized. Campbell presented him with an insurmountable challenge: he had a Gogerddan

Pryse Campbell of Stackpole Court

pedigree, being the grandson of Lewis Pryse, Gogerddan, and he had already been an M.P. for Scottish constituencies since 1754, a member of the government and Lord of the Treasury. With the full support of the powerful Gogerddan family, and the prospect of ministerial aid in the event of any election petition, Pryse Campbell stood virtually invincible. Thomas Johnes had the political astuteness to recognise the strength of Sir Herbert's new adversary: 'Pryse Campbell', he remarked to John Johnes, 'is a much more formidable opponent than Pugh Pryse, as he is very sure to have every influence that government can give'.[13] The choice of Campbell had been a triumphant coup for John Pugh Pryse and changed overnight the Baronet's prospects of retaining the seat.

But at no time did the other gentry underestimate Sir Herbert's capacity to strike back; so often he had been seen to extricate himself from seemingly impossible situations, and no-one believed that he would now submit passively to Pryse Campbell's challenge. Even Lady Lisburne threw herself into the fight against him; during her husband's illness she wrote to James Lloyd of Mabws, warning him to be on his guard against Sir Herbert Lloyd and to see to it that there should not be any division in the ranks of the gentry opposing him. 'The Baronet', she remarked from bitter personal experience, '. . . amidst all the various causes of his present mortification would take new life and courage, if from any precipitate resolution, any desertion . . . should happen in a corps united'.[14]

The field must have appeared daunting to Sir Herbert as he desperately thought out his next move at Peterwell. With only a month to go before the general election, he had very little time in which to use his customary guile or exert pressure on any of the gentry to switch their support from John Pugh Pryse's candidate to himself. He had tried to prevail on John Paynter to help him, but being the fair weather friend he was, he kept a discreet distance up at Hafod. Sir Herbert Lloyd no longer presented a ticket to prestige and power; he

Mabws

was a drowning man and John Paynter had no intention of going anywhere near Peterwell to be sucked into the same whirlpool of political disaster, social disgrace and insolvency. He even refused to be registered as a burgess for Lloyd, and in a pen steeped in poison he informed Lord Powis: 'The Baronet is much displeased that I have not gone to be sworn as a Burgess . . . and he also seems mightily cool in respect of your Lordship'.[15] Even the ever loyal Thomas Johnes the Custos began to show signs of disaffection: 'I have heard nothing from the Baronet for a great length of time', he told John Johnes, 'nor do I suppose I shall, until he wants some assistance from me'.[16]

During the final weeks before the election, Sir Herbert Lloyd remained fuming at Peterwell and, with rising panic, contemplated the odds against him. Yet, there was still fight enough left in him, and he was to sally forth in one last frantic and dramatic bid to reverse his failing fortunes. It must stand as one of the most bizarre acts in the political history of Cardiganshire.

With his usual obstinacy, he had refused to accept the decision of the King's Bench concerning the legality of John Lewes's election as mayor of Cardigan. On the day of the borough election, 24 March 1768, the tension proved too much for his unquiet nature and he stormed out of Peterwell, rounded up his supporters, which were said to be 'upward of 2,000' and ordered them all to ride down to Cardigan because he was 'determined to stand a poll'. It was a ridiculous venture, but typical of the Baronet. His intention was to coerce Ben Davies, his rejected nominee as mayor, to act as returning officer at the election on his behalf, in the hope of obtaining, at worst, a double return.

But Ben Davies, understandably, had had enough. He rode to meet Sir Herbert Lloyd on the road to Cardigan and refused to accompany him to the polls to play the part of an illegal returning officer alongside John Lewes. Without his co-operation, Sir Herbert realized that he could no longer continue with this charade. News of the event spread quickly, which left the Baronet vulnerable to his many enemies and bailiffs who were itching for the opportunity to present him with writs. Sensible of all this, it seems that even Sir Herbert's nerve failed. Fearing the consequences of this illegal act, he turned and rode back furiously to Peterwell, leaving all his unfortunate and bewildered burgesses straddling the road between Cardigan and Lampeter. The whole farcical venture was witnessed by the Reverend John Lloyd of

Alltyrodyn, who informed his brother Posthumus that: 'The Baronet himself, being apprehensive of writs to take him', abandoned the two thousand burgesses 'to shift for themselves'.[17] This unceremonious and ignominious dash back to Peterwell meant that Lord Lisburne and Pryse Campbell now became the new members of Parliament for the County of Cardigan and Cardigan boroughs respectively, 'being chosen without opposition'.

Sir Herbert Lloyd was a stricken man. Stripped of the protection previously afforded to him as an M.P. against bailiffs and other creditors, he desperately sought to salvage his self respect and to hang on to his crumbling estate. But his past misdeeds had so sickened the gentry that nothing short of his total humiliation would now slake their thirst for revenge. Lord Lisburne continued to spearhead the campaign against Sir Herbert Lloyd. In July he wrote to James Lloyd of Mabws proposing that punitive measures be taken against the Baronet for his many dishonourable acts, and that 'some proper resolution be taken to guard and protect the county from his violent and oppressive measures'.[18] But Lloyd was not to be easily quelled by Lisburne. He was too proud and too wily a warrior to be browbeaten by any of the Cardiganshire gentry.

Summoning to the fore all his old arrogance, he once again tried to impose his authority on others and began to interfere in the affairs of the county by attempting to place his own nominees in positions of authority. All this was too much for Lord Lisburne who remarked despairingly to Lloyd of Mabws:[19]

> I am quite shocked to hear of the treatment of you and our other friends received from Baronet. Is it not out Heroding Herod? What can it end in?

It was to end in a manner which Wilmot Vaughan, Lord Lisburne of Trawsgoed, could never have anticipated!

NOTES

[1] D.R.O. Cwmgwili Mss. 109.
[2] Falc. Mss., Nos. 15-19.
[3] D.R.O. Cwmgwili Mss. 109.
[4] ibid.

[5]ibid.
[6]N.L.W. 14215.C.
[7]ibid.
[8]ibid.
[9]P.C. Mss. 3485.
[10]Nanteos Mss., Lisburne to Wm.P. (n.d.).
[11]ibid.
[12]Nanteos Mss., Pryse Campbell to Wm.P., 26 Jan. 1768.
[13]D.C.Mss., T.J. to J.J., 7 Feb. 1768.
[14]N.L.W. 14215.C.
[15]P.C.Mss. 3859.
[16]D.C.Mss., T.J. to J.J., 7 Feb. 1768.
[17]Evans, ed., *Lloyd Letters,* p. 34.
[18]N.L.W. 14216.D.
[19]N.L.W. 143215.C.

Chapter Sixteen

'A NOBLE NINE DAYS FIGHT'

The Devil looks after its own and the unpredictable happened which devastated Lisburne, John Pugh Pryse and Dr William Powell, but which swung open the gate for Sir Herbert to re-enter the political arena in Cardiganshire. On 4 December 1768 Pryse Campbell died unexpectedly at the age of forty three. Such was the mysterious dispensation of providence. For Lord Lisburne and the others it was a 'bitter blow to bear, with bitter tears to shed'. They wept for Campbell, and still more, they wept for themselves.

The cloud which had blotted out this rising star also now descended over the gentry, for there was no obvious successor to Pryse Campbell who would oppose the Baronet in his inevitable bid for this abruptly vacant borough seat. Once again, the gentry were obliged to organise their opposition to Sir Herbert, and John Pugh Pryse, now the M.P. for Merioneth, consulted with Lord Lisburne in London; they decided to leave the choice of a new candidate to Dr William Powell, Nanteos, who was in a position to discuss arrangements with the local Cardiganshire gentry.

Lisburne proposed that Dr William Powell's son, Thomas, should again be offered the nomination: 'Your son', he wrote, 'was our first object'. Once again Thomas Powell declined. But of paramount importance was the need, to quote Lisburne's own words, 'To have a candidate ready supported by government to oppose any attempt from the Baronet'. The son of the former borough member, John Symmons, also put himself forward for nomination, but Lisburne and John Pugh Pryse did not consider that he would present a strong enough threat to Sir Herbert Lloyd.

Despite the general tide of public opinion against the Baronet, Thomas Johnes the Custos had remained remarkably faithful to him; the other gentry had looked upon this dog-like devotion with some surprise. Lisburne noted disapprovingly that, 'the Custos acted like a kind of subaltern to Sir Herbert', and he was at a loss to understand it. Thomas Johnes himself had long realized that he was supporting a lost cause in the teeth of determined opposition. Nevertheless, he was still prepared to assist him in this one last bid for the borough seat; but this time there was a proviso attached to his support. He promised to put forward Sir Herbert Lloyd's application for the nomination for the borough seat on the clear understanding that if it was not accepted, he would then stand down to make room for the Custos's son, Thomas Johnes the younger (later of Hafod). 'I said I would endeavour to bring him [Sir Herbert] in', explained the Custos to John Johnes, 'but if I could not, he must submit, which he said he would'.[1]

When the meeting to decide the candidature was held, not surprisingly, the name of Sir Herbert Lloyd was rejected and they opted unanimously for Thomas Johnes the younger. But Sir Herbert Lloyd refused to stand down in favour of the Custos's son. His promises to do so had, as usual, been nothing but hollow noises. Despite all the opposition, he was determined to contest this by-election. Thomas Johnes was furious. Herbert Lloyd's obduracy completely destroyed

Thomas Johnes, later of Hafod, son of Thomas Johnes the Custos

any chance that Thomas Johnes the younger might have had to win the seat, for the Whig vote would have been split. This act of betrayal on the part of Lloyd finally caused Thomas Johnes to sever all connections with him; but after all the years of cunning and deceit he ought to have known his man. In a letter mingled with deep-felt bitterness and spiked with the plans for revenge, the Custos reported Sir Herbert's treachery to Dolaucothi: 'Both sides have unanimously named my son and he only objects to it . . . this breaks through every engagement; and Duke Gwynne* and myself have left him'.[2]

Thus, his staunchest and most resolute of allies had deserted Sir Herbert Lloyd who, this time, had acted with suicidal improvidence. An enraged and vengeful Thomas Johnes now crossed the Rubicon to join the opposing camp of Lisburne, John Pugh Pryse and Dr William Powell. They welcomed him with open arms, for he brought with him a crucial supply of burgesses in the Lampeter, Llanfair and Pumsaint areas. The Custos was soon to hit Lloyd where it would hurt most; he immediately instructed his brother John Johnes to involve himself in the by-election activities and to campaign vigorously for John Pugh Pryse: 'Make every burgess you can for Mr Pryse of Gogerddan', he ordered. With the defection of the Custos to the Gogerddan camp, the defences of the Cardiganshire gentry were complete. Sir Herbert Lloyd stood a political pariah in his own county; and was forced to look to Carmarthenshire for support in the person of Griffith Philipps, Cwmgwili.

Meanwhile, the plans to adopt Thomas Johnes the younger, as the Whig candidate were aborted, and Lloyd's adversaries decided to look for a new and altogether more powerful candidate who would present an irrefutable challenge to the Baronet. After a wide search they decided upon a complete stranger to the county in the person of Ralph Congreve of Aldermaston in the county of Berkshire. He had no connections whatever with Cardiganshire, but he was possessed of the one essential requisite for success in eighteenth century elections, vast wealth. Congreve himself never even bothered to ride across the mountains of Wales to attend his own election; his whole campaign, lavishly funded, was left to the organisation of the revenge obsessed gentry. Physically present, but with more grit than money, Sir

*Marmaduke Gwynne of Garth.

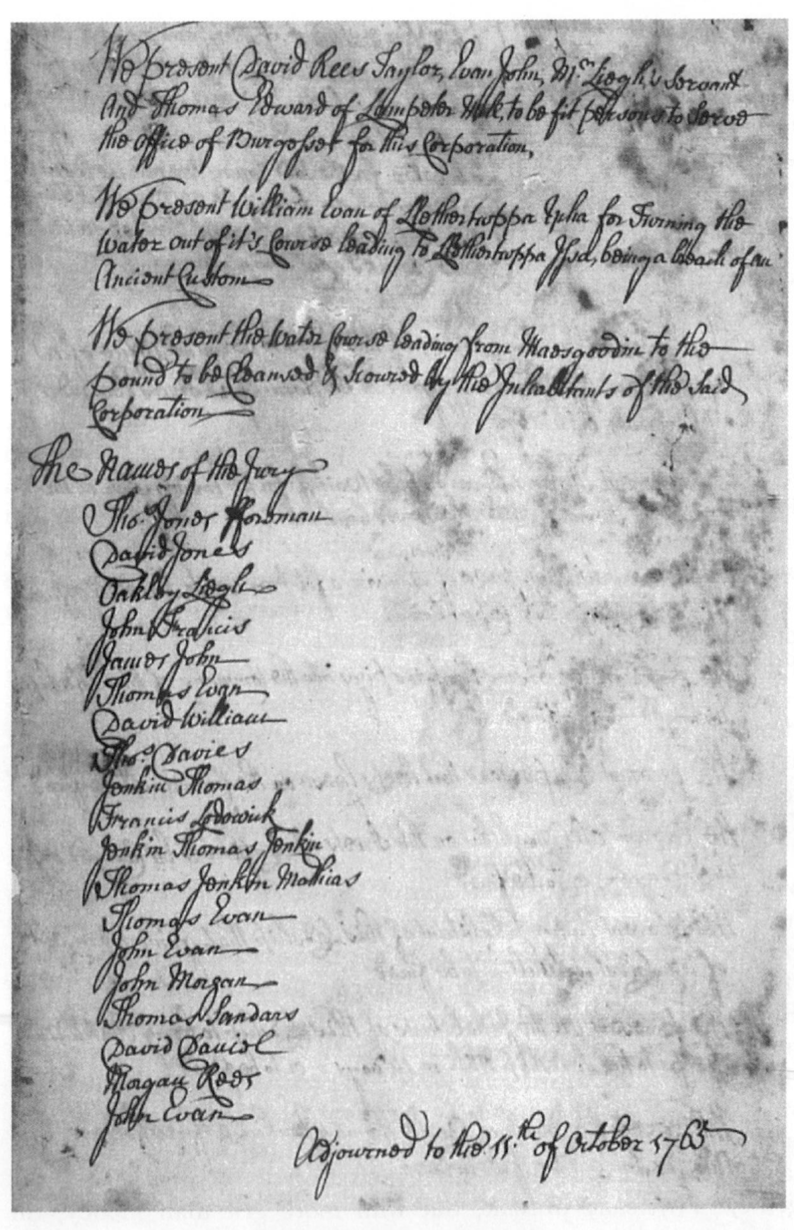

We present David Rees Taylor, Evan John, Mr. Leigh's Servant And Thomas Edward of Lampeter Mill, to be fit persons to serve the office of Burgesses for this Corporation,

We present William Evan of Llethrtroppa Ucha for Turning the water out of it's Course leading to Llethrtroppa Issa, being a breach of an Ancient Custom

We present the water Course leading from Maesgoedin to the pound to be Cleansed & Scoured by the Inhabitants of the said Corporation

The Names of the Jury

Thos. Jones Foreman
David Jones
Oakley Leigh
John Francis
James John
Thomas Evan
David William
Thos. Davies
Jenkin Thomas
Francis Lodowick
Jenkin Thomas Jenkin
Thomas Jenkin Mathias
Thomas Evan
John Evan
John Morgan
Thomas Sandars
David Daniel
Morgan Rees
John Evan

Adjourned to the 15th of October 1765

Lampeter Court Leet Record

The first minute in this record shows the appointment of Oakley Leigh's servant as a burgess in October 1765. Among the list of the jurors Oakley Leigh's name figures prominently.

Herbert Lloyd braced himself for the contest, bravely rallying around him all the support he could possibly muster.

It was to prove a bitter encounter. The by-election itself commenced on 5 January 1769 and continued for nine days, drawing into its vortex the whole of Cardiganshire and many other counties beyond. In Lampeter itself, every last man committed to the support of Peterwell was rounded up and driven to Cardigan to swell Lloyd's numbers at the hustings. At Aberystwyth and its surrounding areas, every burgess who supported the Gogerddan hegemony was bundled into wagons and carts and trundled down to Cardigan, so that for days the coast and inland roads were clogged with this jostling, motley crowd of voters all rumbling to the polls to record their support of their respective patrons. Not that any of them had any political consciousness; all minds would have been filled with the thoughts of free food and drink rather than with the political ramifications of this by-election. From all parts of Wales men wound their way to Cardigan, for as many burgesses as possible were persuaded to ride in from other counties. The poll book shows that Sir Herbert Lloyd polled one hundred and seventy nine voters from Carmarthenshire, one hundred and forty six from Pembrokeshire, and twenty seven from Breconshire. Considering his reputation, this was a remarkable achievement and probably reflects the unflagging industry of such men as Oakley Leigh and Griffith Philipps.

It was a strange situation at Cardigan; Congreve was the invisible candidate and the voters were never even made aware of his christian name; but it was of no consequence, for his interests were strongly represented by Gogerddan, Trawsgoed and Nanteos. These three, blind to everything except the defeat of the Baronet, left no stone unturned; they summoned their supporters from counties as far afield as Denbigh, Merioneth and Montgomery. At the clarion call of Gogerddan, they came like sheep to the polling station where, under the scrutinizing eye of Thomas Lloyd, the Gogerddan appointed mayor, they dutifully cast their votes for the unknown and hitherto unheard of Congreve.

In Cardigan town itself, the beer and wine flowed freely, as was the custom at eighteenth century elections: there were also bright knots and flying ribbons to add a splash of colour to the scene. All this cost money; we know that Congreve was easily able to withstand the expense, but it is remarkable that Sir Herbert Lloyd was able to undertake the election at all. It is possible that the credit obtained in ale houses was by dint of fear and threats from the armed henchmen who flanked him wherever he went.

Inevitably, the nine days at the polls proved to be a time of mounting tension for everyone, but particularly for Sir Herbert Lloyd. Without the support of Thomas Lloyd, the returning officer, his position became increasingly hopeless. Exasperated but impotent against the system, he hovered at the polling stand and repeatedly tried to assess the validity of the votes cast, but he was consistently frustrated by Thomas Lloyd, who absolutely refused to allow him access to the books. The Baronet later claimed that Thomas Lloyd had overtly and shamelessly exerted pressure how and when he pleased for Congreve, by accepting or refusing votes according to his whim. This was probably true, and it was maddening for Sir Herbert, but he was powerless to act against it.

The closing days of the election saw Sir Herbert Lloyd caught in a mood of rising panic, frantically striving for more voters to keep the poll open. His last vain attempts to keep politically afloat were witnessed by one voter, Lewis Evans of Llangathen, who vividly captured the drama of the moment in a letter which he wrote to Richard Knethell, an attorney from Haverfordwest. This contemporaneous account brings into sharper focus the whole election scene prevailing at Cardigan on 15 January 1769:[3]

> I went with a couple of voters to Cardigan on Friday morning at 1. By 2 o'clock Sir Herbert could not make up his tally and desired the Mayor not to shut the books, as he expected more voters on Saturday. But I met Mr Tommy Bowen, and he told me to make up a tally as before; for there were but five good ones before; he laughed and said it was all over, they had not a man left, but they had held out a noble nine days fight.

Normally, at the poll, each candidate was required to produce thirty voters at a time in turns; these then produced their voting tickets, and their name and manner of voting were recorded in the books under the supervision of the mayor. But evidently, Sir Herbert's voters were drying up, since by Friday he was hard pressed to produce batches of five, let alone thirty.

This same letter gives a fascinating account of the despicable conduct of the Baronet who, on the previous Thursday evening, had

An Election Scene
(Hogarth)

indulged in a display of petulant and unedifying behaviour, when he had used an unkempt gipsy lad to ridicule the absent Congreve and harass the gentry acting on his behalf. It was one of the last futile outbursts on the part of a desperate man:[4]

> Sir Herbert gives the gentleman as much trouble as he can and makes all the game he can of Mr Congreve. Thursday evening he had a tinker boy, who had the oddest head of hair as ever I saw, for when I saw him on Friday he had it combed and powdered. He was barefooted and barelegged, with his elbows out through his coat. Some part of his face blacked. Sir Herbert brought him to the Hall door in the evening when the Gentlemen were coming out, and his mob carried him round the town crying 'Behold, what a figure Congreve was'.

But for all the farce and charade, hope was ebbing for the Baronet. By Friday Sir Herbert's chances had receded beyond recovery and a deathly hush had settled over the scene. Lewis Evans commented: 'Congreve was 240 ahead when I came from there on Friday night, and two talleys to be polled that night again, everything was very quiet, no mobbing or rioting'. Inevitably, Sir Herbert's frenzied efforts to procure more voters had failed and he was unable to prolong the agony beyond the ninth day. On Saturday, Thomas Lloyd closed the books and the final result was announced, when Congreve was declared to be elected by a majority of 1950 to 1704 over Sir Herbert Lloyd. The gentlemen of the county had won and it was all over for the 'Bart'.

The poll book for the election shows the pattern of voting.[5] As to be expected, the burgesses from Aberystwyth, Llanrhystud, Cardigan and many other areas under the control of Gogerddan voted for Congreve. But other figures emerge to show that Lloyd had reaped the retribution for past cantankerous outbursts against former friends. His fracas with David Lloyd of Breinog had cost him dearly, for we find voters from Breinog's territory, Llanfihangel Ystrad, voting *en masse* for Congreve. More damaging still was the changed allegiance of Thomas Johnes the Custos; voters from Talley, Caio, Llanfair Clydogau and Cellan had cast their votes for the unknown Congreve rather than 'The great man of Peterwell'. This backlash from the Johnes brothers had proved Lloyd's great downfall, for they had made every effort to whip up support for Congreve, and it was ironic that burgesses originally created by Sir Herbert Lloyd at Lampeter, had now been deflected to support his opponent. In all, one hundred and ninety of these burgesses polled for Congreve, enough to tip the balance against Sir Herbert Lloyd.

The following table is a sample from the poll book, emphasising the Peterwell hold on Lampeter and showing the Gogerddan hold on Cardigan and Aberystwyth.[6]

	Sir Herbert Lloyd	Mr Congreve
CARDIGAN	89	340
ABERYSTWYTH	0	479
ADPAR	11	19
LAMPETER	949	190

Sir Herbert Lloyd, however, perverse to the last, refused to accept the result and he petitioned for a declaration that it was invalid. Two petitions were submitted to the House of Commons, one on behalf of Sir Herbert Lloyd, and the other on behalf of the burgesses of the four contributory boroughs. The allegations contained in the petitions were several. Sir Herbert maintained that the christian name of Congreve was not known to any of the electors, nor mentioned during the entire poll. He also laid claim to the majority of the votes cast, stating that Thomas Lloyd, the mayor, had not examined the legality of each vote cast, and in particular had not ensured that the admission slip of each burgess had been duly stamped as required by Act of Parliament. Sir Herbert accused Thomas Lloyd of allowing many to vote for Congreve who 'had no right or colour' to do so. 'Others', he said, 'had been coerced into supporting Congreve by the gentlemen representing his interest'. The second petition argued that Thomas Lloyd, 'the said mayor, kept open the poll for nine days and admitted several hundreds of people for Congreve, who had no right or pretence whatever, in prejudice . . . to the real burgesses . . . and by unwarrantable acts and practices . . . the petitioners have been deprived of their legal rights and franchises'.[7]

The accusations levelled against Thomas Lloyd, the mayor, in these petitions were lengthy and detailed, and almost certainly they would have been valid complaints on the part of Sir Herbert Lloyd. Thomas Lloyd, the mayor, was a Gogerddan nominee, certain to have acted in favour of Congreve. What is surprising is that Sir

Herbert Lloyd had polled so well in the face of such overwhelming opposition. Defeat by only one hundred and forty six votes illustrates the power he continued to wield despite his isolation by the Cardiganshire gentry.

Sir Herbert Lloyd presented the petitions on 3 February 1769, and they were referred to the Committee of Privileges and Elections for examination and a report to the House of Commons. But they were the last sterile noises of a defeated man. By the end of the parliamentary session on 9 May, no report had been prepared. Nor in fact, was any report ever to appear, for the death of Sir Herbert on 19 August 1769 removed the incentive for any further enquiry into that unique and acrimoniously contested Cardigan by-election of January 1769.

NOTES

[1]D.C. Mss., T.J. to J.J., 2 Jan. 1769.
[2]ibid.
[3]Eaton Evans and Williams Mss. 954.
[4]ibid.
[5]Abermeurig Mss.
[6]P.D.G. Thomas, 'Eighteenth Century . . .', *Ceredigion,* Vol. 5, p. 414.
[7]*J.H.C.*, Vol. 32, p. 177.

Chapter Seventeen

AN ENIGMATIC END

If 1769 began inauspiciously, worse was to follow. The parliamentary defeat at the hands of a total stranger had been a jolt to his pride and sorely injured his dignity; this fight against Congreve had been in the nature of a last ditch stand, where the expense of the nine day poll had swallowed up his remaining assets and much more besides.

The gamble had not paid off. Now at the neap of his misfortunes he had returned to Peterwell defeated, ostracised and, more seriously for him, deprived of the status and benefits afforded to an M.P. As a petitioner, he still enjoyed parliamentary immunity from prosecution for debt, but the clouds had long been gathering, and it could only be a matter of time before the great fiscal storm broke about his head. He had been living dangerously for months; even as long as a year previously, he had been obliged to ride smartly home to Peterwell so as to avoid the service of writs against his person. Now, at last, the long shadow of his original debt to his sister-in-law Elizabeth, had finally caught up with him. Although she herself had died, her relatives had pursued her claim in the courts, where they had been granted an order of distraint to enter Peterwell '. . . to sell and dispose of goods'.[1] To add salt to the wound, the lawyer who had obtained this order was John Jones the Aberystwyth attorney, whom he hated with all his heart. After some fourteen years of devious evasion, it seemed as if he were powerless to stem this onward sweep of retribution.

Lloyd's troubles came not singly. The gentry, not content with electoral defeat in itself, continued to savage him by persisting in their campaign to have him removed from the Commission of the Peace. His most relentless persecutor had now become Thomas Johnes the Custos. Still furious at Lloyd's betrayal over his son, he hounded him mercilessly and resolved to pick him clean of every vestige of respectability or former authority. 'I every day expect to hear out of Cardiganshire about the Commission of the Peace, if we can turn him out', he told John Johnes, 'and there is not the least doubt to be made of it'. All those years of camaraderie and political conspiracy had become twisted into an obsession, not only to destroy him, but if possible to expunge him from the face of Cardiganshire. 'I would be extremely glad of laying hold of him', he thundered, 'and would spend any money to make an example of him'.[2]

Sir Herbert's ears must have been burning at Peterwell but, as usual, he showed no signs of contrition or yielding to events. Indeed, somehow or other, he still managed to strike back and sting Thomas Johnes into exclaiming: 'I do not wonder at the Bart's behaviour; this little, low, dirty resentment is worthy of him'. It is not clear what trick he had played this time, but it was sufficiently discreditable to goad Thomas Johnes into launching the following blistering attack upon him: 'He is perfectly void of all sensations or shame . . . such an infamous wretch I hope never existed nor ever will again'.[3] Strong words for a man who once so befriended him!

These fulminations of Thomas Johnes did not appear to have any effect on Sir Herbert Lloyd; bloody but unbowed, he remained brooding at Peterwell. Impenitent as ever, he continued to ward off his creditors and await the one hope of a reprieve from his present predicament, that of a favourable result to the election petition which he had presented to Parliament on 3 February 1769. He was clutching at straws. Even if he had had support in high places, which he definitely had not, the machinery of government ground too slowly for a man caught in his desperate straits. By the end of the parliamentary session, his appeal had not even been considered.

This winter of defeat gave way to an equally unpropitious spring. The beauty and the freshness of nature's rebirth all around Peterwell could have held little consolation for him. With every avenue in the county bricked up against him, his position became increasingly untenable. He endured it until June when, rather than remain any longer cornered in Cardiganshire, his thoughts turned to London for salvation. There, at least, was a chance, however remote, of deliverance; for estates were known to have been won as well as lost in a single night at the gaming tables.

But such a venture required money. With a face of brass he now turned to John Johnes of Dolaucothi for help. On 26 June, in a very uncertain hand, he scribbled a hasty note to Dolaucothi pleading for money to attempt the only course open to him, the card tables. The brevity and the brusqueness of this letter reflect his desperation and, as far as is known, this is the last written communication from the Baronet. It is a fitting epitaph:[4]

Dear Sir,

You would oblige me very much if you could let me have some bank bills or drafts for cash in London. Favour me with your answer what you can spare. My nephew shall wait for you with the cash. With many thanks. From dear sir,

Yours sincerely,
Herbert Lloyd.

To John Johnes, Esq. Sunday, June 26, 1769
Dolaucothi.

We do not know whether or not John Johnes complied with this request. It is unlikely that he did, for he was very close to his brother the Custos now so implacably opposed to Lloyd. It seems to have been an outrageous appeal, coming so soon on the heels of the bitter feud which had developed between Peterwell and the Johnes brothers. But Herbert Lloyd was, as usual, impervious to circumstances. Whatever the outcome, soon after this letter, the Baronet's great coach swept out of Peterwell avenue and turned for London, on what was to prove an apocalyptic journey.

An account of what happened to him after reaching London has been set out in a highly charged and dramatic fashion by the Lampeter historian George Eyre Evans.[5] It is based almost entirely on folk tradition and conjecture, rather than on documented evidence. It is, nevertheless, interesting to recount the picture of Lloyd as painted by Evans in 1902. Evans claims that at the end of July, Sir Herbert Lloyd travelled to London in his great coach 'armed with his inevitable brace of loaded pistols, without which he never travelled far'. Having reached London, he put up at the Black Bull[6] in Holborn and then made for his club, which was a gambling den situated in the neighbourhood of Brooke Street. Here, 'several nights running did the Baronet take his place at the gaming tables', until on 17 August he was hit heavily by losses, allegedly exceeding £7,000. His nemesis was also overtaking him in Cardiganshire, for news was relayed that floods had washed away his crops and that his pet hunter had cut himself so fearfully against stakes that he had to be put down.

Lloyd had reached the point of no return. 'What could he do?', asks Evans, who also provided the answer. 'On a plea of seeking a little fresh air, Sir Herbert walked out into the small garden to the rear of the gambling den'. When his companions searched for him the following morning, they found him, 'With face upturned to the grey morning . . . shot through the temples by his own hand'. His body was carefully packed in rugs and placed in a coffin covered with canvas. This was then secured on top of his great coach and labelled 'valuable furniture'. In this manner it was transported back to Wales.

On arrival at Peterwell it was met by a reception committee of bailiffs anxious to place their writs on the coffin in order to secure payment for debts. 'There they were', wrote Evans, 'ordered to stay on watch both night and day . . . to prevent the body being removed for burial . . . What was to be done?' Once again Evans provides the answer to his own question. After almost two weeks with Sir Herbert's body lying in the mansion, the valet and the coachman conceived of a scheme to outwit the bailiffs. The Peterwell cellars were opened and the bailiffs were liberally plied with doctored *cwrw* (beer), which quickly made them drunk. While they lay unconscious, the funeral was hastily arranged for that night, 3 September 1769. The tenantry and neighbours were informed, and every man was ordered to bring a torch.

Evans then went on to describe the proceedings in a manner which has seared itself into the folk lore of the locality: 'The coffin was slowly carried out and placed on the bier. What a scene! The mansion with its numerous windows all closely blinded; the flower garden on the roof; the artificial water on each side of the avenue, down which the procession passed through rows of lighted torches; the surpliced vicar at the head supported on either side by the steward and the valet; and the ever increasing number of mourners behind, as torch bearers, two by two, quietly fell into the ranks after the coffin had passed along. The old church of St Peter's lit with candles in sconces was crowded with mourners and silent spectators. After the service, Sir Herbert's coffin was placed in the family vault . . . at length secure from further molestation, where it could with impunity defy all earthly authorities'.

So wrote G. E. Evans and it seems a pity to have to cut across such a fitting finale to the life of the Baronet. Evans claimed to have based his work on 'extremely valuable documents' placed in his hands by Mr Howell Evans, the Chief Constable for Cardiganshire. Unfortunately, there is no trace of these manuscripts in the collection of the G. E. Evans papers in the National Library of Wales, and contemporary evidence does not substantiate this theatrical account of his end.

The exact date of Sir Herbert's departure for London is not known, but he must have left Peterwell shortly after he made his last plea for bank bills to John Johnes on 26 June. We have no account of his activities in London, but it is likely that he spent much of his time at the gaming tables of Holborn. Ironically, the first real evidence of his presence in the capital is provided by his last will and testament dated 13 August 1769 and signed in London. He possibly feared that his end was near, for in it he claimed to be of 'sound mind, but indisposed in body'.[7] The Peterwell estate he left to his nephew John Adams of Whitland, and his final wish was that his 'body is to be buried in the family vault at Lampeter'.

Then, incredibly, the day after he had drawn up his will he entered into a widely publicised marriage with a Mrs Bacon. An announcement of the wedding appeared in *Baldwin's London Weekly Journal* 19 August: 'Married at St George's, Hanover Square, Sir Herbert Lloyd, Bart. to Mrs Bacon, Relict. of Bacon Esq. late of Newtoncap, near Bishop Auckland in the county of Durham'. The *Annual Register of Marriages* also records the marriage, but strangely no record exists in the Registers of St George's itself.

This was an astonishing step for Sir Herbert to have taken, for the marriage would have been bigamous. Lady Lloyd still languished at Foelallt, and there is no evidence of a divorce. The inscription on her tomb at Strata Florida nine years later described her as the 'relict' of Sir Herbert. Divorce in the eighteenth century was a cumbersome affair, obtainable only through the Church Courts and then only if followed by a special Act of Parliament. Bigamy in the eighteenth century was still deemed to be a felony and a capital offence. It is astonishing that even Sir Herbert should have flouted the law in so flagrant a manner and laid himself open to the most dire of consequences.

Under what compulsion did he enter into this bigamous union so late in the day? Was it the last act of a dying man wishing to be united with his mistress? Local tradition ascribed to the Baronet a mistress in London, but there are no written references to support this, and nowhere does the name of Mrs Bacon appear. Could it be that he had found an extremely rich widow prepared to rescue him from his calamitous situation? Or was this his final gesture, a sick charade, flinging convention to the wind, hurling a last futile response at a world that was rapidly closing in upon him? The threat of hanging for bigamy probably held no fear for him, since his life was already forfeit to sickness and disease. His condition was such that he must have known that he would never again see Peterwell with its verdant acres fringed in sylvan splendour. He had left Wales sick, solitary and insolvent, and in July his Swansea cousin, Thomas Popkins, had seen him in London, 'extremely ill and full of remorse'.[8] This was a changed Sir Herbert, for he had never before showed any sign of contrition for his deeds; it indicates the depth of his despair at this time.

But this remorse was shortlived; a few weeks later the would be penitent became a bigamous groom, bidding defiance to anyone and everyone. He had little time left in which to enjoy the company of his bigamous bride, for five days later, he died at the age of forty nine years. The shadowy figure of Mrs Bacon had flitted only briefly across the stage, and she vanished as abruptly as she had materialised, the victim of Sir Herbert's last and greatest deceit.

Even in the manner of his death, the Baronet poses something of a mystery. The *Public Advertiser* for 30 August 1769 announced that on '20 August Sunday night died Sir Herbert Lloyd Bart.' The *Gentleman's Magazine* contains notices of both his marriage and his death on opposite pages dated 14 and 19 August respectively. *Baldwin's Weekly Journal* and the *Middlesex Journal* also record his death, but include a further revealing detail in that, 'he died at Salt Hill on his way to Bath'. This accords with the information given to Thomas Johnes the Custos by Popkins, a few weeks before his death. Sir Herbert had told Popkins that if his health would permit, he would be at Bath in a few days. The significant factor is that all the newspapers record a natural death for Sir Herbert, which is a far cry from G. E. Evans's highly dramatised account of a suicide in the garden of a sleazy gambling den in Holborn.

Had the Baronet shot himself, either deliberately or accidentally, it is highly unlikely that all those eighteenth century newspapers, which so voraciously recorded every tit bit of violence, would have missed or suppressed such a sensational piece of news. The age loved a scandal, and the Baronet was a well known figure. It is not feasible that any person would have had the power to stop the publication of the 'suicide' of Sir Herbert, for the newsheets of the day were saturated with accounts of violence involving fights and beatings, frays, duels, wagon accidents and such like. Therefore, the evidence suggests that Sir Herbert Lloyd died of natural causes at Salt Hill, which is a hamlet near Slough on the route west for Bath, where he had stated he intended to go in order to gain his customary relief from sickness.

G. E. Evans was the first and only writer to suggest that the Baronet took his own life, and it is possible that he sought to revamp history more to his personal taste in order to provide a suitably stormy end to a tempestuous life. It is more likely, however, that he was influenced by a local tradition based upon the unusual events following the Baronet's death; namely, the manner of the body's return from London, the impounding of the coffin, and the midnight burial.

In the eighteenth century, suicide or *felo de se* was a felony of self murder, and suicides were buried without benefit of clergy, sometimes at a spot where four roads met, with a stake through the body.[9] This practice was discontinued by a statute of 1823 which allowed burial in a churchyard, but only between the hours of nine and twelve at night and without a divine service. With the passage of time it would have been quite feasible for the midnight burial of Sir Herbert Lloyd to have been interpreted as an act of burying a suicide, and for a tradition to emerge that the infamous Baronet, filled with remorse for his misdeeds, had fittingly put an end to his existence. The midnight burial was by no means unique to Sir Herbert Lloyd. Indeed, it had been the fashion for royalty to be so buried. Queen Anne's husband, Prince George, was buried by torchlight on 13 November 1708 in Westminster Abbey, 'after the same manner as King Charles II, which was privately at twelve midnight'.[10] Horace Walpole, in a letter to George Montague 13 November 1760, described the funeral of George II also at night as being 'very theatric . . . attended by mourners with lights . . . every seventh man bearing a torch . . . an absolutely noble sight'. G. E. Evans implies that Sir Herbert's midnight burial was a ruse to defeat the debt collectors and that there was a rush to get him interred before the bailiffs recovered consciousness; but it appears to have been a Peterwell family tradition, for his heir and nephew John Adams of Whitland, was also 'buried by torchlight'.[11]

Nevertheless, a fortnight elapsed between the death and burial of Sir Herbert; even allowing three or four days for the coach to transport the body from London to Peterwell, this was a long time, especially during the month of August. It is quite possible that bailiffs had placed writs on the coffin, thereby preventing the immediate interment of the body. But the Peterwell coffers were empty and

August turned into September before Sir Herbert's coffin was finally borne along the stately avenue leading from the mansion to be lain at rest in the vault of his ancestors. Edmunds writing in 1861 stated: 'He was buried at night with great pomp, the road from the mansion to the parish church being lighted with torches'.[12] This must have been a remarkable sight with the coffin covered by a pall of black velvet on a carriage drawn by six horses, caparisoned in black, as was the custom in the funerals of the gentry in the eighteenth century.

In view of all this pomp and splendour, it is ironic that Sir Herbert now commands the same amount of space in the Parish Register as that afforded his meanest tenants. A single line in the Register records: 'Buried. September the 3rd. Sir Herbert Lloyd, Bart.' A scrutiny of the Lampeter Parish Register (see opposite) shows the Baronet ingloriously wedged between small pox victims and common paupers, and he is given the same amount of word coverage as the Sexton. Not surprisingly, the cleric even made an error in entering the month, which he afterwards corrected. It is interesting to note that David Daniel, blacksmith, whom he made his first Portreeve on taking over the Court Leet in 1755, also appears on the same burial page as his master, so that they rose and fell together. Any stone tablet or plaque to his memory has long disappeared, and a visitor to St Peter's Church today will find nothing to remind him of Sir Herbert's existence. Epitaphs to his grandfather, Daniel Evans of Peterwell, his sister Anne and other members of the Maesyfelin family still remain high above the church porch. As for the Peterwell vault, it now lies unmarked beneath a grassy sward surrounded by other old gravestones. Recently a local gravedigger, who had occasion to open one of the adjoining graves, informed the author that during his digging he struck the original wall of the Peterwell tomb and could hear earth and stones rolling into the vault. During the eighteenth century this vault lay inside the church beneath the chancel, but since Sir Herbert's time the church has been twice rebuilt and resited higher up the hill, so that the Peterwell family now lie in the open graveyard with no commemorative plaque to show that they ever existed. It is also ironic that Sir Herbert's name survives only on the memorial tablet to his neglected widow Dame Anne Lloyd at Strata Florida Church. Even in death, Sir Herbert's bones were not to find repose, and it was believed in Lampeter that they had been taken from the tomb and were kept in a loft in the town. The truth of this was confirmed by a member of a

Bur^d. March ye 24th. Elizabeth Linton from Lanwnen
April ye 11th Ann Evan Hugh from Pound.
April ye 26th Elinor Richard a pauper
May ye 11th Nathaniel David from Coedmor
Bur^d. June ye 10th James ye Son of John Thomas
June ye 14th John the son of Thos. David
Bur^d. ye same day Jane Roberts both of the Small Pox
Bur^d. Augt. ye 10th. Sarah Moses of the Small Pox
Bur^d. ye same day Eliz: David Thos. of the Town
Bur^d. 7^ber ye 3^d. Sr Herbert Lloyd Bar^t.
Bur^d. Catherine Jones of the Town 7^ber. ye 15th
Bur^d. 7^ber ye 17th Rachel ye Daughter of Moses Evan
Bur^d. 8^ber ye 1st Evan Thomas of Pant ysgawen
Bur^d. 9^ber ye 8th Eliz: David Wid: from Maeslyn
Bur^d. 9^ber ye 24th Jane Jones of Ty yn yr Eithyn
Bur^d. 10^ber ye 7th John ye son of Morgan Evan

1770

Bur^d. Jan: ye 9th Margaret David from Pencarreg
— Jan: ye 10th David the son of Simon David
Jan: ye 19th Rees the son of Evan D^d David & Joice his wif
Jan: ye 23^d. Evan the son of William Evan Netty Lwyppia
May ye 10th Mary John Rowland widow
June ye 5th Evan David Sexton
July y^e 24th Elinor y^e Daughter of Edmund John
Oo^br. y^e 6th Evan David Rees a pauper
— y^e 28th David Daniel Blacksmith of the Town
December y^e 10th Thos. the son Charles Edmund
and Martha his wife

Burial entry of Sir Herbert Lloyd

The unmarked grave
(St Peter's Churchyard—the site of the Peterwell vault; this lay beneath the chancel of the old Church)

local family who wrote to the historian G. E. Evans in 1902: 'Sir Herbert's bones were taken from the vault by my mother's brother, who was a medical student, and it was in his room that they were found when the old house was pulled down'.[13] Where they are today must remain a matter of pure conjecture.

The demise of the Baronet was, no doubt, a relief to the gentlemen of the county. For over a decade his disreputable escapades and scandalous behaviour had plunged the name of the west Wales squirearchy into disrepute. His cantankerous disposition had put him at odds with most of the gentry and by August 1769 no one grieved his departure. The last days of his life seem to have been lived in much the same defiant tenor as he spent his years in Cardiganshire. The whole sequence of events leading up to his death had so sickened Thomas Johnes that, a fortnight after his funeral, he wrote the following letter to John Johnes expressing his revulsion:[14]

> I can now mention the Baronet, though it is still disagreeable. When I first heard of his death and disposition, it made me quite

> sick, and I could not bear to think of the villain with any degree of temper . . . the villain's death surprised me—I had seen him so often in the Jaws of Death that I imagined it had no power over him.

Such was the impact of his death even on those he had counted as his friends.

NOTES

[1] D.R.O. (Aber.) D.X./3/25.
[2] D.C.Mss., T.J. to J.J., 4 Feb. 1769.
[3] ibid.
[4] D.C.Mss., S.H.L. to J.J., 26 June 1769.
[5] See G. E. Evans, *Lampeter,* pp. 219-232.
[6] Phillips, *Mid-Georgian London,* p. 283.
[7] Pet.Mss., 65.
[8] D.C.Mss., T.J. to J.J., 15 Sept. 1769.
[9] Jowitt, p. 792.
[10] Green, *Queen Anne,* p. 203.
[11] N.L.W. 13660.
[12] *Arch. Camb.,* p. 159.
[13] N.L.W. 13548. C., Cicely Banks Price to G. E. Evans, 10 Aug. 1902.

Chapter Eighteen

THE AFTERMATH

Sir Herbert Lloyd had departed this life generally unlamented, without the eulogies normally afforded in the eighteenth century to a person of his station in life. Nothing was resolved by his death, and the huge debts which he had during his lifetime remained. On 13 August, six days before his death he had drawn up his will; apart from bequests of £2,000 to his niece Martha Adams, £500 to his lawyer, Albany Wallis's son, and a few smaller bequests to servants, the remainder of his estates at Peterwell, Maesyfelin, Foelallt and Llechwedd Deri together with lands in Carmarthenshire and Cardiganshire were bequeathed to his nephew John Adams of Whitland. Significantly, there was no provision whatsoever in his will for his widow Anne Lloyd; this, together with the fact that her coat of arms as a member of the Nanteos family was never incorporated into that of Sir Herbert, shows how incompatible had been their marriage.

There had fallen to John Adams a legacy of trouble. The total deficiencies on the Peterwell and other estates amounted to a staggering £54,000. Peterwell itself had been mortgaged for £14,000 and Maesyfelin for £16,000; the other £24,000 existed as a result of sundry sums owed to individuals including the sum of £1,000 owed to Lady Lisburne.[1] By eighteenth century standards the amount owing was considerable. Enormous as they were, his nephew John Adams in no way allowed these debts to inhibit his own lifestyle as the new owner of Peterwell, and he was soon to be seen following the same improvident mode of living as his thriftless uncle had pursued before him.

The take over of Peterwell was not a smooth one; almost immediately, he was plagued by the unquiet spectre of Maesyfelin, this time rearing its head in the form of a claim against his estate by Edward Ffoy and Elizabeth Sherbourne, the nephew and sister of the late Sir Lucius Christianus Lloyd. They maintained that they, and not John Adams, were the rightful heirs to the Lordship of the Manor of Lampeter. This dispute had to be settled in the King's Bench where Oakley Leigh was required to swear an affidavit that Sir Herbert Lloyd had been in 'lawful and peaceable' possession of both Peterwell and Maesyfelin for many years before his death, and that John Adams was the present 'Lord of the Manor as Devisee in Fee under the last will and testament of Sir Herbert Lloyd'.

The court found for Adams who, with his authority restored and his position reaffirmed, now installed himself as the Lord of the Manor and president of the Court Leet. But his tenure of the mansion became increasingly uncomfortable as the ligature of the many debts tightened and he soon attempted to let the estate for cash. On Lady Day 1771 he succeeded in letting the demesne to one Pilkington on a lease of twenty years at a rental of £240 per annum, but this tenant failed to make the proper improvements and was ejected. On 25 January 1773 Adams raised £7,000 on 'lands in Lampeter and the surrounding parishes' by contracting mortgages with Sir Robert Cunliffe of Chester and James Coulthard of Lincoln's Inn.

In this manner John Adams was able to continue at the mansion. Not content with being a mere squire, he now sought to emulate his uncle by carrying the Peterwell banner to Westminster. It was a bold step. In 1774 he made a strong bid for the Carmarthen Borough seat vacated by Griffith Philipps of Cwmgwili, when his audacity was rewarded with a victory. He retained this seat until 1780. Shielded by his M.P.'s status, he weathered another seven years of debts and claims which poured thick and fast into Peterwell. Throughout it all, he exhibited the same flair for living as Sir Herbert Lloyd. After winning the Carmarthen borough seat, in a splash of munificence which was extraordinary for a man so precariously placed, he donated £4,000 for the building of a new town hall at Carmarthen; this has been described as the 'best application of corruption money ever heard of'.[2]

This lavish spending at Carmarthen only served to weaken further his crippled estate in Cardiganshire, where he was now forced to sell off his lands piecemeal in order to survive. Among the first farms destined to be sold was Llechwedd Deri, that old cornerstone of the Peterwell inheritance and the original home of his enterprising ancestor, David Evans. This passed to William Williams of Pantseiri. Adams could not afford to be sentimental about long held family possessions; in 1774, another ancestral home was disposed of when Foelallt, the residence of his grandfather and one time seat of Sir Herbert Lloyd, was sold to Thomas Johnes the Custos for £3,500.

Foelallt was still occupied by the now ageing Anne Lloyd; there she had remained ever since Sir Herbert Lloyd had left to go to Peterwell in 1755. High above Llanddewi, cloistered by the mountains, she had lived alone pursuing an almost nun-like existence, secure from the storms which had rocked Sir Herbert Lloyd and Peterwell. But with the sale of her only abode, the vibrations had finally reached her. Any fears she might have had of being evicted were allayed by Thomas Johnes the Custos, who showed for Anne a solicitude she had never experienced at the hands of her husband. He gave instructions that 'Lady Lloyd is to enjoy the Vailallt Estate for her life and she must determine the goodness or the badness of the bargain'.[3]

Anne Lloyd was to live only a few more years. She died on 2 August 1778 at Colby in the county of Pembroke at the home of her sister Elizabeth, who had married the Reverend James Philipps. The poignancy which attached to her life continued even unto death. Her will was not immediately discovered, but later found locked away in an old trunk at her sister's home and her maid was required to swear an affidavit confirming the authenticity of the document.[4] Although buffeted by fate during her lifetime, Anne had always nourished within her a brightness of spirit which remained uncrushed and unembittered to the end. A reading of her will conveys an image of dignity and humility. Her desire was to 'be buried in the Abbey Church at Strata Florida, between my first daughter and her father in a decent manner without pomp . . . and no leaden coffin'. These directions contrast starkly with the midnight splendour and ceremony of her husband's funeral nine years previously. Her concern for others was kept alive to the last for in her will she stipulated: 'I desire five pounds may be given or distributed to the poorest housekeepers in and about Tregaron and Rhydbendigaid and three pounds to the most necessitous in and near Llanddewi brefi'.

An inscription to her memory exists in the church at Strata Florida. In the eighteenth century, hyperbole featured prominently in epitaphs, but the tablet to Anne Lloyd seems to reflect her true nature and conforms with the image of her as a person noted for her piety and generosity. It reads: 'Her virtues were eminent, but her pity was without ostentation, hypocrisy or superstition . . . her charity appears by the heartfelt lamentations of the poor and the needy'. Her loss was truly mourned among the less fortunate whom she had helped in life.

Back at Peterwell, John Adams was reaping the whirlwind sown by his uncle: in the courts a string of judgements and writs was being entered up against him by the various creditors of Sir Herbert Lloyd.

The following sample shows how the Baronet had borrowed from all and sundry:[5]

> In the Exchequer: Claims against Peterwell.
> *Michas. Term 1778.* At the suit of Sarah P . . . ps., in debt for £2,000
> *Hilary Term 1779.* At the suit of Evan Jenkins, Gent., in debt for £1,600
> *Easter Term 1779.* At the suit of Edward Vaughan, Esq., in debt for £2,000
> *Hilary Term 1780.* At the suit of James Philipps, D.D., in debt for £6,000
> *Hilary Term 1780.* At the suit of Winfford James, Gent., in debt for £400

In 1780 his term in Parliament was at an end and with it went the bastion which might have protected him against these creditors. Like his uncle before him, he was now obliged to face the consequences of his prodigality and there was nothing for it but to sell the 'great mansion of Peterwell'. Adams reluctantly wrote to John Lewes of Carmarthen: 'I am come to a resolution to dispose of the Lordship, which I will offer for sale to Mr Lovedon'.[6]

'Mr Lovedon' was Edward Lovedon of Buscot Park, Berkshire, who had married Margaret Pryse, the daughter of Lewis Pryse of Gogerddan. Edward Lovedon, seeking to extend his influence in Cardiganshire, had shown an interest in taking over Peterwell, and an agreement was actually reached over the sale of the property. But during this period of negotiation, Adams's affairs gravely deteriorated, and a certain paranoia began to exhibit itself in his correspondence. 'I well know', fumed Adams to Lovedon, 'that every engine of wickedness is set on foot against me, but I hope to defeat their plots'.[7]

Adams had every reason to feel unnerved, for he was now faced with a threat that the bailiffs would seize his valuables to satisfy his many creditors. He was particularly fearful lest the appointment of an unfriendly sheriff would assist in this. To obviate the danger, he arranged for the transfer of many silvers and valuables from Peterwell to London, and requested the assistance of Edward Lovedon in this operation. 'I should be glad to remove the plate from the house and deposit them with your bankers in London', he entreated, 'lest an adverse sheriff might remove them'.[8] The records show that 'tankards, silvers, castors, candlesticks, mugs, coffee pots, salt cellars, punch ladles, spoons' were transported to London for safe keeping.

It was the beginning of the end. Peterwell, bereft of its gleaming silver and handsome accoutrements, and deprived of the means to ensure its upkeep, soon took on the seedy appearance of an impoverished household. Its fate was becoming apparent to onlookers, and at least one visitor to Peterwell was taken aback by the shabby condition of its interior. When in October 1780, John Lewes called at the mansion 'to present bills and accounts' to Adams, he was shocked into remarking: 'I fear poverty is getting the inside of that house very fast from the manner of living I saw there'.[9] Evidently, the inside of the 'great fabric' had now been reduced to a mere shadow of its former magnificence. Added to this, Edward Lovedon, possibly put off by its jaded state, now decided that he no longer wished to purchase the mansion after all and withdrew from all negotiations concerning Peterwell. Nevertheless, John Adams still owed money to Lovedon, for he was forced to submit the corporation books and papers of Lampeter as a 'pledge or collateral security for the payment of six hundred and seventy pounds due by bond and judgement . . . to Edward Lovedon'.

No man had lived more on credit than Sir Herbert Lloyd, and his nephew John Adams had followed the same improvident path. His fall could have been predicted, and it finally came in September 1781 when the entire estate was put up for auction. Every object from the remaining silvers right down to the lowly wooden pails in the dairy was itemised and carefully catalogued, ready to go under the hammer of William Cow the auctioneer. John Lewes took charge of the arrangements and two hundred leaflets announcing the sale were printed by John Ross of Carmarthen.

It was an event which had long been anticipated by gentry and peasantry alike. For years, many had looked towards the great mansion, noting its sliding fortunes and taking satisfaction from the dilapidated appearance of the building and the unkempt state of the luxurious gardens. On the day of the sale, crowds from all over the county and beyond flocked to Peterwell to witness the final humiliating act in the story of the mansion. Detailed inventories of the sale survive, meticulously recording each object, its sale price and its buyer: these provide us with a last glimpse of the life style of the squires of Peterwell before the final dismemberment. We learn that the mansion had a 'middle parlour, and inner parlour, drawing room, study, library, green room, a blue and white room, a red and white room, an unfinished room . . .' and, rather poignantly, 'a nursery'. One room was still referred to as 'Sir Herbert's Room', but its remaining contents consisted only of 'one glass drawer, one mahogany drawer, a tea chest, eight chairs, one cabinet, one regulator, one marble slab, one elbow chair, and one tongs and poker'. 'What a falling off had been there'!

The mansion was stripped entirely of its contents, the windows divested of their curtains, the ornamental pieces taken from the fireplaces, lamps, guns, clocks, bellows, fire irons were numbered for auction. From the laundry room came mangles, flat irons, bolsters, counterpanes and blankets piled high. From the kitchen came spits, fleshforks, candlesticks, and a mortar and pestle. From the dairy came cheese presses, churns, tubs and brass pans. The card tables, carrafes, gold edged wine and ale glasses, and tobacco safe were redolent of earlier and more carefree days. The dusty contents of the dank, dark cellar were revealed; one hundred and eleven bottles of wine fetched £9 14s. 3d., and six porter barrels £1 16s. 0d. The plenitude of barrels, wine coops, decanters and glasses suggests that drink had been a source of comfort for the last owners of Peterwell.

A sale is invariably a melancholy occasion: a callous intrusion into the privacy of a family's past. So it was on 24 September 1781 when the objects which reflected one hundred and fifty years of life at Peterwell were carried out into the cold light of day to be dispersed among the curious strangers who had come to buy. At last, the whole of Peterwell had been washed up on the reef of time. The founder, Thomas Evans, must have looked down ruefully upon the wreckage of his creation, its wealth so wantonly squandered by his descendants.

Of the magnificent stables, all that was left to auction were five saddles and one bridle, one girth, a grindstone and £3 10s. 0d. worth of hay. All that remained of the fine horses were one bay mare sold at £2 10s. 0d. and one pony and foal which went for one guinea. For three days the sale continued; the remaining plate fetched £137 17s. 2½ d. but the bidding was low, and John Lewes bought 391 ounces of silver 'to prevent their going under value at 5/6 per ounce'. Many farmers went away with bargains, carrying with them little bits of the history of Peterwell, many of which must still be in the locality if only they could be recognised. Ben Morris, writing in 1907 claimed

The within is Thos. Wms.'s Bill of —
Expences for myself & horse while
there waiting for Mr. Adams's Ansr.
to Mr. Lewes's Letter about paying
Thos. Evans's Wages &c — being there
2 Nights & a Day — — 0 ~ 5 ~ 4

Black Lyon Lampeter
1781

		s	d
19 Augt.	Supr. Breakft. Dr. & Supr. —	1 ~	8
	Ale —	0 ~	10
	Hay 2 Nights —	1 ~	4
	Corn —	1 ~	6
		5 ~	4

Recd. the Contents in full
Thos. Williams

A claim for expenses by Evan Jenkins, Sir Herbert's agent, during the sale of Peterwell in 1781. Costs for the horse were twice those for himself.

that: 'Many of the treasures of Peterwell are to be found in various houses in the locality . . . settles and vessels . . . the Peterwell clock is now in the possession of Mr J. M. Edwards, Dôl Wen, an exceptional and expensive clock . . . made in Holborn. In my libarary are to be found many books that were in the possession of Sir Herbert Lloyd with his rare book plate on them'.

Rare indeed they must have been, for Sir Herbert Lloyd was anything but a bibliophile. The entire contents of the Peterwell library fetched only £69 10s. 3d., and the meagre selection of books reveals that to Sir Herbert in particular, the pleasures of the flesh assumed greater relevance than the cultivation of the mind. They were in the main classical, legal, historical and geographical volumes, and the inventory is notable for the absence of any books in the Welsh language.

As for the mansion itself, this was initially sold to Thomas Johnes the younger of Hafod and Herbert Lloyd the Attorney of Carmar-

Book Plate of Sir Herbert Lloyd

then, the son of Jeremiah Lloyd and Alice, Sir Herbert's sister. An account of the proceeds of the sale was as follows:

Net proceeds of the Peterwell Estate	£25,023	0s. 6d.
Net proceeds of the Millfield Estate	£25,340	14s. 0d.
Net proceeds of the Gwernvilig Estate	£ 1,495	0s. 0d.
Net proceeds of the Llanborth Estate	£ 973	10s. 0d.
Net proceeds of the Crown Leases	£ 1,050	0s. 0d.
	£53,882	4s. 6d.*
Deficiency to pay incumbrances	£ 2,411	10s. 10d.

The purchase of Peterwell by Thomas Johnes of Hafod and Herbert Lloyd of Carmarthen was never completed; had it been finalised it would have maintained a family connection and possibly changed the destiny of the place. Perhaps Thomas Johnes would have responded to the challenge and channelled his great drive and energy into renovating and improving Peterwell instead of transforming Hafod, thereby changing the course of Cardiganshire history. As it was 'the great fabric' was shuffled from one absentee landlord to another, each one indifferent to its fate, leaving it a victim to time and decay.

In 1781, when Thomas Johnes withdrew from the sale, Peterwell passed into the possession of Albany Wallis, Sir Herbert's London lawyer, who held the principal mortgage on the estate. Wallis was never really interested in Peterwell and its receding fortunes; he was a successful city lawyer with a lucrative practice in Norfolk Street, off the Strand. In any case he was already in the sixty eighth year of his life, far too aged to face that never ending, jolting journey to visit a ramshackle mansion in deepest Cardiganshire. It had only fallen to him because of the profligacy of Sir Herbert in years gone by.

Wallis, unconcerned about Peterwell, lived on to the ripe old age of eighty seven. At his death on 3 September 1800, his fortune, including the abandoned mansion was bequeathed to Lady Bailey of Pall Mall for her life; and after her death it was to pass to her son Colonel Bailey. Lady Bailey wanted no truck with Peterwell; consequently, Colonel Bailey who subsequently added Wallis to his surname, became the next uncaring owner. He took no more interest in the place than

*These figures have been copied as they appear in the Gogerddan Mss.

Albany Wallis, and in 1812 the mansion passed into the ownership of Mr Hart Davis of Bristol, M.P. for Colchester.

The sad fate of Peterwell reinforced the long held belief of the local people that the curse of Vicar Prichard continued to bedevil the place; they saw in the tangled gardens, the untrodden drive and the disintegrating structure the inexorable fulfilment of the Vicar's verse. Their fear of the place was never to be allayed. The mansion fared no better under Mr Hart Davis who sold it to the Harford family of Blaise Castle in Gloucestershire. Under this family, the town of Lampeter was to undergo transformation, but not Peterwell. The Harfords, for some reason, chose not to renovate it, or even to build within its precincts; rather, they erected a totally new residence at Falcondale, one mile away. So Peterwell was left to its memories and ghosts.

Yet, however much the people of Lampeter dreaded the place, cupidity evidently got the better of their fear, for men began to take the stone of the forsaken mansion to build and repair houses in the town. The Lampeter Parish Vestry Book contains the following minute: '28 May 1798, consented to pay £1 10s. 0d. for the carriage of stones from Peterwell to-wards the rebuilding of John Jones, Saddler's House'. We have no means of ascertaining which was John Jones Saddler's House to see if it still stands! But we do know that this was a charity cottage used to house the destitute. How the mighty had fallen, that their great residence of such noble proportions was now being used to shore up the dwelling of one of the town's poorest inhabitants.

By 1802, just twenty one years after the sale, time and men had so pillaged its fabric that Peterwell was described by Sir Robert Colt Hoare journeying through Lampeter as 'an old mansion . . . now dilapidated'. Even while it crumbled into ruin and decay it was still sufficiently impressive to attract comment from travellers and writers. Thomas Evans in his *Cambrian Itinerary* (1801) noted that Lampeter contained 'nothing particularly worthy of observation except the large old seat of Sir Herbert Lloyd, which . . . exhibits a very striking appearance with its four great towers crowned with domes; but it appears to have been long neglected and seldom inhabited'.

At the turn of the twentieth century, Ben Morris, a local historian, recollected nostalgically that in his youth he had spoken to 'very old men living on the edge of the town . . . who well remembered the mansion before its fall, and the most significant feature of attraction in

Falcondale, the new mansion built in 1859 by the Harford family, owners of Peterwell

£ s. d
consented to pay 1.10.0 for the
Carriage of Stones from Peterwell, towards
rebuilding John James, the Sadler's House.
Mr. H. Lloyd is to discharge all other expences.

Removal of stones from Peterwell

their youth was the extraordinary flower garden and fruit trees which grew on its roof'. No doubt, this garden growing wild and unkempt hastened its collapse, for by the beginning of the twentieth century the whole roof had caved in leaving only the outside walls standing like fretwork against the open sky. The years never slackened their hold on its stones, and time mocked Sir Herbert Lloyd's vanity. The poet Dafydd Dafis, Castell Hywel, who had seen it in its heyday, also foresaw its ultimate fate, and his lines convey much of the atmosphere of the place to-day:[10]

I'r llwch aeth pan daeth ei dydd,—a darfu
Ei dirfawr lawenydd;
Y dylluan fudan fydd
Yn gori'n ei magwyrydd.

Troir ei chain lydain aelwydau,—'n erddi
A gwyrddion weirgloddiau;
A mynych yr ych o'r iau
Bawr lawr ei gwych barlyrau.*

*To the dust it went when its time came,
And its great merriment ended.
The silent owl breeds in its walls.
Its beautiful wide hearths
Will become gardens and green hedgerows.
And often the ox from its yoke
Will graze the floor of its magnificent parlours.

Peterwell ruins

After all the grand designs, the lust for power and the pursuit of prestige, this is all that remains of the age of Sir Herbert Lloyd and the House of Peterwell.

NOTES

[1] Gog.Mss.Pet.Bundle.
[2] Spurrell, p. 102.
[3] D.C.Mss., T.J. to J.J., 11 Jan. 1774.
[4] P.R.O.Prob. 11/1047.
[5] Gog.Mss.Pet.Bundle.
[6] Gog.Mss., Adams to J. Lewes, 15 Nov. 1779.
[7] Gog.Mss., Adams to Ed. Lovedon, 6 Dec. 1779.
[8] Gog.Mss., Adams to Ed. Lovedon, 13 Dec. 1779.
[9] Gog.Mss., J. Lewes to Lovedon, 20 Oct. 1780.
[10] Thomas Parry, ed., *Oxford Book of Welsh Verse,* p. 324.

APPENDIX A

MISCELLANEOUS ACCOUNTS RELATING TO SIR HERBERT LLOYD

The Maespwll Story

Ever eager to extend the Peterwell estate, in 1766, Sir Herbert Lloyd attempted to acquire land belonging to Maespwll, a farm adjoining the mansion. After his success in procuring Sion Philip's field, he sought to repeat the same ruse, only this time a valuable piece of Peterwell tapestry was used. The tapestry had adorned the mansion hall and was a treasured possession of the Lloyd family.

According to tradition, Sir Herbert Lloyd sent two of his servants under cover of darkness to lower the tapestry down the chimney of Maespwll. This time, however, the scheme failed because the whole incident was witnessed by a wandering harpist who happened to be sleeping in the loft of an outbuilding. He quickly alerted the occupants who set fire to the tapestry. When Sir Herbert Lloyd and his accolytes arrived, instead of the incriminating tapestry they found only a heap of grey ash. Thus, on this occasion the Baronet was thwarted in his effort to appropriate another man's land.

This story is alluded to by both William Edmunds and George Eyre Evans. According to Evans:

> The story as told here was heard as far back as 1825, only fifty nine years after the event was said to have taken place, by my father, to whom it was told in his boyhood by an intelligent man, who was a servant at Peterwell in the employ of Sir Herbert Lloyd.

The Story of Vaughan Dolgwm

Dolgwm was the residence of Sir Gwynne Vaughan who was High Sheriff for Carmarthenshire in 1773, and whose estates in Carmarthenshire and Pembrokeshire were left to Sir James Cockburn, Bart., the father of Lady Hamilton. Dolgwm is situated in the parish of Pencarreg on the Carmarthenshire side of the Teifi, a few miles from Peterwell. The story was set out in a letter to George Eyre Evans from John Davies, Cefncoed, Blaencwrt in 1900:

> Dyma stori a glywais i fy nhad yn ei hadrodd ganodd o weithie am Syr Herbert Lloyd a Vôn Dolgwmisa. Roedd Syr Herbert Lloyd wedi ffansio rhyw ffarm fach obeiti Felinsych Pencarreg, a fe ddywedodd wrth y ffarmwr bach y myne fe hi oddiarno neu fe gai ei grogi, a fe benderfynnodd ei chymryd hi drwy drais. Fe aeth y ffarmwr bach i ddweyd ei gwyn wrth Mr Vôn Dolgwmisa, yr hwn oedd yn ŵr ac awdurdod mawr ganddo yn yr ardal y pryd hwnw. 'Ho'n wir,' medde Mr Vôn, 'mi af draw i sharad ag e'. Wel fe aeth Mr Vôn drosodd i weld Syr Herbert yn y Palas, a chyda eu bod nhw i mewn, dyma Mr Vôn yn cloi y drws ac ar unwaith yn gofyn i Syr Herbert beth odd e'n feddwl wrth ddwyn y ffarm fach? A chyda hynny dyma fe yn dal revolver go dderbyn a thalcen Syr Herbert ac yn ei orfodi i roi y ffarm nol yn union i'w pherchenog, neu fe gai ei saethu yn gorpws marw yn y man. Ni fu sôn i Syr Herbert gyflawni yr un weithred ysgeler wedi hyn.

Translated:

This is a story which I heard my father tell many hundreds of times concerning Sir Herbert Lloyd and Mr Vaughan Dolgwm. Sir Herbert had fancied a small farm at Felinsych Pencarreg, and he told the farmer that unless he was granted possession of the farm, he would be hanged. He was determined to get it by force. The farmer went to Mr Vaughan, who was a man of great authority in the locality at that time. 'Indeed', said Mr Vaughan, 'I'll go across to have a word with him.' Well, Mr Vaughan went over to the mansion to see Sir Herbert, and as soon as they were inside he shut the door and asked Sir Herbert what he thought he was doing by stealing the small farm. With that, he held a revolver to the forehead of Sir Herbert and forced him to return the farm immediately to its owner or he would shoot him stone dead on the spot. Never again was there any account of Sir Herbert committing a deceitful act.

(N.L.W. 13548 c. John Davies to G. E. Evans, 21 Aug., 1900).

The Story of Siôn Britsh Coch

Of all the tales told, this is the only story in which Sir Herbert emerges in a favourable light. George Eyre Evans was given this story by his father. Siôn Britsh Coch was a notorious character who lived in a cabin by the roadside outside Lampeter. Although extremely ugly, he was highly regarded in the locality for his many acts of charity and his knowledge of country matters. Farmers consulted him about the weather, and he was a welcome guest at harvest suppers, 'where he sang to the tones of an ancient harp, which his fingers lovingly stringed'.

One day late in Autumn, an aged woman by the name of Gwen John came tottering into his cabin. She had no corn to take with her to Lampeter mill for grinding and appealed to Siôn for help. He had no corn himself but he told her to return the following day by which time he would procure some. Knowing that the barns of Llanfechan on the Peterwell estate were full, Siôn, staff in hand, set off thither to beg a sheaf of corn for the old woman. On arrival, the steward of the farm told Siôn that they had nothing in the barn. Not to be outwitted, Siôn Britsh Coch returned to the farm later and helped himself to some corn which he duly gave to the thankful Gwen John.

But Siôn's theft of the corn had been witnessed by the steward who had so rudely repulsed him earlier. The result was that Siôn was committed to appear at the next assize at Cardigan. The evidence to be offered by the steward was deemed by all to be conclusive, and no-one thought that Siôn had any chance of acquittal; but the old man had kept his defence to himself. At the trial he pleaded not guilty, his defence being that since the steward had told him there was no corn in Llanfechan, he could not possibly have stolen what was never there. To the surprise of all Sir Herbert Lloyd, who owned Llanfechan, came forward in the Court to testify that he had overheard the steward make this statement to Siôn Britsh Coch. Therefore, on the evidence of the Baronet, Siôn was aquitted.

This act appears out of keeping with Sir Herbert's character, but in this instance he may have had some sympathy with a fellow rascal. Whatever the reason, G. Eyre Evans maintained that Sir Herbert's image in Lampeter improved as a result of this incident 'so that his tenants would line the streets touching their forelocks when he went by'.

(G. E. Evans, *Lampeter,* pp. 214-217).

The Hanging of Shâms Pant yr Ynn

This is a traditional story told in the New Quay area and it links Sir Herbert Lloyd with the activities of the smugglers who infested the Cardiganshire coastline during this period. Shâms was a local rascal, grossly immoral, who had fathered so many bastards that he was a liability to the area and a burden on the parish. He was also Sir Herbert Lloyd's contact with the smugglers; but Sir Herbert had long been dissatisfied with him on account of his boastful nature and his many indiscretions, which were dangerous traits in an accomplice. One evening, Sir Herbert rode down to Cwmtydu and caught Shâms in the act of selling his wife* to the smugglers. The Baronet saw his opportunity of ridding himself of Shâms. He ordered a make shift gallows to be erected on the beach, and had him hanged there and then as an example to others.

(As related by Mr D. G. Williams, M.A., Llannon.)

Sir Herbert and Siôn Cwilt

According to tradition Peterwell mansion was well supplied with many luxuries such as casks of brandy, French wines, tea, tobacco, sugar, silks and many other fineries supplied by the smugglers. One of the most notable of the Cardiganshire smugglers was Siôn Cwilt, whose name is still associated with the tract of moorland between New Quay and Llandysul. He built himself a *Tŷ Unos* inland from Cwmtydu, living the life of a recluse. At first he dressed as a gentleman, but in time his clothes became worn and patched until his cloak resembled a quilt. Hence the name Siôn Cwilt. People came to fear him and believed him to have associations with the devil.

Among the few visitors who came at dead of night to his cabin, was the infamous Sir Herbert Lloyd of Peterwell. It was also noticed that servants from Peterwell would visit Siôn and return to Lampeter with a waggon fully laden with sacks, bottles and casks. Sir Herbert was not the only member of the gentry to approach the cabin, for it was the centre of a brisk smuggling trade, enabling the finest brandies and wines to appear on the tables of the Cardiganshire squires.

(As related by Mr W. J. Lewis, M.A., Aberystwyth.)

The Donkey

One old character from Llanddewi Brefi told the following anecdote which was recorded in 1868. A man named Thomas William Jerry, a mason, once killed a favourite donkey of Sir Herbert's in error. Whilst out hunting, a fellow workman told him that there was a hare in some furze close by. Jerry fired into the furze, but on approaching he was horrified to find that he had killed the donkey. Because of this incident he was obliged to flee the country and he dared not return for many years.

(John Rowlands, *Historical Notes,* Cardiff, 1866, p. 177.)

*This is an interesting reference to wife selling in Cardiganshire; many examples of this practice existed in England during the eighteenth and nineteenth centuries. Wife sale was regarded by many labouring people as a legitimate and lawful form of marriage. See R. W. Malcomson, *Life and Labour in England 1700-1780,* pp. 103-04; William Marshall, *Customs in Common* (Lond. 1982); Sarah Farley, *Bristol Journal,* 11 Sept. 1784, 6 March 1790.

See Thomas Hardy, *The Mayor of Casterbridge,* cf. Michael Henchard who sold his wife.

The Tyrant

Sir Herbert Lloyd of Peterwell was one of the greatest tyrants of his age. He used to rule the County of Cardigan with a rod of iron. The judges, and bishops were entirely under his control. He was accompanied by his tenants to all fairs. They were always armed with stout staves and woe to anyone who offended their master. He used to attend Cardigan Assizes with a bodyguard of Lampeter men carrying so many large staves that the Shire Hall of Cardigan appeared like a grove of trees.

(*Pembrokeshire Antiquities,* 14 Jan., 1888.)

Free Wine

There is an amusing account of two men who were bold enough to play a trick on Sir Herbert. On one occasion, during the Baronet's absence from the town, two of his servants dressed up in his clothes and went to the Star Inn at Lampeter where they consumed a large quantity of wine on Sir Herbert Lloyd's account. The owner of the Star believed the men to be friends of Sir Herbert and willingly served the drinks. The mistake was only discovered when an irate Sir Herbert Lloyd returned from London.

(John Rowlands, *Historical Notes,* 1888.)

To Gaol of His Own Volition

Alice M. Harfod, the wife of the owner of Falcondale wrote a letter to George Eyre Evans in 1904 describing the fear generated by Sir Herbert Lloyd among the people of Cardiganshire. She states that she well remembered the old houses of Llanfechan and Foelallt and she had heard men say that Sir Herbert Lloyd was held in such awe, that if he sent any poacher or other law breaker to gaol, they willingly walked the thirty miles alone to deliver themselves up.

(N.L.W. 13485C., Alice Harford to G. E. Evans, 17 July, 1904.)

Kicking the Church Door

Ben Morris, a local historian recorded the following story by a very old man, Thomas Evans of Caeronnen in his cottage on the evening of Thursday, 6 July, 1905.

Thomas Evans stated that his father was once in a church service in Cwmann where Sir Lucius Lloyd was one of the congregation. When the cleric was beginning his sermon, Sir Herbert Lloyd happened to pass the building. He stopped, got down from his carriage and began to kick the church door and create a disturbance. Sir Lucius walked slowly out and caught Sir Herbert by the collar, demanding what he meant by behaving so atrociously and preventing worship? He then ordered: 'Go home you immoral devil for fear God will knock you down insensible here'. Sir Herbert Lloyd turned and went away without saying another word.

(Notes by Ben Morris, N.L.W. 13486C.)

Falling Mortar

A mason was once employed to carry out repairs on the Peterwell estate. One day he was required to see to the roof of the mansion. While doing so a lot of mortar fell down on Sir Herbert Lloyd, who was strutting below in the courtyard. He was furious and lost his temper with the workman. 'Come down you rascal and go home', he shouted. 'Do you think I pay ten pence a day for you to destroy my suit of clothes worth five pounds?'.

(N.L.W. 13486C.)

The Clock Face from the Coffin Plate

Despite the spectacular funeral, Sir Herbert Lloyd's grave was not left intact. One wintry evening, a man from the neighbourhood broke into the Peterwell vault and removed the brass name plates from Sir Herbert's coffin. They were then bought by a watch maker who fashioned them into the brass face of a grandfather clock. This very clock was some years ago in the possession of a blacksmith in Cellan.

(N.L.W. 13486.)

Destroying the Registers

During an outburst of temper Sir Herbert Lloyd is said to have burned the Parish Registers of Cellan . . . 'in order to answer his own purposes the better'.
(The Registers of Cellan are in fact missing.)

(N.L.W. 13486)

Oxen and Horses

Sir Herbert was a man of influence and great authority in his locality and it appears that he was not averse to using it. His word was law and he ruled his subordinates and tenants with a rod of iron. His mode of life at Peterwell was on a scale similar to that of the old barons. When he went back and forth from Lampeter to Llandovery on his way to London, his tenants would accompany him all the way as an escort to help him along with their horses and oxen.

(G. Jones, *Enwogion Sir Aberteifi,* p. 109.)

The Peterwell Chest

Recently during her quest for information on Sir Herbert Lloyd, the author visited the home of an old Lampeter family who once lived close to the mansion of Peterwell. She was told by the owner that a large black oak chest had been in the possession of the family for many generations, and this was in fact the box which had held the body of Sir Herbert Lloyd on his journey from London. The box had been kept in a barn for many years and used as a store. However, in 1950, the owner decided that the chest was responsible for a run of bad luck because of its unpleasant associations. She accordingly had it cut up and burnt.

Destruction of the Lampeter Charter

One story relates that Sir Herbert Lloyd discarded his mistress for the favours of another. In order to avenge herself, she then destroyed the 'Lampeter Town Charter'.

(N.L.W. 13486.)

His Body Labelled 'Valuable Furniture'

There are dramatic accounts of the journey of Sir Herbert's body from London to Peterwell in August 1769. Mr Howell Evans, the Chief Constable for Cardiganshire described the event in a letter to George Eyre Evans in 1900.

'Sir Herbert Lloyd was surrounded with debt both in London and at home. His coffin containing his body was packed up in rugs and quietly smuggled away, and on the way people believed it to have been a valuable piece of furniture carefully packed and taken home from London. One of his servants had been dispatched home to announce the day his body would come. You will remember that he had parted with his wife at this time, but he had a lady friend in London who generously supplied him with the necessaries of life'.

(N.L.W. 13548.)

An accursed stone?

An interesting sequel to the story of the Curse of Maesyfelin was related to the author by Major Herbert Lloyd Johnes, formerly of Dolaucothi and a direct descendant of the Peterwell family. Apparently a carved stone from the Maesyfelin mansion was unearthed and taken to Dolaucothi. This stone lay for many years in the grounds of the mansion, but when a new library wing was built in 1928 the stone was placed in the wall of the building. It is ironic that by to-day hardly a trace remains of Dolaucothi.

APPENDIX B

MEDICAL RECORDS OF JOHN LLOYD OF PETERWELL

(Original spelling retained)

		£	s.	d.
1754	Dr Wm. Price			
Oct. 16	Lavender Drops			6
Nov. 3	A Bottle of Hartshorn Drops			6
Feb. 7	A Bottle of Diacodium		1	0
	Sugar Candy			8
9	Sperma Cety 1 oz.			4½
	A Bottle of Cinamon Water		1	3
	Linseed			2
	Oil of Sweet Almonds			9
	Pectoral Syrup			6
	Chymical Oil of Sulphur		1	0
	Hartshorn Drops			6
	Gum Dragon			4
	Saffron		1	0
20	Tincture of Rhubarb Madm. Lett.		1	3
28	A Bottle of Stomachick Drops Do.		1	0
April 9	The Rhubarb Repeated Madm. Lett.		1	3
26	A Bottle of Hartshorn Drops Mr. Lloyd		1	0
	A Large Blister for the Back		1	6
27	2 Cephalick Plaisters for the feet		2	0
	Healing Plaister for the Blister Spread		1	6
	A Purging Potion		1	6
	A Paper of Purging Powder		1	0
28	A Large Pot of Digestion Balsam		2	0
	A Large Pot of Blistering Ointment		2	6
	2 Blisters for the Legs		2	0
	A Pint Bottle of Mint Water		1	0
	Alealine Salts		1	0
29	Grains per Mr. Peat			4
30	The Purging Potion Repeated		1	6
	4 Saline Nervous Draughts		4	0
	Double the quantity of Digestive Balsam		4	0
	The Purging Powder Repeated Two Papers		2	0
	½ oz. Camphire Madm. Lett.		2	0
May 1	An Emolient Clyster		2	6
	A Pipe & Blader fixt.			6
	4 Saline Nervous Draughts Repeated		4	0
	The Healing Plaister for the Back Repeated		1	6
	Healing Plaister for the Leggs Spread		1	0
2	Drawing Plaister for the Back Spread		1	6

		£	s.	d.
	Drawing Plaister for the Legs Spread		1	0
	A Pint Bottle of Camphorated Julap		3	6
3	4 oz. Lavender Water		2	0
	A Bottle of Smelling Salts			8
	Drawing Plaisters Spread for the Arms		1	0
4	Drawing Plaisters Spread for the Arms and Legs		2	0
	A Large Blister for the Back		1	6
5	Drawing Plaisters Spread for the Arms and Legs		2	0
	One Wide Mouth Bottle			6
	Drawing Plaister Spread for the Back		1	6
6	2 Large Blisters for the Wrists		2	6
	A Pot of Balsamick Linctus		1	0
7	A pound of Sweet Almonds		2	0
	Drawing Plaister for the Back		1	6
	A pint bottle of Balsamick Julap		3	0
8	6 Saline Nervous Draughts		6	0
9	The Balsamick Julap Repeated		3	0
	A Large Pot of Yellow Balsam		2	6
10	The Yellow Balsam Repeated		2	6
	4 oz. Sweet Almonds			6
	1 oz. Sperma Cety			4
11	The Balsamick Julap Repeated		3	0
	Syrup of Balsam		1	0
	Pectoral Syrup			8
	Caraway & Aniseed Each 1 oz. per Mr. Peat			4
	le Campane Brimston Each 2 oz. per Do.			10
	Turmerick Liquorish Powder 2 oz. per Do.		1	1
	The Yellow Balsam Repeated		2	6
	An Anodyne Stomachick Draught Mrs. Lloyd		1	6
	A Saline Stomachick Draught Mrs. Lloyd		1	0
13	A quart Bottle of Pectoral Apozem		2	6
	A Large Bottle of Balsamick Mucilage		2	0
14	An Astringent Draught		1	0
	The Mucilage Repeated		2	0
	2 oz. of Manna Mrs. Lloyd		1	4
	A Paper of Pectoral Powder			6
	Linseed			2
	Burnt Hartshorn			8
15	Hartshorn Drops		1	0
	A Paper of Astringent Ingredients		1	6
	2 Astringent Clysters		5	0
16	2 Papers of Astringent Ingredients		3	0
	2 Astringent Clysters Repeated		5	0
	2 Cordial Draughts		2	0
17	A Bottle of Lavender Drops		1	0
18	A Box of Cordial Electary		1	0

		£	s.	d.
	2 Cordial Boluses		2	0
	The Cordial Electary Repeated		1	0
	Cordial Boluses Repeated		2	0
	1 oz. Candied Ginger			4
19	6 Cordial Boluses Repeated		6	0
	Paper of the Astringent Ingredts, Repeated		1	6
20	A Bottle of Tincture of Bark		1	6
	1 Paper of the Astringent Ingredts. Repeated		1	6
23	2 Large Pieces of White Leather		-	-
24	An Anodyne Clyster		2	6
	A Pipe & Blader fixt.			6
26	6 Papers of Cordial Testaceous Powders		2	0
	A Box of Purging Pills		1	6
	Tincture of Assafoetida		1	6
	Lavender Drops Repeated		1	0
	2 Large Cephalick Plaister for the feet with Gall		4	0
	A Cordial Nervous Draught with Mask		2	6
29	The Plaisters for the feet Repeated		4	0
30	The Clyster Repeated		2	6
	A Plaister Spread for the Back		-	-
June 1	A Nervous Powder for three Doses		1	6
	A Box of Cordial Confection		2	6
	The Clyster Repeated		2	6
	A Pipe & Blader fixt.			6
	The Cordial Testaceous Powders Repeated		2	0
2	The Clyster Repeated		2	6
	The Plaisters Repeated for the feet		4	0
3	A Quart Bottle of Pectoral Apozem		2	6
	12 Papers of Cooling Powders		2	0
	1 Pound of the Best Hartshorn Shavings		2	0
4	The Pectoral Apozem Repeated		2	6
5	An Emolient Anodyne Clyster as per Dr. Jenning		2	6
	A Solutive Mixture with Manna for Many Doses		2	4
	10 Specifick Boluses		7	6
	4 Papers of Antihectick Powders		2	0
	Hallys Powder: fresh 2 oz.		3	0
	Powder of Bark			6
	12 Papers of Cooling Powders Repeated		2	0
6	¼ oz. Camphire		1	0
	Tincture of Bark Repeated		1	6
7	A Bottle of Anodyne Drops		1	0
	Hartshorn Drops Repeated		1	0
	Extract of Bark		1	0
8	The Clyster Repeated		2	6

		£ s. d.
	The Pectoral Apozem Repeated	2 6
10	The Clyster Repeated	2 6
	The Pectoral Apozem Repeated	2 6
	3 Specifick Draughts	3 0
11	4 Specifick Draughts Repeated	4 0
	½ a pound of Diachylon Plaister	1 0
12	The Clyster Repeated	2 6
	6 Papers of Cooling Powders Repeated	1 0
	Lavender Drops Repeated	1 0
13	Yellow Balsam a Boxfull	2
	A Pot of White Cerat	1 3
	6 Papers of Cooling Powders Repeated	1 0
14	4 Specifick Draughts Repeated	4 0
	6 Papers of Cooling Powders Repeated	1 0
15	The Emolient Clyster Repeated	2 6
	The Pectoral Apozem Repeated	2 6
	6 Papers of Cooling Powders Repeated	1 0
16	The White Cerat Repeated	1 3
18	The Emolient Clyster Repeated	2 6
	6 Papers of Cooling Powders Repeated	1 0
21	The Emolient Clyster Repeated	2 6
	The White Cerat Repeated	1 3
	The Emolient Clyster Repeated	2 6
	The Pectoral Apozem Repeated	2 6
23	The Emolient Clyster Repeated	2 6
24	The Pectoral Apozem Repeated	2 6
	3 Cordial Diuretick Draughts per Madm.	3 0
	Diuretick Drops	4
		£14 0 10

Attendance &c. what you please.

July 2nd. 1755 Recd. of Herbert Lloyd Esqr. the Sum of Nineteen Pounds five Shillings in full of this Bill and all Demands . . . per me Wm. Price.

APPENDIX C

A RENTAL OF THE PETERWELL ESTATE
(Original spelling retained)

	Acres (*NM = Not Measured*)	*Rent 1767*			*Rent 1777*			*Rent 1779*		
Undergrove	122	24	0	0	24	0	0	24	0	0
Pant y Kirill	NM	8	0	0	8	0	0	8	0	0
Glancroyddin	NM	14	0	0	14	0	0	14	0	0
Letty Twppa isa	53.1	8	0	0	8	0	0	14	0	0
Tŷ Poeth	72.2	2	10	0	2	10	0	7	10	0
Castell Buged	NM	20	0	0	20	0	0	21	0	0
Llanfair Parish										
Penysarn	NM	8	0	0	11	0	0	11	0	0
Llwyn	NM	11	0	0	25	0	0	25	0	0
Cellan Parish										
Penysingrig	NM	3	10	0	3	10	0	3	10	0
Penygraig	NM	10	10	0	10	10	0	13	10	0
Glanyffrwd	NM	10	10	0	10	10	0	11	10	0
Gilvin	NM	2	2	0	2	2	0	2	2	0
Cwmcoy	NM	5	5	0	5	5	0	5	5	0
Llanwnen Parish										
Blaenywain Ycha	NM	18	0	0	18	0	0	36	0	0
Blaenywainganol	NM	21	0	0	21	0	0	21	0	0
Cartybrodir	NM	3	15	0	3	15	0	4	10	0
Llanwenog										
Abernant y Llan	NM	2	10	0	3	3	0	3	15	0
Tanygraig	NM	4	4	0	6	0	0	8	0	0
Llwyn Killin Bach	NM	15	0	0	15	0	0	21	0	0
Pwll y Quarry	NM	6	6	0	6	6	0	8	10	0
Tynyporth	NM	3	0	0	3	0	0	3	0	0
Tŷ Cam	NM	10	0	0	10	0	0	19	10	0
Gwar prys cynwidd	NM	10	10	0	10	10	0	10	10	0
Keven Rhyddlan Ycha	NM	12	15	0	12	15	0	25	0	0
Keven Rhyddlan Ganol	NM	12	15	0	12	15	0	25	15	0
Llechwedd y Cwn	NM	26	0	0	26	0	0	210	0	0
Lampeter Town										
Black Lyon		20	0	0	20	0	0	20	0	0
House & Garden		2	2	0	2	2	0	2	2	0
House & fields do. Chas. Edmunds		8	0	8	8	0	8	11	0	0
House 8 field do. Evan ab David		8	0	0	8	0	0	11	10	0
House		1	10	0	1	10	0	1	10	0
House		3	0	0	3	3	0	3	3	0
9 houses in all										
2 shops at Lampeter		5	15	6	5	15	6	5	15	6
2 shops again										

	Acres	Rent 1767	Rent 1777	Rent 1779
Lampeter Tolls of Fairs	15 15 0	15 15 0	15 15 0	
Sgubor Lane		12 0 0	12 0 0	12 0 0
House & fields				
Sheldon Leigh	15 15 0	15 15 0	15 15 0	
House & fields				
Thos. Edwards		5 5 0	5 5 0	6 7 6
Lower Stock asses 8 colts		6 0 0	6 0 0	12 0 0
Field by Lampeter Bridge	NM	1 10 0	1 10 0	2 0 0
House & fields				
Mr. Thos. Jones		12 0 0	12 0 0	12 0 0
House		1 10 0	1 10 0	1 10 0
Doley Bont	NM	3 0 0	3 0 0	4 0 0
House, Josey Jenk.		0 15 0	0 15 0	0 15 0
7 Houses etc. Ja. Ja. Sadler				
House 8 field		0 11 0	0 11 0	0 11 0
Tucking Mill Field	NM	3 10 0	3 10 0	3 10 0
Glynhŷr	NM	10 10 0	10 10 0	11 0 0
Drefach	NM	8 8 0	9 0 0	14 0 0
Aberkerdinen	NM	5 5 0	5 5 0	6 6 0
Velyn Vawr	NM	8 0 0	10 0 0	15 0 0
Gwain Ammy	NM	12 12 0	12 12 0	12 12 0
Moelfre	NM	12 12 0	12 12 0	12 12 0
Cappely	NM	14 0 0	17 0 0	23 0 0
Maesdir	NM	30 0 0	33 0 0	33 0 0
Henfedde	NM	25 0 0	25 0 0	40 0 0
Llwyn Llwyd	NM	10 0 0	10 0 0	17 0 0
Danrallt goch	NM	12 0 0	12 0 0	12 0 0
Olwen	NM	20 0 0	22 1 0	22 1 0
Blaen Cwm Rees	NM	4 0 0	4 0 0	5 10 0
Cors y Vrane	NM	10 0 0	10 0 0	10 0 0
Funon da Vras	NM	5 5 0	5 5 0	7 7 0
Cae da Bowen	NM	10 0 0	10 0 0	13 10 0
Pencarreg Parish				
Velyn Vach	NM	20 0 0	20 0 0	32 0 0
Blaen y Cwm	NM	7 7 0	7 7 0	7 10 0
Cwrt y graig	NM	4 0 0	4 0 0	4 4 0
Dangoedythig	NM	15 0 0	20 0 0	20 0 0
Faly vole	NM	8 0 0	8 0 0	15 0 0
Gallysherdrem ycha & Ysa	NM	7 0 0	7 0 0	11 0 0
Glyn Ddu	NM	0 10 0	0 10 0	0 10 0
Coedythig	NM	23 0 0	23 0 0	34 0 0
Killygell Ycha	NM	16 16 0	16 16 0	25 0 0
Killygell isaf	NM	17 17 0	17 17 0	30 0 0
Park y Rhose Glanthig	NM	3 10 0	3 10 0	3 15 0
Llanybyther Parish				
Gwarygraig & Bwlchgwynt	NM	20 15 0	22 10 0	22 10 0
Eskyrliving	NM	4 8 0	4 8 0	7 7 0
Llanybyther mill		10 0 0	10 10 0	12 0 0
Noyadd	NM	15 0 0	20 0 0	20 0 0
Penybont & Cotts	NM	15 0 0	17 0 0	20 0 0
Hendre Eynon	NM	4 4 0	4 4 0	10 0 0

	Acres	Rent 1767			Rent 1777			Rent 1779		
Blaen Gwain Henfod	NM	6	6	0	6	6	0	10	10	0
Glangofariog	NM	10	10	0	10	10	0	24	0	0
Pitchings of 14 fairs		14	0	0	14	0	0	14	0	0
Tolls of 14 fairs		24	0	0	24	0	0	24	0	0
Llanvihangel ar arth Parish										
Rhiw livid	NM	12	0	0	12	0	0	20	0	0
Ochor y Rhose Goch	NM	4	10	0	4	10	0	6	10	0
Gwar & Allt	NM	5	5	0	5	5	0	8	8	0
Rhydylan	NM	15	0	0	16	0	0	20	0	0
Pilbach	NM	1	5	0	1	5	0	1	7	0
Rhos Goch	NM	11	0	0	11	0	0	14	10	0
Bwlch Genersarph	NM	11	11	0	11	11	0	14	0	0
Llansawel Parish										
Penylan	NM	40	0	0	40	0	0	55	0	0
Red Lyon		4	0	0	4	0	0	4	0	0
Rhuglyn	NM	12	0	0	15	0	0	15	0	0
Wayon	NM	8	0	0	10	0	0	10	0	0
Llansawel Mill		9	9	0	9	9	0	10	10	0
Llanycrwys Parish										
Cae Gwyn	NM	10	0	0	12	0	0	14	0	0
Derlwyn & Pant y Squarnog		16	16	0	16	16	0	20	0	0
Penbrin Parish										
Lamborth	NM	17	0	0	17	0	0	30	0	0
Trevor	NM	3	10	0	3	10	0	4	10	0
Pwll y Whywed	NM	3	0	0	3	0	0	6	0	0
Temple Barr	NM	3	0	0	3	0	0	7	0	0
Park y Brag	NM	6	0	0	6	0	0	8	0	0
Lamborth Mill		6	0	0	6	0	0	9	0	0
(Sir Herbert received the estate as an Escheat)										
Ystrad Parish										
Gwern Vylig	NM	50	0	0	50	0	0	50	0	0
Gelly Gwefrwch	NM	15	0	0	15	0	0	15	0	0
Troedyrhiw	NM	2	10	0	2	10	0	3	10	0
Millfeed	NM	20	0	0	20	0	0	20	0	0
Pantsarn Hill	NM	7	0	0	7	0	0	14	0	0
Lletty Twppa Ycha	NM	6	0	0	6	0	0	7	0	0
Llwyn Ieir	NM	8	8	0	8	8	0	10	0	0
Pound	NM	2	2	0	2	2	0	4	4	0
Glandulas	NM	18	0	0	18	0	0	25	0	0
Lampeter Mill		52	0	0	52	0	0	52	10	0
Great Stockers & Island	NM	10	0	0	10	0	0	10	0	0
Maes y Cwdyn	NM	1	10	0	1	10	0	1	15	0
Silian Parish										
Dyffryn	NM	30	0	0	30	0	0	40	0	0
Danyfforest	NM	3	2	6	3	2	6	4	4	0
Bettws Bledrws Parish										
Coedypark	NM	40	0	0	40	0	0	60	0	0
Llanvair vach	NM	26	0	0	26	0	0	26	0	0
Foesydwn	NM	10	0	0	10	0	0	18	0	0
Penygraig & Penybont	NM	10	10	0	10	10	0	21	0	0

	Acres	*Rent 1767*			*Rent 1777*			*Rent 1779*		
Llanerchaeron Parish										
Melyn y Cwm	NM	10	0	0	10	0	0	10	0	0
Castell Kenddu	NM	14	14	0	14	14	0	20	0	0
Park Mawr	NM	5	5	0	5	5	0	6	0	0
Ystrad Parish										
Brongelin	NM	16	0	0	16	0	0	16	0	0
Baily Bach	NM	5	0	0	5	0	0	7	10	0
Castell Drainog	NM	4	0	0	4	0	0	6	6	0
Flaenbant	NM	8	10	0	13	0	0	13	0	0
Llanbadarn Tref Eglwys Parish										
Nantcoy	NM	10	0	0	15	0	0	21	0	0
Baily Coch	NM	15	0	0	15	0	0	20	0	0
King's Park	NM	2	0	0	2	0	0	2	12	6
Penybont	NM	15	0	0	15	0	0	22	0	0
Cayo Parish										
Garthswyd	NM	13	0	0	16	0	0	26	0	0
Druslwyn heligh	NM	6	6	0	6	6	0	9	0	0
Maesdroidin Vach	NM	16	0	0	16	0	0	16	0	0
Glantwrch & Aberbinewid Mill and Sands	NM	30	0	0	30	0	0	60	0	0

APPENDIX D

INVENTORY OF THE EFFECTS AT PETERWELL SALE 1781
(Original spelling retained)

Lots No.		*Prices Fetched* £	s.	d.
1	One Wine Coop	2	2	0
2	9 Elbow Chairs	1	11	6
3	3 Window Curtains	1	7	0
4	1 Square Mahogany Side Table	4	0	0
5	1 Mahogany Knife Case	1	4	0
6	1 Mahogany Dining Table	3	0	0
7	1 Tea Chest	3	5	0

STUDY

		£	s.	d.
1	Fender, Tongs, Poker & Fire Irons	0	5	6
2	5 Mahogany Chairs	1	5	0
3	1 Desk and Bookcase	5	5	0
4	1 Mahogany Writing Table	2	2	0

CLOSET WITHIN STUDY

		£	s.	d.
1	1 Ink Stand &c.	0	5	0
2	1 Marble Book & Instruts	0	2	6

MIDDLE PARLOUR

		£	s.	d.
1	1 Mahogany Side Table	4	0	0
2	1 Wine Coop	1	5	0
3	11 Green Chairs	1	2	0
4	2 Mahogany Tables	3	3	0
5	1 Mahogany Dum Waiter	0	5	0
6	1 Barmr.	0	10	6
7	3 Window Curtains	1	10	0
8	1 Grate	1	1	0
9	1 Tongs and Poker	0	1	6
10	Earthen Ware and Images	0	5	0
11	Fender	0	4	0

INNER PARLOUR

		£	s.	d.
1	2 Small Pembroke Tables	2	2	0
2	1 Mahogany Tea Table	0	18	0
3	8 Mahogany Chairs	3	8	0
4	1 Grate and Fire Irons	1	7	0
5	1 Fender	0	5	0
6	Small Cabinet & Mahogany Pail	1	1	0
7	1 Mahogany Screen	0	7	6
8	3 Window Curtains	1	11	5
9	4 Ornamental Pieces	1	1	0

DRAWING ROOM

		£	s.	d.
1	8 Mahogany Chairs	4	0	0
2	3 Mahogany Tables	2	6	0
3	1 Bellows	0	3	0
4	Grate and Fire Irons	1	11	6
5	1 Brush	0	0	6
6	1 Tea Chest	0	7	6
7	11 Pieces ornament China	0	14	0
8	2 Card Tables	3	3	0

NURSERY

		£	s.	d.
1	1 Bed Stead & Curtains	3	0	0
2	1 Bed 1 Pilow at 9d.			
3	2 Old Blankets Counter Pane	0	4	0
4	1 Deal Table	0	4	0
5	8 Chairs	0	16	0
6	1 Round Table	0	2	6
7	1 Trivet	0	1	0
8	1 Oak Drawer	1	10	0
9	1 Sett Fire Irons & Canister	0	4	6
10	1 Tongs	0	1	6
11	Mahogany Table	0	7	6
12	1 Fender and Bellows	0	3	6

PASSAGE LEADING TO DRAWING ROOM

		£	s.	d.
1	Table 10/6; Glass Lamp 5/-	0	15	6
2	Clock	4	4	0
3	Mahogany Table	0	3	0

GREEN ROOM

		£	s.	d.
1	Damask Bedsted and Curtains	3	3	0
2	1 Mahogany Drawer	0	12	0
3	1 Settee	0	10	6
4	6 Mahogany Chairs	1	10	0
5	1 Table	0	4	0
6	1 Matrass	0	12	0
7	1 Bed Bolster at 11d.			
8	3 Blankets & Counterpane	1	7	0
9	Glass and Painting	2	2	0
10	2 Window Curtains	0	15	0
11	Set Fire Irons and Fender	0	7	0
12	Dressing Box	0	9	0
13	2 Feet Carpets	0	5	0
14	1 Glass and Dressing Table	1	1	0

THOS. DAVIES'S ROOM

		£	s.	d.
1	4 Beds at 6d.			
2	1 Desk Bed	0	10	6
3	Two Bed Steds	1	0	0
4	3 Chairs	0	6	0
5	1 Chest	0	15	0
6	2 Old Blankets and Rug	0	3	0

MR. ADAMS'S ROOM

		£	s.	d.
1	Mahogany Buroe	2	2	0
2	6 Mahogany Chairs	1	10	0
3	1 Walnut Drawer	0	12	0
4	1 Mahogany Table & Glass	1	15	0
5	1 Bedsted and Curtains & Window Do.	5	5	0
6	1 Bed Bolster & Pillows at 1s. p. lb.			
7	1 Matrass	1	0	0
8	3 Blankets	0	10	6
9	1 Counter pane	0	18	0
10	1 Night Stool	0	7	0
11	2 Feet Carpets	0	2	0
12	1 Bed at 6d. p.			
13	1 Swing Glass	0	5	0
14	Set Fire Irons	0	6	0
15	1 Bellows	0	3	0

IN CLOSET

		£	s.	d.
16	1 Chair and two Fenders	0	1	6

ROOM NEXT MR. ADAMS'S

		£	s.	d.
1	Bed Sted & Curtains	2	2	0
2	1 Wash Stand	0	10	6
3	1 Chair	0	1	6
4	1 Bed & Bolster at 9s. p.			
5	1 Counter pane	0	13	0
6	2 Blankets	0	6	0
7	1 Foulding Table	0	7	0

LAUNDRY

		£	s.	d.
1	1 Mangle	0	7	0
2	One Stove	0	15	0
3	6 Flat Irons	0	9	0
4	2 Beds & 2 Bolsters, 3 Pillows at 8s. p.			
5	2 Ironing Tables	0	8	0
6	1 Lady's Saddle	1	0	0
7	2 Old Blankets & Quilt	0	2	6

SIR HERBERT'S ROOM

		£	s.	d.
1	1 Glass Drawer	2	2	0
2	1 Mahogany Drawer	2	2	0
3	1 Tea Table	0	7	0
4	8 Chairs	3	16	0
5	1 Cabinett	2	2	0
6	1 Regulator	3	3	0
7	1 Marble Slab	0	10	6
8	1 Elbow Chair	0	1	6
9	1 Tongs and Poker	0	2	6

CLOSET

		£	s.	d.
1	2 Globes			
2	1 Marble Mortar	0	7	0
3	1 Chair	0	1	0

SERVANTS ROOM

		£	s.	d.
1	3 Bedsted & Curtains	1	10	0
2	3 Beds & 3 Bolsters at 7d.			
3	1 Elbow Chair	0	2	6
4	2 Grates	1	11	6
5	1 Stile			
6	1 Drawer	0	4	0
7	1 Stove	0	5	0
8	Old Boxes & Gun			
9	2 Bottle Stands	0	2	0

BLUE AND WHITE ROOM

		£	s.	d.
1	1 Blue & white Bedsted & Curtains	0	15	0
2	2 Beds & Bolsters at 10d. p.			
3	2 Old Blankets	0	3	0
4	1 Old Chair & piece of a Chest	0	5	0

PASSAGE

		£	s.	d.
1	1 Chest	0	10	0
2	1 Desk Bed	0	10	6

RED AND WHITE CURS. ROOM

		£	s.	d.
1	2 Bedsteds & Curtains	4	10	0
2	2 Beds, 2 Bolsters & 2 Pillows wt. at 11d. p.			
3	1 Old Chair	0	2	0
4	4 Blankets and two Quilts	0	10	0

MR. JENKINS'S ROOM

		£	s.	d.
1	2 Bedsteds, 1 Pair Curtains	2	2	0
2	5 Blankets, 1 Quilt	0	15	0
3	2 Beds, 2 Bolsters & 2 Pillows wt. at 9d. p.			
4	1 Mahogany Chest	0	15	0
5	1 Oak Drawrs	0	5	0
6	1 Commode	2	2	0
7	1 Wash stand 5/-, 3 Chairs 18/-	1	3	0
8	1 Night Chair, Glass and Picture	0	10	0

UNFINISHED ROOM

		£	s.	d.
1	1 Marble Commode	2	2	0
2	2 Old Chairs	0	2	6
3	1 Bedsted	0	7	6
4	4 Saddles	2	0	0

STEWARDS ROOM

		£	s.	d.
1	1 Buroe & Book Case	3	0	0
2	1 Bedsted & Curtains	1	10	0
3	1 Drawrs	0	5	0
4	2 Chairs	0	2	0

SERVANTS HALL

		£	s.	d.
1	1 Deal Table and Settle	0	10	0
2	1 Bench & Chair	0	2	6
3	1 Old Drawrs and Grate	0	7	6
4	2 Potts	0	8	0
5	Pott Hooks	0	1	0

KITCHEN

		£	s.	d.
1	Shelf Dresser & Drawrs			
2	One Deal Table	0	5	0
3	Two Trays	0	10	0
4	One Teaboard	0	5	0
5	2 Chairs	0	6	0
6	1 Leaden Tray			
7	1 Sett Brig Irons	0	10	0
8	1 Chane 10/6, 2 Trivetts 5/-	0	15	6
9	2 Flesh Forks 1/-, Gun £1.1s.	1	2	0
10	1 Spitt & 5 Candlesticks	0	4	0
11	1 Regulator	1	10	0
12	1 Bellows & Fire Screen	0	10	6
13	Marble Mortar & Pistle	0	7	6

DAIRY

		£	s.	d.
1	1 Cheese Press	0	5	0
2	1 Table	0	7	6
3	1 Tub, 1 Churn	0	5	0
4	1 Brass Pan	0	7	6

BREWING KITCHEN

		£	s.	d.
1	Three Coppers	7	0	0
2	One Knive	0	12	0
3	1 Brass Pan	1	16	0
4	4 Pails & 2 Tubs	0	6	0
5	1 Jack & Old Iron			

BUTLERS PANTRY

		£	s.	d.
1	One Cupboard	0	4	0
2	One Table	0	1	0
3	One Tray	0	7	6
4	1 Tobacco Safe	0	1	0
5	1 Tray	0	1	6
6	2 Plate Warmers	0	8	0
7	1 Knife Box	0	4	0
8	4 Bottle Stands	0	2	8
9	24 Knives & Forks	0	15	0
10	24 Do.	0	15	0
11	1 Handboard	0	6	0
12	8 Stewpans	1	15	0
13	Copper Saucepans	0	5	0
14	Pewter 87 lb. at 6d. p.	2	3	6
15	Coffee Pot 2/6, Chair 2/-	0	4	6

STAIR CASE

		£	s.	d.
1	One Lamp & Cord	0	7	6

LINNEN

		£	s.	d.
1	9 Doileys	0	2	3
2	8 Table Cloths	1	10	0
3	17 Do.	9	7	0
4	52 Napkins	1	14	8
5	20 Towells	0	6	8
6	15 Pillow Cases	0	1	3
7	25 Sheets fine	7	7	0
8	19 Pair of Sheets	7	12	0
9	1 Quilt	0	14	0
10	1 Dressing Box	1	1	0
11	Remnants of Paper			
12	2 Pieces of fine Cotton for a Bed at 3s. p. yd.			

CELLAR

		£	s.	d.
1	6 Porter Barrells	1	16	0
2	3 Tubs	1	4	0
3	9 Barrells	1	7	0
4	1 Cage	0	1	0
5	One Glass Lanthorn	0	5	0
6	9 Dozn. & 3 Bottles of Wine	9	14	3

STABLE

		£	s.	d.
1	1 Saddle, 2 Bridles & 1 Girth	0	12	0
2	Bay Mare	2	10	0
3	Pony & Foal	1	1	0
4	Hay	3	10	0
5	Grind Stone	0	5	0

GLASS CUPBOARD

		£	s.	d.
1	Three ornamental Pieces for a Chimney Piece	0	5	0
2	5 Lamps	0	15	0
3	1 Desart Service	0	15	0
4	1 Old Lamp	0	4	0
5	11 Gilt edged Glasses	0	7	0
6	8 Gold egd. Do.	0	4	0
7	9 Gold edgd. Ales	0	4	6
8	36 Ales & Wines	0	10	6
9	16 Jelly Glasses	0	4	0
10	40 Wash hands	0	16	8
11	1 Tray	0	7	6
12	6 Pewter Water Plates	0	15	0
13	4 Water Dishes	1	0	0
14	4 Dozn. Pewter plates	2	8	0
15	1 Sconce	0	5	0
16	10 Carraffs & 22 Wine Glasses	0	11	5
17	11 Water Glasses	0	4	7
18	9 Decanters	0	11	3
19	Earthen Tureen	0	3	0
20	Earthen Water Plates	0	5	0
	Amount of the Plate Sold as p. this Book	138	17	2½
	Do. of the Books as p. Do.	69	10	3

	£	s.	d.
Do. of the China Delph Pewter & Glass	22	19	4
Do. of the Linnen	31	16	10
	£263	3	7½
391 ozs. 7 dwts. of Silver Plate Bot. by J. Lewes to prevent their going under Value at 5s./6d. p. ounce	107	12	0
	£370	15	7½

Novr. 20th 1781. The above is a Just Acct. as Sold and Valued by me Wm. Cow, Aucr.

AN INVENTORY OF THE BOOKS AT PETERWELL
(Sold in 1781 with the names of the purchasers and the prices paid)

Name of Book	*Purchaser*	£	s.	d.
Pope's Homer iliad, 5 Vols.	Mr. Benjamin Davies	0	7	8
Gay's Poems, 2 Vols.	Mrs. Prutheroe	0	5	6
The North Britton, 2 Vols.	Lady Mansell	0	3	7
Blackstone's Commentaries, 4 Vols.	Mr. David Edwards	3	10	0
Bolinsbrooke's Works, 5 Vols.	Mr. Geo. Lewis	4	11	0
Ives's Voyage with compleat Cutts, 1 Vol.	Mr. John Geo. Phillips	0	132	0
Pine's Horace, 2 Vols.	Dr. Brown	1	15	0
Middleton's Life of Cicero, 2 Vols.	Mr. Ross	0	13	0
Anson's Voyages, 1st Ed., 1 Vol.	Mr. Jno. Geo. Phillips	0	19	0
Burnet's History of his Own Time, 2 Vols.	Dr. Brown	0	18	0
Tomson's Works, 2 Vols.	Mr. Ross	1	4	0
Beauchanan's Latin Poems, 2 Vols	Dr. Brown	0	9	0
Gronovius's Cicero, 4 Vols.	Dr. Brown	0	10	6
St. Evremonds Works in Ffrench, 2 Vols	Mrs. Davies	0	10	0
Demostenes, 1 Vol.	Mr. Ross	0	18	0
Dr. Hawksworth's works of Swift, 12 Vols.	Mr. Ross	5	0	0
England Illustrated, 2 Vols.	Mr. Herbert Ball	1	10	0
Chambers's Dictionary, 2 Vols.	Dr. Brown	1	13	0
Boss's Greek Septuagint, 1 Vol.	Do.	0	11	0
Quintus Curtius, 1 Vol.	Do.	0	8	0
Universal History, 44 Vol.	Mr. Ross	9	0	0
Langhorne's Plutarch, 6 Vol.	Mr. Geo. Lewis	1	7	6
Sir Walter Rowley's History of the World	Dr. Brown	0	8	6
Collins's Peerage & Baronetage, 11 Vols.	Mr. Ross	0	18	6

Name of Book	*Purchaser*	£	s.	d.
Atlas Geographical History of the World	Mr. Herbert Ball	0	13	0
Middleton's Life of Cicero & Orations, 5 Vols.	Mr. Ross	1	8	0
Rapin's History of England, 20 Vols. (1 wanting)	Do.	3	4	0
Burn's Ecclesiastical Law, 4 Vol.	Mr. Richd. Howells	0	17	6
Johnson's Shakespear, 8 Vols.	Mr. Dd. Williams	1	14	6
History of the Popes, 3 Vols.	Mr. Ed. Edwards	0	6	6
The Works of Tacitus, 2 Vols.	Mr. Barnikel	1	10	0
Poems of Edmund Waller, 1 Vol.	Richd. Jones Esqr.	0	12	6
Salmon's Geographical Grammar	Mr. Dd. Rees	0	5	0
Sir Wm. Temple's Works, 4 Vol.	Mr. James Hughes	1	7	0
Do.'s works in folio, 2 Vols.	Richd. Jones, Esqr.	0	15	0
Gibson's Farriery, 1 Volume	ready money	0	8	0
Michael Drayton's Works, 1 Vol.	Mr. John Lloyd	0	8	6
Shaw's Travels, 1 Vol.	Mr. Ross	0	7	6
Lord Shaftbury's Characteristic, 3 Vol.	Dr. Brown	0	4	0
Sir Isaac Newton's Chronology, 1 Vol.	Do.	0	2	0
Bentley's Sermons & Boyle's Lectury, 1 Vol.	Revd. Mr. Rogers	0	2	0
Rapin's History of Engld. in two Vols.	Mr. Herbt. Ball	0	15	6
Cave's Life of Christ, 1 Vol.	Mr. Gwynne	0	6	3
Bishop Beveridge's Works, 2 Vols.	Mr. Ross	0	10	6
The Clergyman's law	Mr. Gwynne	0	1	10
The 2nd. Edit. of Do. with improvemt.	Mr. John Lloyd	0	6	2
Evelin of Fforrest Trees	Dr. Brown	0	3	3
Coke's Reports, 7 Vols.	Mr. Ross	1	1	0
Bakon, on Government	Mr. Herbt. Lloyd	0	3	3
St. Cyprian's Works	Mr. Ross	0	2	3
History of England in 3 Vols.	Mr. Dd. Williams	0	13	0
Ovid Variorum, 4 Vols.	Dr. Brown	0	9	0
Camden's Brittania	Mr. Ross	0	3	0
Livi, 6 Vols.	Do.	0	3	6
A folio Bible	Do.	0	9	6
Law of Parliament & Tythes	Do.	0	1	6
Lloyd's Poems, 1 Vol.	ready money	0	3	0
Proceedings of the House of Peers	Mr. David Edwds.	0	1	6
14 Volumes Statutes at large (incorrect)	Dr. Ed. Lewes Esqr.	1	15	6
Churchill's works & a Book called the Ghost	Mr. Spurrel	0	3	1
Esob's Fables	Miss Tayler	0	1	10
Baker's History	Mr. Ross	0	2	6
Baskeville's Milton	Mr. Morgn. Lewis	0	15	6
The Gardner's Dictionary	Mr. Ross	0	6	3
A French Common Prayer & Testament	Mr. Spurrel	0	2	0

Name of Book	*Purchaser*	£	s.	d.
Chillinsworth's Works	Mrs. Williams	0	1	7
Bacon's Abridgmts., 3 Vols.	Mr. Nathl. Morgans	0	16	0
Hale's Pleas of the Crown, 2 Vols.	Mr. Dd. Edwards	0	15	0
British Magazines, 4 Vols.	Lady Mansell	0	3	6
Gentlemen's Magazines, 5 Vols.	Mr. Spurrel	0	5	0
London Magazines, 7 Vols.	Mr. Jas. Thomas	0	7	0
European Settlements in America, 2 Vols.	Mr. Ball	0	3	6
England's Gazetteer & A Geographical Dictionary	Jn. Hancock	0	4	0
An Old Book	for ready money	0	0	3
The remaining odd Volumes, and other Books of difft. Languages	Mr. Ross	5	5	0
		£69	10	3

APPENDIX E

LAMPETER PARISH AND ITS CARE OF THE POOR

(As illustrated by selected extracts from the records of the Parish Vestry Books).

WEEKLY PARISH PAY TO PAUPERS

Jenkin Thomas Mason - many Children	2 „ 0
David John Shoe-Maker and his Wife Pauper	1 „ 6
Tho. David Wm. Weaver being very poor	2 „ 6
David Hugh Tyngrithin being very poor	2 „ 6
Jane John Clynhir	1 „ 0
Mary Price	1 „ 0
Saxton	1 „ 0
Old Rees Cryer	1 „ 0
Tho. David Lewis	1 „ 0
Rees Pentrebach	1 „ 0
Jenkin David Rees Barber	2 „ 0
John Griffith's wife Pauper	1 „ 0
Susan Rees Pauper	1 „ 0
Betty william Lewis Town	1 „ 0
John Evan Tynyffynon being half blind	1 „ 6
Betty John Thomas Cooper having many Children	1 „ 0
Saml. David Samuell wife	1 „ 0
Evan David Simon	1 „ 0
David Thos. Richard	1 „ 0
Saml. Thos. Richard	1 „ 0
David Richard Pauper	1 „ 0
Mary Jenkin John Pauper	1 „ 0
Mary her Daughter being Wife to Tho. Rees Labr.	1 „ 0
Thomas William Clynhir	1 „ 0
Mary David Jenkin Henry'd Fach	1 „ 0
Evan John Stay-Maker having many Children	1 „ 0

THE LAST DEMANDS OF JOHN DAVID, PAUPER

To John David Evan 7 weeks at 1/6 per week	0	10	6
Do for maintaining and nursing him in his last time	1	1	0
Do for wine and vinigar	0	0	11½
Do for his Coffin	0	9	0
Do for diging his grave	0	0	6
Do for bring him from Clwyd Jach to Cwmkees	0	2	0

HIGH INFANT MORTALITY

A New Bier for the Burying of Children. and a New Shovel and other Instruments belonging to the digging Graves to be properly repaired.

	£	s	d
A New Shovel	0	3	0
A New Bier for Children	0	16	0

FINAL COSTS OF EVAN THE IDIOT

to Evan David for Evan y Idiot	5	2	0
to Do 5 Yards Cloth at 2/3 per yard	0	11	33
Coffin to Do	0	10	6
To the Saxton for Diging the Grave	0	1	0
Ale at the burial	0	1	6

THE POOR RATE KEPT RISING

Ordered an Additional one Shilling in the Pound in the Poor's Rate, with the 4/6 already allow'd on Easter Monday last, being 5/6 in the Whole.

SEA WATER FOR THE SICK

ordered Hannah the Niece of the late Rees Evans of Ffynon-Vair 4/ to enable her to go to the Sea Side, in order to procure her Health.

Likewise ordered to Evan Evans Shoe-Maker 1/6 ℘ Week for keeping the Apprentice Boy during his Illness and to defray expences for procuring Sea Water to him.

CASH AND CORN FOR THE SICK

allowed to Thomas David William Weaver owing that his Wife is Ill and unable to earn her Bread one Peck of Peel-Corn and 2/- in Money towards her Support.

CARE OF THE SICK
(No cure—No pay)

ordered that Marg^tt David should be endeavoured to be cured of her disagreeable and Strange Malady, in as moderate a manner as possible. Mr Thomas the Surgeon has undertaken her case for 2 Guin^s no cure = allowed, which was previously & no pay —

KEEPING DOWN THE COSTS

As very few of the Parish^rs attended, we thought proper to have another Meeting, touching the cure of the Boy by Courtnewydd—

Dr Griffiths undertakes to cure the Young Man, as moderately as possible. ——

BLIND AND VERY ILL

ordered a Peck of Barley 5/6. to Jane of Tynyffynon being Blind, and very Ile of a Feaver ——

TO BE NURSED AS CHEAPLY AS POSSIBLE

Authorised the Church Wardens and
overseers of the Poor to provide for
Thomas Evan Glover, and to have him main
tained and nursed with a proper Family
during his Illness, and that as Cheap as
possible.

MATERNITY GRANT

Agreed with Evan Thos. Ap David for the
lying in of Eliz.th Evan, and keeping the Child
of the same from Monday to Saturday 16 Shillings
for the midwife and all.

AS MODERATE AS POSSIBLE

authorised the Church Wardens to settle
and accommodate Mary Evan (who is big with
with Child or Children) with some or one of the Parishrs
as moderate as possible.

HELP IN KIND—CLOTHING

Ordered to old David Richard one Blanket, price 5/ D°. 2 flannen shirts one Pair of Stockings, and a pair of Woodenshoes.

allow'd Two flannel Shirts for Evan the Best.

Likewise allow'd to the Widow of James Rees Philip one Flannel Smock and one Pair of Shoes.

ordered the Ch: Wardens and Overseers to attend and examine the Child of Stephen Abel that they may guess, how much Clothing or Wearing Apparel is Necessary for him at present

ordered a Flannel Shift for the Wife of John Lewis of Glenduar, and also to deduct 3 p Week of their Weekly all=owance towards procuring a Blanket; otherwise We must compel them to come and reside in this Parish,.

PARISH HELP IN KIND—FOOD

ordered a Peck of Corn to old
Tho. D. William Pauper.

ordered before, by some of the Parish[rs]) to Simea
David Simeon, one Peck of Peelcorn, and one
Qr of Barley.

ordered 6d. p. Week more for old Diana
Widow of Tho. Dd. William untile Corn
is come cheaper.

BARLEY AND WOOL

allowd to Evan John of Pantyrhwch
half Teal of Barley, and also one stone
of Wool for making flanel to himself
his Wife and Children.

LEATHER ALLOWED

ordered 20. lb of Leather to Thos. John Thomas
of the Town, and the Overseers are to pay
for the same, his Wife being very Ill.

Ordered to John Thos. Edward Town
the sum of £ 2.0.0 to buy Leather
and he promises not to trouble the Paris
ioners again for a long time, and also
to reimburse us of the above £ 2.0.0

WOOL

ordered 22. lb of Wool for Sarah Thomas Cwrtnewydd
towards making two Blankets & some
other Necessaries.

THATCH

Ordered to repair the House of Susan Rees, and to
thatch the Roof of the same.

allow'd two thraves of Thatch
the House of old Nel Jenkin Rhydderch
at 1/6 per Thrave.

URGENTLY REQUIRED—A BLANKET

Allow'd the Widow of Isaac David 5/- towards getting a Blanket, and the Ch: Warden had paid her immediately.

QUARTER OF A YARD SHORT

allowed a Coat and Breeches for Evan David of Llandewy brevy, the Cloth for a Coat is already had and provided except one Quarter of a Yard;

OLD BETTY LEWIS'S FEATHER BED

Ordered the Church Wardens and Overseers of the Poor to take care of old Betty Wm Lewis's Feather Bed at Dropeh as the Parishrs allow her 1/6d p. Week

FIRING

Likewise ordered to allow John D. Evan 7/ towards providing firing- and says that he will ask no more untill Allsaint's Day.

HELP FOR AN APPRENTICE

N.B. John Thomas of Gwarcoed has agreed to the Parish^rs to keep, Cloath, and maintain (a opposite Vestry) John the Son of the late William James of Llangyby, during the Time of his Apprenticeship or 'till he arrives Sixteen years of Age, for the sum of five Pounds vizt £ 2.0.0 the 1st year, and £ 1.0.0 yearly untill the said sum of £ 5.0.0. is paid him.

SIXPENCE UNTIL SHE CAN FIND SERVICE

Ordered 6^d ℘ Week to Hester Isaac late of Pany Gock until she wile hire herself and fix in service

PARISH HELP FOR A YOUNG BLIND GIRL

allow'd to Hannah William of Tongr: allHach 1/ ℘ W. during her Illness, she being ab^t 15 years of age.

ORDERED FROM HOUSE TO HOUSE

Ordered Eliz^th the Daug^r of the late Thos Evan Thomas to be provided for in the Parish that is to say, to go from House to House &c.

FROM FARM TO FARM

Ordered the Church-Wardens to settle Evan the Ideot in the same place with one of the Farmers, as moderate as possibly they can. —

A SETTLEMENT IN DISPUTE

We the Inhabitants at the Above Vestry) have Agreed to procure the best Intelligence, whether William Thomas Rees can make himself a legal Parishioner here, or not, and we are deter= mind to get the best Advice we can in that Case, before we will admit him to have his Maintenance here

ONE SHILLING A WEEK

We the Parishioners then present have orderd to Advance to the following Paupers, so much ℔. Week

John D. Lewis — 1/ ℔. Week
John Griffiths Wife 1/ ℔. Week
Elizth Moses. — 1/ ℔. Week

ILLEGAL SETTLERS WERE RUTHLESSLY REMOVED

Ordered the Church-Wardens to procure a Removal to the Bastard Children of Eliz.th Samuel Davies to their legal & respective Parish or Parishes, as they are two Children.

Whereas Thomas Evan, his Wife & Children are removed from the Parish of Llanwenog to this Parish, but we are inform'd that he has not gained a legal Settlem.t here,

Likewise order'd to remove James David (who resides at present with David Davies of Wern) from this Parish before he can gain his Settlement here.

REWARDS FOR CATCHING FOXES AND KILLING CROWS

We Allow to Every Farmer throw the whole parish for every Crow killed upon their Tenements and no where else. One penny for every Crow or One Shilling per Dozn to be paid.

allow'd 10/- to Evan Thomas Cooper for destroying the Crows (young & old if possible) in the rookery on Peterwell Farm, particularly in the Pigeons House Field.

Ordered to pay and discharge for diff.t Bills for killing Foxes in this Parish.

QUESTION OF RELEASE FROM GAOL

ordered the Ch: Wardens to consult wi Mr. H. Lloyd, and to have his Opinion in re= =gard to the liberation of Jenkin George from Cardigan Goal,

RELEASE AGREED

ordered to agree for the releasement of Jenkin Jenkins from Prison, provided that his Liberty can be obtained on reason= =able terms.

AT A COST OF £3-3-0

Agreed with Jenkin Jones of Rhydyrhals for £3. 3.0 for the liberation of Jenkin Jenkins from Cardigan Goal; and also the fees of the Goal is to be discharged.

ASSISTANCE FOR A SAILOR

allow'd to John Evan of the Greyhound /6 Sixpence p^r. Day for maintaining and Wat= =ching a Sailor, who was accidentally taken Ille, in his way home to Leverpool; his Sickness and ailing detained him, on Wednesday the 25th of last Month.

NEGLECTING HIS WIFE

impowered the Overseer of the Poor to provide a Horse for Cathrine the Wife of Evan Thomas Mazor. and to apply immediately to a Magistrate for a Warrant to apprehend the said Evan Thomas, to shew cause, why he does not provide for his Wife, and settle her in a comfortable habitation.

PAID TO LEAVE THE PARISH

allow'd a Flannen Shirt for Tho.s D.s late alltgoch and also 2/ in his Pocket to go and Work abroad.

RICHARD JOHN—MADE ACCOUNTABLE

agreed with David Evan of Pentrebach's Wife for the lying in of Deborah Evan, who is pregnant of Richard John, for the Sum of £ 1. 1. 0.
and if the said Richard John does not allow £1.10.0 per Ann: towards the maintenance of his Child or Children, he is to be dealt with according to Law.

CORPORAL OATH

(Pregnant girls were made to swear before a magistrate as to the father of the child)

Ordered the Church Wardens and Overseers of the Poor to convey Eliz^th Evan (being in a state of Pregnancy) before a Magis=trate, in order to make her Corporal Oath who the Father of the Child or Children is and at the same time to apply for a Warrant to apprehend the said Father.

A BOND OF INDEMNIFICATION

We have agreed to accept of a Bond of Indemnification for — — from Joseph David and John David, for the Nursing, keeping and maintaining, the Child or Children that is likely to be born of the Body of Mary John maid servant at Ffynonvair; the said Joseph David is the Father of the said Child or Children as she, the said Mary John, have sworn before a Magistrate, that he is the Father of the said Child; the said Joseph David and John David are the Children of Simon David Carpenter, who lives by Alltyrodyn, in the Parish of Llandyssil.

SARAH STEPHEN ABEL IN A DEPLORABLE CONDITION

ordered the Church-Wardens and Overseers of the Poor to agree for the keeping and maintaining of Sarah Stephen Abel (not above 4/ ℔ Week) as she is in a very deplorable condition.

ONE WEEK LATER—HER DEATH

At a Vestry held in the Parish Church of Lamp^{r} and Adjourn'd to the House of Danl. Evans April 21/ 1790.

Necessity urged the Parish^{rs} to meet this Day in order to settle the Child of Stephen Abel as the Mother was Buried this Evening — and so have ordered the Child to the care of David Davies of Cwmkenryd for 1/6 ℔. Week, untill intelligence can be had from his Father from London.

THE CHILD LEFT BURDENSOME ON THE PARISH

ordered Wm Thomas the Overseer to apply to Henry Jones of Tyglyn Esqr. for a Warrant of complaint on Stephen Abel Morgan who has a Child left burdensome on this Parish, without having gained his legal Settlement here;

Agreed with Enoch Nathaniel of the Parish of Llanwenog to go up to London, and to execute the above Warrant and compel the said Stephen Abel Morgan to make an Affidavit of his Parish, before one of his Majesties Justices of the Peace, allowing him for his expence on his Journey the Sum of one Pounds and one Shilling, also another Guinea, provided that he can execute the Commission given him, otherwise no more.

THE FATE OF STEPHEN ABEL'S SON

allow'd a Flanel Shirt to the Son of Stephen Abel at Cwmhenry.

Ordered a Coat, Waistcoat, Breeches Stockings, and pair of Woodenshoes for the Son of Stephen Abel.

ordered the Son of Stephen Abel to be employed from Farm to Farm. and from House to House within the Parish.

Agreed with Evan Evans of Abergwmelle the present Ch. Warden & Overseer of the Poor to keep, and maintain Wm. Son of Stephen Abel for the Term of Seven Years, the Parishrs have allowd. a Suit of Cloaths and two Shirts for him, and no more.

THE MEAGRE ESTATE OF ELIN RHYDDERCH

We have on the above Day
Authorised the Ch: Wardens & Overseers of
the Poor to sell off the Effects & Furniture
of the late Elin.r J. Rhydderch, and the Whole
amounted to 16/5½.

allow'd to Jenkin Edwards for the Coffin —	10.6
Do. to David Evan's Wife for attending ~~two Weeks~~	5.6
	16.0

We are willing to accommodate John James
Sadler with the House of the late Elin.r Jenkin
Rhydderch, untill such time as we can fur=
=nish him with a superior one.

E. W. Williams Vic.r

AND ONE SHILLING TO THE SEXTON'S WIFE FOR WASHING HER CORPSE

ordered Mr. D. Jones late
Church Wardens to pay to old Sarah
David 1/ for washing the Corpse
of the late Elin.r J. Rhydderch.

ACCOUNT OF THE POOR

Acco.t of ye Poor

	£	S	D
To the Soxton for Digging 3 Graves ..	0	1	6
Relief to 4 Passengers	0	2	0
To Anne Ellis	0	5	0
Journey to Dihewid and to Newqey ..	0	3	0
Journey to Lloyd Jack	0	1	0
For washing the Clothes of Elin Edward	0	1	0
Two shirts to Evan Morgan's apprentice	0	6	5
one Shirt to Evan D.d Landewi	0	3	6
Pare of Stokings & a Hat to Evan the Ideot	0	1	6
Peck of Peelcorn to mary Dan.l ...	0	3	0
Pare of stockins to Joseph Evan	0	1	0
Relief to Stragler from Penbrockshire	0	2	4
to the Child of Tho. Evan Tho. for one Year	2	0	0
The Rent of mary Daniel ...	0	15	0
Rent of Elinor Jenkin	0	10	0
To 3 Passengers	0	1	6
County Stock	5	3	4½

Oakley Leigh

The signature of Oakley Leigh, Sir Herbert Lloyd's most trusted servant who, as church warden, assisted with the distribution of poor relief over a number of years.

BIBLIOGRAPHY

MANUSCRIPT SOURCES

British Library. Additional Manuscripts:

Bute Mss.: 5226D.I. 209; 5726 f.208.

Grenville Mss. 54321 f.1.

Hardwicke Papers: 35603 f.108; 35603 f.282; 35604 f.131; 36132 f.196.

Newcastle Mss.: 32855 f.346; 32856 f.52-3; 32857; 32819 f.248; 32893 f.300; 32901 f.359; 32894 f.513-4; 32968 f.23; 32973 f.21; 32976.

Public Record Office:

Chancery Proceedings: C2023149/2; C123499317; C123496340.

Hearth Tax Returns: E179 219/94 1669-70. Llanbeder.

Home Office Papers: 49/1.

State Papers: 37/4.

Wills:

Ieuan Gwyn of Moelifor, Llanrhystud. Prob. 11/259; Daniel Evans of Peterwell. Prob. 11/435; Sir Charles Cornwallis Lloyd, Prob. 11/637; Sir Lucius Christianus Lloyd, Prob. 11/777; Dame Anne Lloyd, Prob. 11/1047.

National Library of Wales:

Abermeurig Mss.: An incomplete copy of the Poll Book of the Cardigan Borough Election.

N.L.W. 17080E. Account of Election Petitions, 1729-59.

Alltlwyd Mss.: N.L.W. 14, 215C,(2); 14, 215C(3); 14216D; Letters of Lord Lisburne to James Lloyd of Mabws.

Bishops Transcripts: Llangennech 176 and 1711.

Cardiganshire Quarter Sessions Records: Order Books 1 and 2.

Cardigan Gaol Files: Wales 4/897/1-9.

Crosswood Mss.: Series 3:23. Lord Lisburne to Lord Chancellor.

Cwrtmawr Mss.: 182B. List of freeholders for the Manor of Lampeter 1760, 717B; 803.

Derry Ormond Mss.: 63-4, Lease of Foelallt.

Dolaucothi Mss.: Letters of Thomas Johnes, Sir Herbert Lloyd, Francis Skyrme, Eliza Lewis, Jeremiah Lloyd.

Eaton Evans and Williams Mss.: 3792. Legal document relating to partition of Peterwell estate; 954, Letter describing the 1769 by-election, 7125, Writ from King's Bench against Sir Herbert Lloyd.

Edwinsford Mss.: 3152. Documents pertaining to the Llanfair estate.

Falcondale Mss.: 15-19. Lampeter Court Leet Records.

George Eyre Evans Mss.: N.L.W. 7957; 13493; 13519B; 13664C; miscellaneous letters and notes relating to Peterwell.

Gogerddan Mss.: (Peterwell Bundle, Parliamentary Box.) Letters of Rev. John Lloyd of Rug, John Adams, John Lewis. Medical Records of John Lloyd of Peterwell. List of plate, books, and sale contents of Peterwell.

Llanstephan Mss.: N.L.W. 120, 145. Extended version of the Deportment of the Gentry.

Llanwennog Parish Register 1722-1812. N.L.W. 14929E.

Lucas Mss.: 2876. Letter of Sir Herbert Lloyd to Bishop of St David's.

Nanteos Mss.: Will of Richard Steadman; Letters of John Pugh Pryse, Pryse Campbell, Lewis Pryse, Sir John Philipps, the Rev. John Lloyd of Rug, the third Lord Lisburne, Wilmot Vaughan, the fourth Lord Lisburne, John Symmons.

Powis Castle Mss.: 3246, 3247, 3416, 3725, 3910. Letters of John Paynter: 3245, 3983, letters of Thomas Johnes: 2995, 3189, 3246, letters of Sir Herbert Lloyd.

Peterwell Mss.: 11, Court of Chancery action against Mary Lloyd of Peterwell, 26, Will of Walter Lloyd; 38, Mortgages relating to Peterwell; 65, Will of Sir Herbert Lloyd.

Trevecka Mss.: Diaries of Howel Harris.

Trevecka Letters: 572, Howel Harris to Sir Herbert Lloyd; 1295, Howel Harris to James Erskine.

IN OTHER REPOSITORIES

Berkshire County Record Office:

Pryse Mss.: Rev. John Lloyd of Rug to Thomas Lloyd.

Dyfed Record Office:

Aberystwyth Office, Peterwell Box, DX/3/2 to DX/3/25.

Legal documents relating to the Peterwell and Maesyfelin estates.

Carmarthen office; Derwydd Mss. H.I. Paintings listed by Joseph Gulston.

Cawdor Mss. Book A. p. 28, Golden Grove Book.

Cawdor Vaughan Box: 17/507, Illtyd Evans to Richard Vaughan describing the rejection of Sir Herbert Lloyd by the militia.

Cwmgwili Mss.: 109. Sir Herbert Lloyd to Griffith Philipps.

4347, Fountain Hall Pedigree.

St. Peter's Church, Lampeter:

Lampeter Parish Register, 1695-1746. Baptisms.

Lampeter Parish Register, 1746-1805. Deaths.

Lampeter Parish Register, 1755-1812. Marriages.

Lampeter Parish Vestry Books.

Jesus College Archives:

Accounts relating to fees paid by John and Herbert Lloyd of Peterwell.

PRINTED PRIMARY SOURCES

(i) Official Sources

Calendar of Home Office Papers, (George III) 1760-65, (Published in Liechenstein, 1967).

Calendar of the Committee for the Advance of Money (Domestic) 1642-56, (London, 1888, Parts I and II).

Calendars of State Papers (Domestic) 1649-1650, 1651-1652. (London, 1875).

Calendars of the Committee for Compounding 1643-1660, Vols. I-V.

Genealogies of Cardiganshire, Carmarthenshire and Pembrokeshire Families, *West Wales Historical Records,* Vol. I, 1910-11.

Green, Francis, *A Calendar of Deeds and Documents* (1921).

Journals of the House of Commons, Vols. VII and XXXII.

The Population Act II. George IV c. 30. *Abstract of the Answers and Returns, Parish Register Abstract,* Vol. III, 1831.

(ii) Unofficial

Annual Register—A view of the History, Politics and Literature of the Year 1763.

Anon. 'A True Character of the Deportment of the Principal Gentry within the Counties of Carmarthen, Pembroke and Cardigan', *Cambrian Register,* 1796.

Cylchgrawn Cymdeithas Hanes y Methodistiaid Calfinaidd.

Davies, J. H. (ed.), *Morris Letters 1728-1765,* Aberystwyth, 1907.

Evans, G. E. (ed.), *Lloyd Letters,* Aberystwyth, 1908.

Evans, G. E., *Aberystwyth and its Court Leet,* Aberystwyth, 1902.

Foster, I., *Alumni Oxoniensis* (1500-1714), Oxford, 1888.

Rowlands, John, *Historical Notes on the Counties of Glamorgan, Carmarthen and Cardigan* (1866).

Jones, M.H. (ed.), *Trevecka Letters,* Caernarvon, 1932.

Owen, Hugh (ed.), *Additional Morris Letters,* London, 1947.

Phillips, J. R., *Sheriffs of Cardiganshire,* Carmarthen, 1868.

'Pembrokeshire Parsons', West Wales Historical Records, Vol. 1, 1910-11.

Theakston, L. E., & Davies, J. (eds.), *Lloyd Family Pedigrees,* Oxford, 1913.

Williams, A. H. (ed.), *John Wesley in Wales, 1739-1790,* London, 1976.

(iii) Newspapers and Periodicals

Baldwin's London Weekly Journal
Gazeteer
Gentleman's Magazine
Gloucester Journal
London Evening Post
London Gazette
Lloyd's Evening Post
Middlesex Journal
Pembrokeshire Guardian
Public Advertiser
St. James' Chronicle

(iv) Unpublished Thesis

Beynon, Oswald, 'The Lead Mining Industry of Cardiganshire, 1700-1830', M.A. Thesis, 1938.

PRINTED BOOKS

(For reasons of space, only books referred to are included)

Blackstone, William, *Commentaries on the Laws of England, 1793-95.*
Bradley, A. G., *Highways and Byways in South Wales.* (Brecon, 1903).
Cottu, Charles, *The Administration of Criminal Justice in England, 1882.*
Davies, J. H., *The Letters of Lewis, Richard, William and John Morris,* 1907.
Defoe, Daniel, *Tour Through England and Wales.* (London, 1959).
Evans, G. E., *Lampeter.* (Aberystwyth, 1905.)
Evans, J., *Letters Written During a Tour of South Wales.* (London, 1804).
Evans, T., *Cambrian Itinerary.* (London, 1801).
Godley, D. A., *Oxford in the Eighteenth Century.* (London, 1908).
Green, D., *Queen Anne.* (London, 1971).
Hay, D., Linebaugh, P., Thompson, E. P., *Albion's Fatal Tree.* (Bristol, 1975).
Hughes, J., *Methodistiaeth Cymru.*
Ilchester and Brooke, H. L., *Life of Sir Charles Hanbury Williams.* (London, 1928).
Inglis-Jones, E., *Peacocks in Paradise.* (London, 1971).
Jones, D. G. *Blodeugerdd o'r Ddeunawfed Ganrif.* (Cardiff 1936).
Jowitt, E., *The Dictionary of English Law.* (London, 1959).
Meyrick, S. R., *History and Antiquities of the County of Cardigan.* (Brecon, 1810).
Morgan, E., *Life and Times of Howel Harris.* Holtwell, 1852).
Parry, T. (ed.), *Oxford Book of Welsh Verse.* (Oxford, 1967).
Phillips, H., *Mid-Georgian London.* (London, 1964).
T. J. Ll. Prichard, *The Adventures and Vagaries of Twm Shôn Catti,* 1828.
Rees, Rice, *Canwyll y Cymry.* (Wrexham 1867).
Rees, T., *A Topographical and Historical Description of Cardiganshire.* (1810).
Richards, T., *A History of the Puritan Movement in Wales* 1639-53. (London, 1920).
Saunders, E., *A view of the state of religion in the Diocese of St. David's about the beginning of the Eighteenth Century.* 1731.
Spurrell, W., *Carmarthen and its Neighbourhood.* (Carmarthen, 1879).
Whitefield, G., *Journals.* (London, 1960).
Wellington, D., *Cofiant Daniel Rowland.* (Carmarthen, 1905).

Articles

Edmunds, W., 'On Some Old Families in the Neighbourhood of Lampeter.' *Arch. Camb.* 1861.
Jones, E. D., 'The Gentry of South Wales in the Civil War.' *N.L.W.J.,* 1959.
Lewis, W. J., 'Some of the Freeholders of Cardiganshire in 1632.' *Ceredigion,* 1956.
Roberts, G., 'Methodistiaeth Cynnar Gwaelod Sir Aberteifi.' *Ceredigion,* 1964.
Thomas, D.Ll., 'Lewis Morris in Cardiganshire'. *Y Cymmrodor,* Vol. 15, 1902.
Thomas, P.D.G., 'Eighteenth Century Politics in the Cardigan Boroughs Constituency.' *Ceredigion,* Vol. 5, 1967.

ABBREVIATIONS

Add.Mss.	Additional manuscripts.
A.M.L.	*Additional Morris Letters,* ed. Owen.
B.L.	British Library.
B.C.R.O.	Berkshire County Record Office.
D.C.	Dolaucothi.
C.C.H.M.C.	*Cymdeithas Cylchgrawn Hanes y Methodistiaid Calfinaidd.*
Cymm.	*Y Cymmrodor.*
D.R.O.	Dyfed Record Office.
Gog.	Gogerddan.
Falc.	Falcondale.
H.H.	Howel Harris.
H.T.R.	Hearth Tax Returns.
J.J.	John Johnes.
T.J.	Thomas Johnes.
J.H.C.	*Journal House of Commons.*
L.P.R.	Lampeter Parish Register.
L.P.V.B.	Lampeter Parish Vestry Book.
N.L.W.	National Library of Wales.
N.L.W.J.	National Library of Wales Journal.
N.M.W.	National Museum of Wales.
P.C.	Powis Castle.
Pet.	Peterwell.
P.R.O.	Public Record Office.
S.H.L.	Sir Herbert Lloyd.
S.D.U.C.	St David's University College
T.C.A.S.	*Transactions of the Cardiganshire Antiquarian Society.*

INDEX

(Note: Appendices are not included in the index)

PERSONS

A
Acton, John, 160
Adams, John, 140, 207, 209, 214-21
Adams, Martha, 214
Anne, Queen, 72, 168, 209

B
Bacon, Mrs, (of Newtoncap)
Bailey, Lady, 222
Ball, John, Grogwynion, 139, 145, 168
Bowen, Daniel, Mayor of Cardigan, 28, 29
Bowen, Tommy, 198
Bragge, Elizabeth, 39, 54
Bulkeley, William, 99
Bute, Earl of, 180

C
Campbell, General, 68
Campbell, Pryse, Stackpole Court, 187, 188 (portrait), 191
Carbery, Earl of, 2
Charles I, 14, 15
Charles II, 209
Charlotte, Princess, 140
Charlton, John, 147
Collins, John, 177, 178
Congreve, Ralph, 195-202
Coulthard, James, 215
Cow, William, 218
Cromwell, Oliver, 11, 16, 18, 20
Cunliffe, Sir Robert, 215

D
Dafis, Dafydd, Castell Hywel, 224
Daniel, David, Blacksmith, 84, 210
Davies, Ben, Glancuch, 187, 190
Davies, David, Maespwll, 93
Davies, J. H., 162
Davies, Lloyd, Pontfaen, 163
Davis, Hart, 223
Defoe, Daniel, 174
Dyer, John, Aberglasney, 84

E
Edmunds, William, 73, 160, 210
Egmont, Lord, 39
Erskine, James, M.P., 54
Evans, Daniel, of Peterwell, 21, 22, 23, 80, 210
Evans, David, of Llechwedd Deri (Founder of Peterwell), 14, 15
Evans, Erasmus, 21
Evans, Evan (Ieuan Brydydd Hir), 144, 171
Evans, Francis, 93
Evans, George Eyre, 202-09, 212
Evans, Howell, 206
Evans, Illtyd, 140
Evans, Letitia, 22, 23, 78
Evans, Lewis, Llangathen, 198, 200
Evans, Mary, of Peterwell, 22
Evans, Sarah, of Peterwell, 51
Evans, Theophilus, 36
Evans, Thomas, London Attorney, 65
Evans, Thomas, of Peterwell, 11, 16, 17, 18, 19, 219

F
Fielding, Sir Henry, 177
Fielding, Sir John, 177
Frederick, Prince of Wales, 53
Ffoy, Emma, 73, 214
Fox, Henry, 38
Fychan, Ieuan Gwyn, of Moelifor, 21

G
George I, 77
George II, 44, 45, 77, 209
George III, 39, 140, 141, 180
Gerard, Colonel, 15
Gibbon, Edward, 35
Glandynin, William, 103
Grafton, Duke of, 186
Grenville, George, 172, 180, 182
Grubb, Mr, 141
Gwynne, Marmaduke, of Garth, 23, 51, 53, 84
Gwynne, Roderick, of Glanbrân, 84

H
Halifax, Lord, 141
Hanbury Williams, Sir John, 38
Handel, George Frideric, 48
Harding, Frances, 8, 9
Hardwicke, Lord, 76, 80, 124, 125
Harford, Alice, M., 107
Harris, Howel, 35, 46, 47, 48, 49, 50, 52, 53, 55, 59, 60, 62, 78, 163 (Ref. to 'Cried for Sir Herbert)
Heath, Roy, 164
Herod, 191
Hoare, Sir Robert Colt, 223
Hugh, David, Tynrithin, 99
Hugh, Mary Evan, 38
Hughes, John (The Methodist), 52, 53, 63

I
Inglis-Jones, Elisabeth, 62 (Notes), 96 (Notes)

J
Jenkin, Philip, 162
Jenkins, Evan, 217
Jenner, Dr Edward, 100
Johnes, John, of Dolaucothi, 84, 115, letter from Sir Herbert; 129, threat from Abermâd; 137, 141, indifference to Sir Herbert's baronetcy; 171, Refusal to go to Bath; 195, burgess making of Congreve
Johnes, Thomas, of Abermâd, 67 Esgair Mwyn fracas; 68, 125, 126, 172, in Fleet prison; 129, 131, release from gaol
Johnes, Thomas, the Custos, 25, 26, portrait; 37-8, gambling; 39, 63, 68, 84, 116, 122, rivalry with Trawsgoed; 124, 125-37, support of Sir Herbert; 193, 194, 195-201, rift with Sir Herbert; 215
Johnes, Thomas, son of the Custos, later of Hafod, 167, 194, portrait; 195, 222
Jones, David, of Deri Ormond, 175
Jones, D. Gwenallt, 11
Jones, Griffith, 47, 57
Jones, John, of Crynfryn, 84, 107, 114, 139, 176
Jones, John, Saddler, 223
Jones, Richard, 63
Jones, Theophilus, 13
Jowitt, Earl, 162

K
Kilvert, Francis, 8
Knethell, Richard, 198
Knight, Elizabeth, 39
Knight, Richard, of Croft Castle, 39

L
Le Heup, Elizabeth, 44
Le Heup, Isaac, M.P., 44
Leigh, Blanche, 84
Leigh, Bridget, 9
Leigh, John, 86
Leigh, Oakley, 84, 89, 98, 153, 167, 182, 197
Lewis, Eliza, of Llannerchaeron, 165
Lewes-, Erasmus, 33, 46
Lewes, John, 187, 217, 218
Lisburne, The Third Viscount, 25, 41, 63
Lisburne, Lady, 189
Lloyd, Alice, (sister of Sir Herbert), 23, 74
Lloyd, Dame Anne, 56, portrait; 57, 59, 60, 210, 215, 216, death of
Lloyd, Sir Charles, of Maesyfelin, 72, 117, portrait
Lloyd, David, of Breinog, 84, 145, 171, 176, 200
Lloyd, Elizabeth (née Bragge), 40, 41
Lloyd, Elizabeth (née Le Heup), 80, 82, 117
Lloyd, Dame Frances, of Maesyfelin, 73, 74, 108
Lloyd, Sir Francis, of Maesyfelin, 2, 5, 7, 15
Lloyd, Griffith, Principal, Jesus College, Oxford, 33
Lloyd, Sir Herbert, of Peterwell, 14, birth; 33-6, education; 37, made a J.P.; 38, gambling; 39, marriage; 46-54, friendship with Howel Harris; 57, second marriage; 63, tyrannical conduct; 67, Esgair Mwyn affair; 69, lost his status as J.P.; 82-95, Lord of the Manor; 126-31, vendetta against Abermâd; 140-51, baronetcy; 151-65, Black Ram affair; 167, ill health and irascibility; 197-201, parliamentary defeat; 207, third marriage; 208, death; 210, burial; 221, his library
Lloyd, Herbert, of Carmarthen, 221, 222
Lloyd, John, of Peterwell, 23, birth; 33-6, education; 43, portrait; 44, election to Parliament; 44, marriage; 77-9, illness; 80, death.
Lloyd, John, of Alltyrodyn, 60, 144, 169
Lloyd, James, of Mabws, 118, 183, 184, 189, 191
Lloyd, Jeremiah, 74, 84, 103
Lloyd, John, of Llangennech, 22
Lloyd, John, of Rug, 43, 75, 76

Lloyd, Sir Lucius Christianus, of Maesyfelin, 35, 39, 63, 72, 73, 74
Lloyd, Sir Marmaduke, of Maesyfelin, 1, 3, portrait; 46, 72
Lloyd, Oliver, Mayor of Tregaron, 17
Lloyd, Richard, of Mabws, 27
Lloyd, Thomas, Mayor of Cardigan, 198, 199, 200, 201, 202
Lloyd, Walter, of Peterwell, 14, 23, 24, portrait; 25, 26, 27, 28, 29, 30, 38, 41, 72, 73
Lluyd, Edward, 100
Llwyd, Francis, 116, 117
Lovedon, Edward, 217, 218

M
Meredith, Rees, 46
Meyrick, William Rush, 125
Montague, George, 209
Montague, Lady Mary Wortley, 100, 181
Morgan, Ann, 64, 91
Morgan, David, 65
Morgan, Herbert, of Hafod Uchtryd, 21
Morgan, John, 65
Morgan, Robert, Iron Master, 114
Morris, Ben, 223
Morris, Lewis, Llewelyn Ddu o Fôn, 46, 65, 66, 67, threatened by Sir Herbert; 68, 69, 70, 71, 100, description of health; 101, 102, 124, 127, 128, 131, 143, death; 171, 174
Morris, Richard, 133, 174
Morris, William, 69
Myddleton, William, 28

N
Nash, Richard, 168
Newcastle, Duke of, 79, 122, 124, 132, 133, 137, 142, 180
Norton, Sir Fletcher, 182, 183

O
Owen, John, 127
Owens, of Orielton, 28

P
Paynter, John, of Hafod, 71, 107, 139, 145, 146, 147, 148, 149, 163, 166, 168, 171, 176, 186, 189, 190
Pelham, Henry, Prime Minister, 69
Philip, Siôn, 60, 151-64
Philipps, Griffith, of Cwmgwili, 181, 182, 195, 197, 215
Philipps, Rev. James, 216, 217
Philipps, Sir John, Picton Castle, 35, 43, 74, 76, 120, 134
Pilkington, 215
Pitt, William, The Elder, 180
Popkins, Thomas, 52, 208, 209
Powell, Thomas, of Nanteos, 25, 27, 29, 30, portrait; 74, 193
Powell, Dr William, of Nanteos, 67, 68, 70, portrait; 71, 124, 131, 177
Powis, Lord, 69, 71, 146, 166, 172, 177, 190
Price, David, 36
Price, Dr William, Lampeter Physician, 77, 78, 79, 80, 81
Prichard, Rev. Rees, Vicar of Llandovery, 2, 7, 72, 223
Prichard, Samuel, 2, 6, 8, 11
Prichard, T. J. Ll., 7, 13
Pryse, Sir Carbery, 65
Pryse, John Pugh, of Gogerddan, 41, 74, 76, 84, 131, 132, 133, 134, 135, 137, election to county seat; 181-203 campaign against Sir Herbert
Pryse, Lewis, of Gogerddan, 188, 217
Pryse, Margaret, of Gogerddan, 217
Pryse, Thomas, of Gogerddan, 27, 131
Pugh, John, 64

R
Rees, Mary, 162
Rees, Rice, editor of *Canwyll y Cymry,* 11
Rhydderch, John, 33
Rice, of Dinefwr, 140, 168
Richard, Edward, of Ystrad Meurig, 55, 57
Rigby, Richard, 38
Rockingham, Second marquess of, Prime Minister, 180
Ross, John, 218
Rowland, Daniel, Llangeitho, 47, 48, 49, 51, 52, 55, 59, ejection from Church; 60, 84

S
Seward, William (Methodist martyr), 52
Sherbourne, Elizabeth, 214
Skyrme, Francis, of Llawhaden, 126, 129, 174
Smith, Adam, 35
Squire, Bishop of St. David's, 59, 60, 143
Stedman, Anne, 46, 55
Stedman, Averina, 57
Stedman, Richard, 41, 53, 55
Symmons, John, Llanstinan, 76, 134, 193

V
Vaughan, Edward, of Greengrove, 84
Vaughan, Gwyn, 68
Vaughan, Wilmot, The Fourth Viscount Lisburne, 79, 122, 123, portrait; 125, 131, 132, 134, 139, 177, 184, 185, portrait; 187, 191, 193, 195

W
Wallis, Albany, 183, 222
Walpole, Horatio, 74
Walpole, Sir Robert, Prime Minister, 25, 29, 51, 74
Watson, Thomas, M.P., 132, 137
Wesley, Charles, 51, 81
Wesley, John, 35, 62, 81
Wilkes, John, 180
William III, 72
Williams, Eliezer, 11
Williams, Evan, 65
Williams, William, Pantseiri, 215
Williams, William, Pántycelyn, 49, 52, 60
Williams-Wynn, Sir Watkin, 28, 43, 74
Whitefield, George, 35, 47, 49, 52, 80
Woodward, John, 158

Y
Young, Arthur, 167

PLACES

A
Abermâd, 68, picture; see also Thomas Johnes, Abermâd
Aberllolwyn, 128
Aberystwyth, 16, 27, 64, 68, 114, 137, 181, 183
Adpar, 137, 201
Alltyrodyn, 191

B
Bala, 49
Balliol College, Oxford, 35
Banc-y-Warren, 159, 160
Bath, 94, illustration; 95, 109, 139, 166, 168, 170, illustration; 171, 173, illustration; 174, illustration; 208, 209
Betws Bledrws, 47
Berwick-on-Tweed, 137, 184
Black Bull, Holborn, 205
Black Lion Inn, Lampeter, 27, 28, photo; 212, expenses; 220, 221
Blaise Castle, 223
Bodleian, Oxford, 35
Brongest, Home of Oakley Leigh, 85, photo
Bristol, 76, 95
Bronwydd, 127
Brynhyfryd, 45
Burton, 21

C
Caio, 84, 200
Cambridge, 33
Cardigan, 17, 23, 27, 28, 41, 53, 73, 76, 137, 157, 201
Carmarthen, 9, 41, 49, 73, 140, 215, Town Hall; 217
Cellan, 200
Colby, 216
Colchester, 223
Coldbrooke, 38
Cors Caron, 55
Croft Castle 39, 40, illustration; see also Thomas Johnes the Custos
Cwmann, 54

D
Dolaucothi, 130, illustration
Denbigh, 197

E
Esgair Mwyn, 65, 67, 68, 69, 70, 124, 126, 133, 146

F
Falcondale, 223, 224, illustration
Ffair Rhos, 52
Foelallt, 29, 33, 41, 42, illustration; 47, 48, 49, 55, 57, 60, 80, 82, 215

G
Galltfadog, home of Lewis Morris, 65
Garth, 51, 53
Glyncorrwg, 55
Gogerddan, 75, illustration
Green Dragon, 82
Great Abbey Farm, 61, illustration
Greyhound, The, 82
Gunthorpe Manor, 44
Gwinten, 5

H
Hafod, 25, 139, 146, 147, 167, 186, 222
Hereford, 16, 187
Holborn, 205, 207

L
Lampeter, 1, 5, 7, 9, 11, 37, 82-96, Court Leet; 91-111, Parish Vestry; 106, Medieval Church; 106, 201
Llanbadarn, 167
Llanbadarn Church, 143
Llancrwys, 84
Llanddewibrefi, 33, 54, 55, 59, 216
Llandeilo, 166
Llandovery, 2, 5, 7, 8, 97
Llanfair, 16, 19, 38, 39
Llangeitho, 47, 48, 50, 55
Llanfihangel Ystrad, 200
Llanrhystud, 200
Llanstinan, 29
Llanwenog, 38
Llanybydder, 127
Lledrod, 60
Llechwedd Deri, 14, 15, 19, 23, 47, 80, 215
London, 38, 80, 89, 168, 183, 204, 205, 209, 217
Ludlow Castle, 2

M
Maesyfelin, 1-12, Curse of; 72, decline of; 82, passed to Peterwell

N
Nag's Head, 82
Nantcwnlle, 33
Nanteos, 31, illustration
Nant yr Hogfaen, 6
Norfolk, 44, 117
Norwich, 117

O
Oriel College, Oxford, 1
Oxford, 8, 33, 35, 36

P
Pant-y-Weil, 6
Pencarreg, 7, 84
Peterwell, 1, 11, 12, illustration of Avenue; 14 seq. rise of; 21, expansion of; 74, acquisition of Maesyfelin; 82, Sir Herbert's rule at; 214, inherited by Adams; 217, sale of; 223, descriprion of decay; 226, photo of ruins
Pontrhydygroes, 168

S
Salt Hill, 208
Severn, 158
Ship, The, 82
Shrewsbury, 160
Slough, 209
St James's Palace, 78
Strata Florida, 41, 55, 57
Strata Florida Church, 210, 216
St George's, Hanover Square, 207
Swan, The, 82

T
Talley, 200
Three Horse Shoes, 82
Trawsgoed, 121, illustration
Tregaron, 15, 25, 37, 57, 63, 148, 216
Tresaith, 52
Tunbridge Wells, 95, 166

W
Westminster, 25, 44, 45, 83, 120, 180

Y
Ysbyty Ystwyth, 65
Ystrad Meurig, 55, 144

SUBJECTS

A
Aberystwyth Court Leet, 27
Annual Register, 141
Annual Register of Marriages, 207

B
Badging (of the Poor), 98, 99, Vestry Record; 101, illustration
Bailiff, 83, 85
Baldwin's Weekly Journal, 208
Beldam (Bethlehem), 78
Black Ram (Siôn Philip incident), 151-63
Burgesses, 27, creation of; 28, 83, 84, creation of; 176, 196, Court Leet Record; 201
Burial (of Sir Herbert), 209, 210, 211, Church Register entry
By-election (1769), 194-202

C
Cambrian Itinerary, 223
Canwyll y Cymry, 2, 7, 11

Cardigan Gaol, 52, 63, 67, 107, 127, 155, 157, 162, 177
Carmarthenshire Militia, 139
Chairing the Member, 136
Circulating School (at Foelallt), 57
Civil War, 9, 14, 21
Cockfighting, 35, 47, 109, illustration; 111
Committee of Privileges and Elections, 29, 202
Communion Vessels (gift of Mrs Lloyd, Peterwell), 44, illustration; 45
Crows (destruction of), 109
Court of Chancery, 116, 117, 119
Court Leet, 27, 83, 84, 86, 87-96, 197, 215
Curse of Maesyfelin, 4-12

D
Drovers, 83, 102, 174, 175, 176
Drych y Prif Oesoedd, 36

E
Elections, 27-9, 41-3, 133-37, 180-98, 199, illustration; 200, 201, 202
Election Feast, 134, 135, illustration
Emergency Baptisms, 38, 39
Esgair Mwyn dispute, 64-71
Estrays (Rights of), 93

F
Fevers, 99
Fairs, 47, 89
Fleet Prison, 127, 128, 129, 131, 181
Font, (Medieval, originally in St Peter's Church), 110 illustration; 111
Food, of the Poor, 102; of the Gentry, 100
Foxes (destruction of), 109

G
Gambling, 35, 37, 38, 73, 170 illustration; 174, illustration; 204, 205
Gloucester Journal, 113, 118, 177, 184
Gentleman's Magazine, 78, 209
Golden Grove Book, 22, 140
Gout, 165, 166, 169, illustration
Gray's Inn, 21
Great Sessions, 151-64

H
Habitations (of the Poor), 97, illustration; 101
Hanging, 64, 153, 159, 160, 161, illustration; 162, 164
Health (of the Poor), 99-102
Hearth Tax, 19

I
Immunity (from prosecution for M.P.'s), 181, 203
Infant mortality, 14, 41, 99
Infanticide, 103
Inner Temple, 36
Interludes, 47, 109

J
Javelin Men, 149, 157
Jesus College, Oxford, 21, 33, 34, illustration; 35, 36
Justices of the Peace, 25, 36, 37, 63, 85, 139, 143, 145, 149, 158, 186

K
King's Bench, 190, 214
King's Patent, 148, 149

L
Library (of Sir Herbert), 221
London Chronicle, 141
London Evening Post, 137
London Gazette, 140

M
Medicines (of the eighteenth century), 77-79, see also Appendix B
Memorial Ring, 80, illustration; 81
Methodist Revival, 35, 46-62
Middle Temple, 1
Mob violence, 67, 125-28
Murder, 103

N
North British Dragoons, 68

P
Parish Vestry, 83, 89, 99, 100, 101, illustration; 104, 105, 111, see also Appendix E
Patronage, 142, 143, 144
Paupers, 97-111, see also Appendix E
Peace of Paris, 60
Petitions, 29, 201, 202, 204
Poaching, 105, 107
Polling, 190, 199, illustration; 200, 201
Portreeve, 84, 90, 210
Pound, 93, 95
Public Advertiser, 208
Punishments, 37, 83, 90-2

Q
Quarter Sessions, 37, 69, 83, 85, 102, 105, 167, 178

R
Racing, 35
Riot Act, 51
Relief (by the Parish), 104-05
Roads (condition of), 167, 169

S
Scot's Greys, 68
Sale (of Peterwell), 218-22, see also Appendix D
Seven Years War, 180
Shrouds, 99, see also Appendix E
Smallpox, 92, 100, 210 211
Stamp Act, 180
Steward, 83
Stocks and Whipping Post, 91, illustration; 155
St Mary's Church, Cardigan, 76
St Peter's Church, Lampeter, 41, 72, 82, 106, illustration; 202, 206, 210, 212, illustration
Suicide, 103, 208
Swearing, 90

T
Travel (hazards of), 166, 169

V
Vagrants, 37, 108, illustration

W
Wakes, 47
Welch Fusiliers, 68
Whipping, 64, 91, 92, illustration
Window Tax, 97
Wine, 165, illustration